The law of stamp duties on deeds and other instruments : containing the Stamp Act, 1891, the Stamp Duties Management Act, 1891, and acts amending the same : a summary of case law ...

E. N. Alpe

The law of stamp duties on deeds and other instruments : containing the Stamp Act, 1891, the Stamp Duties Management Act, 1891, and acts amending the same : a summary of case law ...
Alpe, E. N. (Edmund Nicholas)
collection ID ocm23805143
Reproduction from Harvard Law School Library
First published in 1890 under title: A digest of the law relating to stamp duties on deeds and other instruments. Includes index.
London : Jordan, 1894.
xxiii, 333 p. ; 19 cm.

The Making of Modern Law collection of legal archives constitutes a genuine revolution in historical legal research because it opens up a wealth of rare and previously inaccessible sources in legal, constitutional, administrative, political, cultural, intellectual, and social history. This unique collection consists of three extensive archives that provide insight into more than 300 years of American and British history. These collections include:

Legal Treatises, 1800-1926: over 20,000 legal treatises provide a comprehensive collection in legal history, business and economics, politics and government.

Trials, 1600-1926: nearly 10,000 titles reveal the drama of famous, infamous, and obscure courtroom cases in America and the British Empire across three centuries.

Primary Sources, 1620-1926: includes reports, statutes and regulations in American history, including early state codes, municipal ordinances, constitutional conventions and compilations, and law dictionaries.

These archives provide a unique research tool for tracking the development of our modern legal system and how it has affected our culture, government, business – nearly every aspect of our everyday life. For the first time, these high-quality digital scans of original works are available via print-on-demand, making them readily accessible to libraries, students, independent scholars, and readers of all ages.

biblio life
old books. new life.

The BiblioLife Network

This project was made possible in part by the BiblioLife Network (BLN), a project aimed at addressing some of the huge challenges facing book preservationists around the world. The BLN includes libraries, library networks, archives, subject matter experts, online communities and library service providers. We believe every book ever published should be available as a high-quality print reproduction; printed on-demand anywhere in the world. This insures the ongoing accessibility of the content and helps generate sustainable revenue for the libraries and organizations that work to preserve these important materials.

The following book is in the "public domain" and represents an authentic reproduction of the text as printed by the original publisher. While we have attempted to accurately maintain the integrity of the original work, there are sometimes problems with the original work or the micro-film from which the books were digitized. This can result in minor errors in reproduction. Possible imperfections include missing and blurred pages, poor pictures, markings and other reproduction issues beyond our control. Because this work is culturally important, we have made it available as part of our commitment to protecting, preserving, and promoting the world's literature.

GUIDE TO FOLD-OUTS MAPS and OVERSIZED IMAGES

The book you are reading was digitized from microfilm captured over the past thirty to forty years. Years after the creation of the original microfilm, the book was converted to digital files and made available in an online database.

In an online database, page images do not need to conform to the size restrictions found in a printed book. When converting these images back into a printed bound book, the page sizes are standardized in ways that maintain the detail of the original. For large images, such as fold-out maps, the original page image is split into two or more pages

Guidelines used to determine how to split the page image follows:

- Some images are split vertically; large images require vertical and horizontal splits.
- For horizontal splits, the content is split left to right.
- For vertical splits, the content is split from top to bottom.
- For both vertical and horizontal splits, the image is processed from top left to bottom right.

THE

Law of Stamp Duties

ON

DEEDS AND OTHER INSTRUMENTS.

Seventeenth Edition. Price [illegible]

A HANDY BOOK ON THE FORMATION, MANAGEMENT, AND WINDING UP OF JOINT STOCK COMPANIES. By JAMES M. JORDAN, Registration and Parliamentary Agent, and F. GORE BROWNE, M.A., of the Inner Temple, Barrister-at-law.

"This is eminently a practical book... we cannot sufficiently commend it; for a book containing so much useful information in so handsome a form." — *Law Notes*

Price 10s. 6d., for Cash to Order; by Post 11s.

CONCISE PRECEDENTS UNDER THE COMPANIES ACTS, 1862 to 1890. By F. GORE-BROWNE, M.A., of the Inner Temple, Joint Author of "A Handy Book on the Formation, Management, and Winding Up of Joint Stock Companies."

Containing numerous Precedents of Memoranda and Articles of Association, Agreements with Vendors and other Preliminary Contracts, Underwriting Letters, Commission Notes, &c., Forms of Debentures and Trust Deeds, Schemes of Winding Up and Reconstruction of Companies and Arrangements with Creditors, Contracts, Resolutions and Petitions to Reduce Capital, to Alter Memorandum of Association and to Wind Up, Notices of Motion and various Pleadings in Actions, and numerous other Forms for various purposes.

THE COMPANIES ACTS, 1862 to 1890; The Life Assurance Companies Acts, 1870 to 1872; The Stannaries Acts, 1869 and 1887; The Forged Transfers Acts, 1891 and 1892; and other Statutes and Statutory Enactments relating to or affecting Joint Stock Companies formed under The Companies Acts 1862 to 1890, with Cross References and a full Analytical Index. By WILLIAM S. FOWKE, of Lincoln's Inn, Joint Author of "The Secretary's Manual."

This is the only book published containing the Text of the numerous Acts governing and relating to Joint Stock Companies. It contains Twenty or so complete Statutes, besides other Acts and portions of Acts affecting Companies, with Cross References, Notes, and a full Analytical Index. It will be found a most useful companion volume to the preceding.

THE NEW LAW OF TRUSTS.

Price 6s. net, by Post 6s. 6d.

THE TRUSTEE ACT, 1893. An Act to Consolidate Enactments Relating to Trustees, together with The Trustee Act, 1888, and The Trust Investment Act, 1889, with Explanatory Notes, the Rules of the Supreme Court under the New Act, Numerous Forms, and a Complete Index. By ARTHUR REGINALD RUDALL, of the Middle Temple, and JAMES WILLIAM GREIG, LL.B., B.A. Lond., of Lincoln's Inn, Barristers-at-law.

Price 6s. net, by Post 6s. 6d.

THE LAWS TO COPYHOLD ENFRANCHISEMENT UNDER THE COPYHOLD ACT, 1894: containing the Text of the Act with Explanatory Notes, Comparative Tables of Repealed Statutes, Minutes of the Board of Agriculture, Scales of Compensation under the Act, Numerous Forms, and a full Analytical Index. By A. R. RUDALL and J. W. GREIG, Authors of the foregoing.

JORDAN & SONS, Publishers, London.

LAW OF STAMP DUTIES

ON

DEEDS AND OTHER INSTRUMENTS

CONTAINING

The Stamp Act, 1891

The Stamp Duties Management Act 1891,

AND ACTS AMENDING THE SAME,

A SUMMARY OF CASE LAW, NOTES OF PRACTICE AND ADMINISTRATION
TABLES OF EXEMPTIONS, THE OLD AND NEW DEATH DUTIES
AND THE EXCISE LICENCE DUTIES

BY

E. N. ALPE,

OF THE MIDDLE TEMPLE, BARRISTER AT LAW
OF THE SOLICITOR'S DEPARTMENT, INLAND REVENUE

FOURTH EDITION.

LONDON
JORDAN & SONS
120 CHANCERY LANE AND 8 BELL YARD, TEMPLE BAR

1894

Contents.

	PAGE
PREFACE TO THE FOURTH EDITION	vii
PREFACE TO THE SECOND EDITION	vii
PREFACE TO THE FIRST EDITION	ix
TABLE OF CASES CITED	xi
ABBREVIATIONS OF REFERENCES TO REPORTS	xxiii
INTRODUCTION	1

THE STAMP ACT, 1891:—

Arrangement of Sections	5
PART I—Regulations Applicable to Instruments Generally	15
PART II—Schedule of Duties and Regulations Applicable to Particular Instruments	44
General Exemptions from all Stamp Duties	203
PART III—Supplemental	204
Rules as to Composition for Stamp Duties	215
List of Enactments Repealed	217

THE STAMP DUTIES MANAGEMENT ACT, 1891:—

Arrangement of Sections	220
Text of Act	222
List of Enactments Repealed	240

APPENDIX.

	PAGE
SPECIAL EXEMPTIONS IN STATUTES NOT OTHERWISE RELATING TO STAMP DUTIES	242
TABLE OF STATUTES IN APPENDIX	263
DUTIES IMPOSED BY ACTS NOT OTHERWISE RELATING TO STAMP DUTIES	266
EXAMPLE OF ASSESSMENT OF SETTLEMENT DUTY	270

TABLES OF DEATH DUTIES.

DEATH DUTIES BEFORE AUGUST 2, 1894 —

1 PROBATE AND ADMINISTRATION DUTIES	274
2 ACCOUNT DUTY	275
3 LEGACY DUTY	276
4 SUCCESSION DUTY	278
5 TEMPORARY ESTATE DUTY	280

DEATH DUTIES IMPOSED BY THE FINANCE ACT, 1894 —

1 ESTATE DUTY	283
2 LEGACY DUTY	286
3 SUCCESSION DUTY	287

EXCISE LICENCES, TABLE OF	289
INDEX	309

PREFACE TO THE FOURTH EDITION

IN the preparation of the Fourth Edition of this work the text has been carefully revised, and notes of the most recent cases bearing on Stamp Law have been added. The changes in the Death Duties made by The Finance Act, 1894, will be found on pages 281 to 288

MIDDLE TEMPLE LIBRARY,
November, 1894

PREFACE TO THE SECOND EDITION.

THE Consolidation of the Acts relating to Stamp Duties Duties by The Stamp Act, 1891, and The Stamp Duties Management Act, 1891, renders a new edition of "A Digest of the Law relating to Stamp Duties" necessary, and it is now issued under the title of "THE LAW OF STAMP DUTIES ON DEEDS AND OTHER INSTRUMENTS."

The changes in the law effected by the new Acts are not considerable The obsolete duties charged under the heads "Admission to the Inns of Chancery" and "Schedule or Inventory" have been allowed to drop out, and statutory confirmation has been given to several points of practice established at Somerset House in favour of the taxpayer. The change of language in Section 14 (4) of The Stamp Act, 1891, respecting the admissibility of instruments in evidence, and the introduction of the word "whatsoever" into Section 59, are of importance, while the sections of the older Acts have been amalgamated or rearranged with a free hand, and textual alterations are very numerous.

The plan adopted in the Digest (taken from the old Stamp Laws) of grouping the sections containing particular regulations under the heads of charge to which they relate has been continued, as being the most convenient for handy reference.

The Notes, Appendices, and Index have been corrected and revised, and, for the convenience of practitioners, Tables of the Death Duties and the Excise Licence Duties have been added.

MIDDLE TEMPLE LIBRARY,
September, 1891.

PREFACE TO THE FIRST EDITION

THE absence of a Digest of the Stamp Laws brought brought down to date, and supplemented by Notes on Practice and Administration, has often been remarked. The important changes in Stamp Duties made by The Customs and Inland Revenue Acts of 1888 and 1889, and The Revenue Act of 1889, have not been fully noticed in new editions of existing treatises, and no attempt has of late been made to condense the Case Law upon stamp questions in a short and concise summary. The Author has made a humble effort to supply these wants.

The accuracy of the Notes on Practice scattered through the book may be relied upon, and it is hoped they will give the Profession information upon many points of everyday occurrence in official experience which is now obtainable only by correspondence or adjudication. Debateable questions have been avoided, and if anywhere it should seem that the Author has expressed an opinion of his own, it will be found on inquiry that he has quoted a dictum uttered from the Bench or contained in a Text Book of acknowledged authority.

The Acts relating to the Stamp Duty on the Capital of Limited Companies and to Composition for Stamp Duties have been included, although perhaps they are not strictly Acts relating to Stamp Duties "on Deeds and other Instruments" to which the volume professes to extend.

Middle Temple Library,
October, 1890.

TABLE OF CASES CITED.

	PAGE
ABBOTT v STRATTEN, 3 Jones & Latouche, 616	210
ADAMS v. MORGAN, 12 L R, Ir Ex 1	35, 77
ALBERT AVERAGE ASSOCIATION, re, L. R. 13 Equity, 529	55
ALLEN v. MORRISON, 3 M. & R 71; 8 B & C 565	19, 152
ALSAGER'S SETTLEMENT, re, 10 L T R. 238	194
AMES v HILL, 2 Bosanquet & Puller, 150	56
ANGLO EGYPTIAN NAVIGATION COMPANY v RENNIE, 10 L R. C. P. 271	59
ARTHUR'S ESTATE, re, 14 Ch D 603, 49 L J, Ch 556	194
ARUNDELL v. BELL, 52 L J, Ch 537, 49 Jurist, N L 345; 31 W. R 477	105
ASHBY v ASHBY, Moore & Payne, 186	79
ASHLING v BOON, 64 L T R 193, 39 W R.	26
ASQUITH v GRIFFIN, 48 J P 724	300
ATKINSON v FELL, 5 M & S 240	64
ATTENBOROUGH v COMMISSIONERS, 11 Ex. R 461, 25 L J, Ex 22	59, 163
ATTORNEY-GENERAL v. BROWN, 3 Ex. R 662, 18 L. J, Ex 336	105, 141, 170
ATTORNEY-GENERAL v GILPIN, 6 Ex 193	16, 245
ATTORNEY-GENERAL v LAMPLOUGH, 3 Ex. Div, C A 214	303
ATTORNEY-GENERAL v MILFORD DOCKS COMPANY, 69 L T R 443	205
ATTORNEY-GENERAL v PHILLIPS, 19 W. R 1146	245
AUSTRALASIAN MORTGAGE &c Co. v COMMISSIONERS, 16 Rettie, 64, 26 Sco. L R 47	74, 76
BACON v SIMPSON, 3 M & W 78	17
BALDEY v PARKER, 2 B & C 37	19
BARBER v CALLOW, 41 J P 823	294
BARKER v SMARK, 7 M & W 50	170
BARRY v GOODMAN, 2 M & W. 768	55
BEAVEN, re, 2 L J, Ch 536	189
BEECHING v WESTBROOK, 8 M & W 411, 1 Dowling, N S 18	54, 55
BELCH v COMMISSIONERS, 4 Rettie, 592	2, 104

	PAGE
BELFORT, in re THE, L R, 9 Probate, 215	29, 34, 41, 97
BIRKBECK FREEHOLD LAND SOCIETY, ex parte, 24 Ch. D 119	210
BLACKWELL v M'NAUGHTEN, 1 Q B. 127; 1 A. & E, N S 127	55
BLANDY v HERBERT, 9 B & C 396	105
BLEWITT v TRITTON, Law Times 9th July, 1892	34
BLOUNT v. PEARMAN, 1 Bingham, N. C 408	144
BOASE, in re, CROFTON v CROFTON, 50B L J, Ch 135	82, 84
BOASE v JACKSON, 3 B & B 185	144
BOULTON v COMMISSIONERS, 5 Ex 82	19, 147
BOWEN v ASHLEY, 1 New Reports, 274	19
BOWEN v FOX, 2 M. & R 167	54
BOWKER v WILLIAMSON, 5 Times L R. 382	34
BOWLBY v BELL, 3 M G & S 284	61
BRADLAUGH v DE RIN, 3 C P 286, 18 L T R, C. P 904	23, 82
BRAY v HANSON, 8 M & W 668	56
BRAITHWAITE v HITCHCOCK, 10 M & W 494, 2 Dowling, N R. 444; 6 Jurist, 976	37, 125
BRICE v BANNISTER, 3 Q B. D. 569, 38 L T 739	77
BRISTOWE v SEQUEVILLE, 5 Ex R. 275, 19 L. J, Ex 289	35
BRITISH INDIA STEAM NAVIGATION COMPANY v COMMISSIONERS, 7 Q B D 165, 50 L J, Q B 517; 44 L T R 378	2, 80, 170
BROOKS v DAVIS, 3 C. & P 186	188
BROOKS v ELKINS, 2 M & W 74, 2 Gale, 200	79
BROWN v VAWSER, 4 East, 584	131
BRYANS v NIX, 4 M & W 775	85
BUCK v ROBSON, 3 Q B D 687; 39 L T R., Q B 325	77
BULL v O'SULLIVAN, 6 Q B D 209	77
BURLINSON v HALL, 12 Q B D 347	170
BUSSEY v BARRETT, 9 M & W 312	189
CALDWELL v DAWSON, 5 Ex R 1, 14 Jurist, 916	170
CALLOW v LAWRENCE, 3 M & S 95	78
CAMPBELL v LOADER, 34 L J, Ex 50	34
CAMPBELL v STRANGEWAYS, 3 L R., C P Div 105, 42 J. P 39	292
CANNING (LORD) v RAPER, 1 E & B 164, 22 L J., Q B 87	169
CARRINGTON v ROOTS, 2 M & W 248	61
CARUS-WILSON v GREENE, 18 Q. B D 7	70
CASHBOURNE v DUTTON, Selwyn, N P 371	79
CHADWICK v CLARE, 14 L J, C P 233; 1 C B 700; 9 Jurist, 539	53
CHANDOS, MARQUIS OF, v COMMISSIONERS, 6 Ex R 464	31
CHANTER v DICKENSON, 12 L J, C P 147, 5 M & G 253, 2 Dowl, N R 83, 6 Scott, New Reports, 182	59

TABLE OF CASES

	PAGE
CHANTER v JOHNSON, 11 M & W 408, 14 L. J, Ex. 239	131
CHAPLIN v CLARK, 4 Ex. R 407	53
CHARLES v HILL, 26 L R, Ir. 603	269
CHATFIELD v COX, 18 Q. B 321, 21 L J, Q. B. 279	68
CHILDERS v BOULNOIS, 1 D & R 8	55
CHOLMONDELEY, in re, 1 C & M. 149	15
CHOLMONDELEY v DARLEY, 14 L J, Ex. 328; 14 M & W 344	17
CHRISTIE v. COMMISSIONERS, 2 Ex 46, 36 L J, Ex 11	2, 113
CITY OF GLASGOW BANK v. COMMISSIONERS, 8 Rettie, 391, 18 Sco. L R 242. (*See* Liquidators of City of Glasgow Bank, &c.)	
CLARK v BULMER, 11 M & W. 242	59
CLARKE v. ROCHE, 3 Q B. D 170, 37 L T. R 633	34
CLAY v CROFTS, 20 L. J, Ex. 361	55
CLAY v YATES, 25 L. J., Ex 237, 1 H & N 73	59
CLAYTON v BURDENSHAW, 5 B & C 41	18, 143
COATES v PERRY, 3 B & B 45	170
COMMISSIONERS v. ANGUS & Co, LIMITED, 23 Q B D 579, W R 1889, 60	1, 2, 32, 102, 106, 118, 132
COMMISSIONERS v GLASGOW & SOUTH WESTERN RAILWAY Co, 5 Appeal Cases, 315	2, 32, 107
COMMISSIONERS v MORTGAGE INSURANCE CORPORATION, LIMITED, 21 Q B D. 352	32
CONSERVATORS OF RIVER THAMES v COMMISSIONERS, 18 Q B D. 279, 56 L. J., Q B 181; 56 L. T R. 198	32, 87, 104
COOPER v FLYNN, 3 Ir L R 473	144
COPPOCK v BOWER, 4 M & W 361, Horn & Hurlston, 340	37
CORDER v DRAKEFORD, 3 Taunton, 382	3, 18, 143
CORNISH v. SEARELL, 8 B. & C 471	56
COTTERELL v APSLEY, 6 Taunton, 322	59
COWAN v STEWART, 10 Rettie, 4th Series, 735	37
CRISP v ANDERSON, 1 Starkie, 35	37
CROPTON v. CROFTON, in re Boase, 56 L J, Ch. 135	82, 84
CROSBY v. WADSWORTH, 6 East, 602	61
CROSSMAN v THE QUEEN, 18 Q B D. 256	104
CROWTHER v SOLOMONS, 6 C B 758	37
CURRY v EDENEOR, 3 Term Reports, 524	3, 58
DAKIN v WATSON, 2 Crawford & Dix, Cir Rep 225	57
DAVIS v WILLIAMS, 13 East, 232	19
DE PARQUET v PAGE, 15 Q B 1073, 20 L. J, Q. B. 28, 15 Jurist, 148	55
DOE D BINGHAM v CARTWRIGHT, 3 B & Ald 326	54
DOE D COPLEY v DAY, 13 East, 241	19, 144
DOE D CROFT v TIDBURY, 14 C B 304	3, 19

	PAGE
DOE D DOWNE v GOVIER, 5 L T R. 37	17
DOE D FRANKIS v FRANKIS, 11 A & E 792, 3 Perry & Davison, 565	56
DOE D FRYER v COOMBES, 12 L. J, Q B 36, 3 A & E 687, 6 Jurist, 930	37
DOE D LINSEY v EDWARDS, 5 A. & E. 95	56
DOE D MANIFOLD v DIAMOND, 4 B & C 243, 6 D & R. 328	103
DOE D MERCERON v BRAGG, 8 A & E 620, 3 Neville & Perry, 644	170
DOE D PRIEST v WESTERN, 2 Q B 249, 11 L J, Q B. 17	115
DOE v SCRUTON v SNAITH, 8 Bingham, 146, 1 Moore & Scott, 230	170
DOE D ST JOHN v HORE, 2 Espinasse, 724	36
DOE D WRIGHT v SMITH, 8 A & E 255; 2 Jurist, 854	56
DOE D WYATT v STAGG, 9 L J, C P. 73, 3 Jurist, 1981	3
DRANT v BROWN, 3 B & C 665	54
DURIE'S EXECUTRIX v FIELDING, 30 Sco L R 371	36, 76
EDGAR v BLICK, 1 Starkie, 464	55
EDMONDS v BLAINA FURNACES CO, 36 Ch D 215	171
EMMERSON v HEELIS, 2 Taunton, 38	19
ENGLISH, SCOTTISH, and AUSTRALIAN CHARTERED BANK, in re [1893], 1 Ch, C A 385, 42 W R. 4	150, 153
EVANS v PROTHERO, 20 L J, Ch 448, 21 L J, Ch 772	35
EVANS v ROBERTS, 5 B. & C 836	60
FAIRCLOUGH v ROBERTS, 54 J P 241	290
FALMOUTH, EARL OF, v THOMAS, 1 Crompton & Meeson, 89, 3 Tyrwhitt, 26	61, 106
FIELDER v RAY, 4 C & P 63	59
FISHER v CALVERT, 27 W R 301	77
FISHER v LESLIE, 1 Espinasse, 426	55
FISHWICK v MILNES, 4 Ex R 824, 19 L J, Ex 153	55
FITZGERALD'S TRUSTEES v MELLERSH, Law Times 16th January, 1892	41
FLATHER v STUBBS, 2 A & E 614	242
FOLEY (LORD) v COMMISSIONERS, 3 Ex 263	1
FOSTER (JOHN) & SONS, LIMITED, v COMMISSIONERS [1894], 1 Q B, C A 516, 63 L J R 173, 69 L T. R 817, 9 R 149	22, 32, 103, 108
FOWLER v MONMOUTHSHIRE CANAL CO, 4 Q. B D 334	93
FRASER v BUNN, 8 C & P 704	55
FREEMAN v COMMISSIONERS, 6 Ex 101	18, 108
FRITH v ROTHERHAM, 15 L J, Ex 133, 10 Jurist, 208	170
FURNESS OR ULVERSTON RAILWAY COMPANY v COMMISSIONERS 33 L J, Ex 173, 10 L T R 101	20, 21, 103, 111

	PAGE
GARBUTT v WATSON, 5 B & Ald 613	59
GARLAND, ex parte, 7 Times L R 121	303
GATTY v FRY, 2 Ex Div 265	77
GIBB v COMMISSIONERS, 8 Rettie 4th Series, 120	104
GILCHRIST v HERBERT, 26 L T R 381	34
GINGELL v PERKINS, 4 Ex R 720, 19 L J, Ex 129	105, 141
GLEN v DUNGAY, 4 Ex R. 61	144
GLOVER v GILES, 18 Ch. D 180	43
GLOVER v HALKETT, 26 L J, Ex 416, 2 H. & N, Ex 490, 3 Jurist, N S 1083	54
GOODSON v FORBES, 1 Marshall, 525	19
GOULD v COOMBS, 14 L J, C P 175, 1 M G & S 543, 9 Jurist, 494	55
GOWAN v GOWAN, 17 Ch D 778	194
GREAT BRITAIN STEAMSHIP PREMIUM ASSOCIATION v WHITE, 29 Sco L R 104	178
GREAT WESTERN RAILWAY CO v COMMISSIONERS [1894] 1 Q. B., C A 507, 63 L J R 405; 9 R 184	32, 102, 111
GREEN v DAVIS, 1 C. & P 451	79
GRENFELL v. COMMISSIONERS, 1 Ex Div 242, 45 L J, Ex 465	161
GREY v SMITH, 1 Campbell, 388	35
GRIFFIN v WEATHERBY, 3 Q B 753, 18 L T R., Ex. 881	81, 82
GUARDIANS OF BANBURY UNION v ROBINSON, 12 L J, Q B 327; 4 A & E, N S 919	256
GURR v SCUDD, 11 Ex R 190	1, 59
GUYER v REG., 53 J P. 436	300
HADGETT v COMMISSIONERS, 3 Ex Div 46, 37 L T R 612	18, 63
HALL v URBAN SANITARY AUTHORITY OF DERBY, 16 Q B D 163	66
HAMPSHIRE v WICKENS, 7 Ch D. 661	147
HARLEY v WILKINSON, 4 Campbell, 127, 4 M & S 25	17
HARNETT v MILES, 48 J P 155	300
HARRIS v BIRCH, 9 M & W 59, 11 L J., Ex. 219	171
HEAP v HARTLEY, 42 Ch. D. 461, 58 L J Ch. 790	105
HEGARTY v MILNE, 23 L J, C. P. 151, 14 C B 627, 18 Jurist, 496	54
HELBY v MATTHEWS, 1894 2 Q B 262	60
HENNIKER v HENNIKER, 22 L J, Q B 94, 1 E & B 54	104, 137
HERON v GRAINGER, 5 Espinasse, 269	3, 58
HESELTINE v SIGGERS, 1 Ex R 856	61
HILL v RANSOM, 12 L J, C P 275	4, 55
HOBBS v CATHIE, 6 Times L R 292	84
HOLMES v SIXSMITH, 7 Ex R 802, 21 L J, Ex 312, 16 Jurist, 619	37

TABLE OF CASES

	PAGE
HORSFALL v HEY, 2 Ex R 778, 17 L. J, Ex. 266	16, 58, 103
HORTON, in re, 8 Q B D 434	93
HOWARTH v MINNS, 51 J P 7	291
HOWES v INLAND REVENUE, 24 W R. 407 & 897, 45 L J, M C 86, 1 Ex. Div 385	305
HUBBARD v JACKSON, 4 Bingham, 390, 3 C & P 134	78
HUDSON v SPOOTER, 55 J P 325	301
HUDSPETH v YARNOLD, 19 L J, C. P 321; 9 C B. 625; 14 Jurist, 578	53
HUGHES v BUDD, 4 Jurist, 654, 8 Dowling, 478	54, 59
HUMBLE v MITCHELL, 11 A & E 205	61
ISRAEL v ISRAEL, 1 Campbell, 499	55
JACKSON v HILL, J P 5th January, 1884	58
JACKSON v STOPHERD, 4 Tyrwhitt, 330	64
JAMES v CATHERWOOD, 2 Espinasse, 528, 7 Term Reports, 241	85
JAMES v NICOLAS, 50 J P. 292	292
JAMES v SHORE, 1 Starkie, 426	19
JAY v WARREN, 1 C & P 532	56
JOHNSON v BLENKINSOPP, 5 Jurist, 870	58
JOHNSON v DUKE OF MARLBOROUGH, 2 Starkie, 313	38
JONES v FLINT, 9 Parry & Davidson, 594	60
JONES v JONES, 1 Crompton & Meeson, 74	38
JONES v RIDER, 4 M & W 32	252
JONES v SIMPSON, 2 B & C 318, 3 D & R 545	76
KELLAWAY v McDOUGAL, 45 J P 207	305
KNIGHT v BARBER, 16 L J, Ex 18, 16 M & W. 66, 10 Jurist, 929	54, 61, 99
LANGDON v WILSON, 7 B & C 640, 2 M & R 10	55
LANT v PEACE, 3 Neville & Parry, 329	197
LAVERY v PURSELL, 39 Ch D 508	61
LAWRENCE v BOSTON, 21 L J, Ex 49, 7 Ex R 28	4, 170
LAZARUS v COWIE, 11 L. J, Q B 310, 3 A & E, N S 459	78
LEAROYD v BRACKEN [C A 1894], 1 Q B 114, 9 R 154	93, 100
LEE v BUTLER [1893], 2 Q B 318	60
LEE v GASKELL, 19 Q B D 701	61
LEE v GRIFFIN, 30 L J, Q B 252, 1 Best & Smith, 272	59
LEEDS v BURROWS, 12 East, 1	70
LEEDS v LANCASHIRE, 2 Campbell, 205	17
LEIGH v BANNER, 1 Espinasse, 403	61
LEVY v ABERCORRIS SLATE AND SLAB COMPANY, 37 Ch D 260	171
LEWIS v TAYLOR, 16 East, 49	278

LIDDIARD v GALE, 4 Ex R 416, 19 L J, Ex. 160	57
LIMMER ASPHALTE PAVING CO. v COMMISSIONERS, 7 Ex 211, 41 L J, Ex 106; 28 L T R. 683	2, 3, 18, 87, 104, 105
LIQUIDATORS OF CITY OF GLASGOW BANK v COMMISSIONERS, 8 Rettie, 391; 18 Sco. L R 242	111
LONDON, BRIGHTON, & SOUTH COAST RAILWAY COMPANY v. FAIRCLOUGH, 2 M & G. 675, 3 Scott, N. R 68	38
LONDON AND COUNTY BANKING CORPORATION v. RATCLIFFE, 6 Appeal Cases, 730	36
LOOME v. BAILEY, 3 L. T. Rep, N. S 406	300
LOVELL v HILL, 6 C. & P 238	80
LOVELOCK v FRANKLAND, 16 L J, Q B. 182, 8 A & E 371	18, 143
LUCAS v JONES, 13 L. J., Q B 208; 5 A. & E, N. S 949	188
LYSAGHT v. WARREN, 10 Ir L R. 269	170
MACLEOD v. COMMISSIONERS, 12 Rettie, 1045, 22 Sco L R. 674	113
MARC v ROUY, 31 L T R, Q B 372	23, 82, 84
MARINE INVESTMENT COMPANY v HAVISIDE, 5 L R., H. L 624, 42 L J C 178	37
MARSHALL v GREEN, 1 C P. 35	60
MARSHALL v. POWELL, 16 L J, Q B. 5; 11 Jurist, 61	55
MASSEY v NANNEY, 3 Bingham, N C. 478	103
MATHESON v ROSS, 2 House of Lords Cases, 286	35
MAXWELL v COMMISSIONERS, 4 Rettie, 1121	169
MAYFIELD v. ROBINSON, 14 L J, Q. B 285; 7 A & E, N. S. 486	16
MAYFIELD v WADSLEY, 3 B & C 266	61, 106
MEEK v BAYLISS, 31 L J, Ch 448	171
MELANOTTE v TEESDALE, 13 L J, Ex 358, 13 M & W 216	56
MILLER v DENHAM, 5 Q B D. 467	88
MISA v CURRIE, 1 App Cas. 554	78
MOFFAT v EDWARDS, 1 C & M 16	56
MOORE v GARWOOD, 4 Ex R 681; 19 L J, Ex. Ch 15	53
MORGAN v PIKE, 14 C B 473	29, 174
MORLEY v HALL, 2 Dowling, 494	1, 56
MORRIS v DIXON, 4 A. & E 845, 6 N & M 438	252
MORRIS v LEE, 1 Strange, 629; 5 Modern, 362	80
MORTGAGE INSURANCE CORPORATION, LIMITED, v COMMISSIONERS, 21 Q B D. 352, 57 L. J, Q. B. 630; 36 W R 833	2, 79
MORTGAGE INSURANCE CORPORATION, LIMITED, v COMMISSIONERS (Policy case), 57 L J, Q B 179	183
MORTIMORE v COMMISSIONERS, 22 L J, Q B 94, 1 E & B 54; 2 Hurlston & Coltman, 628, 10 L T R 657	1, 111, 169
MOUNSEY v STEPHENSON, 7 B & C 403	87

	PAGE
MUIR v KEAY, 23 W R 700, 44 L J, M C 143, 10 Q B 594	305
MULLER v HUTCHINSON, 3 C & P 92; 7 B & C 639, 1 M & R. 522	55
NEWBY v HARRISON, 1 J & H 393	105
NICOLL v GREAVES, 33 L J, C P 259, 17 C. B., N. S 27	58
NIXON v ALBION MARINE INSURANCE COMPANY, 2 Ex 338	37
NORRIS v IRISH LAND COMPANY, 8 E & B 512	43
NOWLAND v ABLETT, L J, Ex 155, 2 C M. & R 54	58
OHLSON, ex parte, 55 J P 117	303
ONSLOW v. COMMISSIONERS, 24 Q. B. D 584, 59 L J., Q B 321, 1891, 1 Q B, C A. 239	32, 193, 271
OPENSHAW v OAKLEY, 53 J P 740	302
ORME v YOUNG, 4 Campbell, 336	186
PARKER v STANILAND, 11 East, 362	60
PARMITER v PARMITER, 30 L J, Ch 508, 1 J & H 135	252
PARPY v DEERE, 5 A & E 551, 2 H & W 395	20, 21, 143
PEARSON v COMMISSIONERS, 3 Ex 242	142
PEATE v DICKEN, 1 C M & R 422; 5 Tyrwhitt, 116	55
PHILLIPS v COMMISSIONERS, 2 Ex 399	113
PHILLIPS v MORRISON, 13 L J, Ex 212, 12 M & W. 740	1
PINNER v ARNOLD, 2 C M & R. 613, Tyrwhitt & Granger, 1	16, 59
PONSFORD v WALTON, 3 C P. 167	35
POOLEY v GOODWIN, 4 A & E 94, 1 H & W 567	112
POTTER v COMMISSIONERS, 10 Ex R 147, 23 L J, Ex 345, 18 Jurist, 778	32, 104, 105, 113
POWELL v LONDON AND PROVINCIAL BANK [1893], 1 Ch. 610; 69 L. T. R 421	36, 106
PREUSSING v ING, 4 B & Ald 204	76
PRICE v THOMAS, 2 B & Ad. 218	3, 143
PRUDENTIAL ASSURANCE SOCIETY v CURZON, 8 Ex R 97, 22 L J, Ex 85	29
PUNNETT, ex parte, 16 Ch D 233	106
PYLE v. PARTRIDGE, 15 L J, Ex 129	171
RAMSBOTTOM v DAVIES 4 M & W 584, 7 Dowling, 175; Horn & Hurlston, 464	19
RAMSBOTTOM v TONBRIDGE, 2 M & S 434	54
RAMSBOTTOM v WORTLEY, 2 M & S 445	54
REARDON v SWADEY, 4 East, 188	56
REG v COMMISSIONERS OF I R, ex parte Ohlson	303

TABLE OF CASES.   xix

	PAGE
REG v GILCHRIST, Car. & M 224	257
REG v INGHAM, 21 Q B D. 47	15
REG. v KELK, 12 A. & E 559	152
REG. v LEE, 9 Q B. D. 394	38
REG. v. McINERNEY, 30 L. R, Ir. 49	152
REG. v MORTON, 42 L J, M C. 58	131
REG. v OVERTON, 18 Jurist, 134, 1 Crown Cases Reserved, 308, 23 L J, M C 29	188
REG v REGISTRAR OF JOINT STOCK COMPANIES, 21 Q B D. 131	43, 117
REG v STRACHAN, 7 Q. B 463	200
REG. v TYLER, 56 J. P 118	38
REG v. WORTLEY, 21 L J, M C. 44, 15 Jurist, 1137	57
REX v BOARDMAN, 2 Moo & R 147	188
REX v HALESWORTH, 3 B. & A. 717	66
REX v HAWKESWORTH, 1 Leach, C. C. 811, 2 East, P C 955	37
REX v. PRESTON, 5 B. & Ad. 1028	43
REX v RIDGWELL, 6 B. & C 666	2
RICHARDS v. BANKS & PRESTON, 52 J P 23	307, 308
RILEY v. WARDEN, 2 Ex R. 59	57
RIPPENER v. WRIGHT, 2 B & Ald. 478	36
ROBERTS v ELLIOTT, 11 M. & W 527	45
RODWELL v PHILLIPS, 9 M & W 501; 11 L J, Ex 217	61
ROOTS v LORD DORMER, 4 B. & Ad 77; 1 N & M 667	19
ROTHSCHILD & SONS v COMMISSIONERS [1894], 2 Q. B 142	74, 76
ROYAL LIVER FRIENDLY SOCIETY v. COMMISSIONERS, 5 Ex 78	16, 244
RUTTY v. BENTHALL, 2 C P. 488	35
SADLER v JOHNSON, 16 M. & W 775	58
SAINSBURY v MATTHEWS, 4 M & W 343	60
SANVILLE v. COMMISSIONERS, 10 Ex R 159, 23 L. J, Ex 270	195
SAYER, in re, 10 C P. 569	64
SCHULZE v. STEELE, 54 J. P 232	298
SCHUMANN v. WEATHERHEAD, 1 East, 537	17
SCOVELL v. BOXALL, 1 Glyn & Jameson, 396	61
SEMPLE v. STEINAU, 8 Ex. R. 622, 22 L J., Ex 224	57
SHARMAN v SANDERS, 12 C B 166	57
SHARPLES v RICKARD, 2 H & N, Ex 57, 26 L. J, Ex 382	33, 82
SHELLARD, ex parte, in re Adams, L R 17 Eq 109	77
SIBREE v. TRIPP, 15 L J, Ex 318	79
SKRINE v ELMORE, 2 Campbell, 457	16, 57, 58, 187, 189
SMITH v CATOR, 2 B & Ald. 733	58
SMITH v. MAGUIRE, 1 Foster & Finlason, 199	125
SMITH v MASON & Co LIMITED [1894], 2 Q B 363, 58 J P 342	303
SMITH v. SURMAN, 9 B & C 561	60

	PAGE
SOUTH v FINCH, 3 Bingham (New Cases), 506	16, 58
SOUTHGATE v BOHN, 16 M & W. 34	59
SPAWFORTH v ALEXANDER, 2 Espinasse, 621	188
SQUIRE, ex parte, 4 Ch D 47	35
STEPHENS v LOWE, 2 Moore & Scott, 44	17
STONELAKE v BABB, 5 Borroughes, 2673	34
STUCLEY v. COMMISSIONERS, 5 Ex. 85	18, 193, 194
TAYLOR v CROWLAND GAS & COKE COMPANY, 16 Jurist, 728	93
TAYLOR v ORAM, 10 W R 800, 1 H & C 370; 31 L. J, M C 252	305
TAYLOR v STEELE, 16 L. J, Ex 177, 16 M & W 665, 11 Jurist, 806	56
TEAL v ANTY, 2 B & B 99, 4 Moore, 542	61
TEMPEST v KILNE, 3 C B 249	61
TEXAS LAND AND CATTLE COMPANY, LIMITED, v. COMMISSIONERS, 26 Sco. L R. 51	214
TODD v KERRAGE, 8 Ex R 151, 22 L J., Ex. 1	58
TOTTENHAM v ROYAL BANK OF SCOTLAND, 9 R 223	78
TRIPP v ARMITAGE, 1 M & W. 687	59
TROUP v COMMISSIONERS, 7 Times L. R. 610	113
TURNER v POWER, 1 Moody & Malkin, 113, 7 B & C. 625	55
ULVERSTON OR FURNESS RAILWAY COMPANY v COMMISSIONERS, 2 H & C 855, 33 L J, Ex 173, 10 L T. R. 161	20, 21, 103, 111
VALLANCE v FORBES, 6 Rettie, 1099	2, 29
VAUGHTEN v BRINE, 1 M & G 359, 1 Scott, N R 258	54
VEALE v MITCHELL, 30 L. T R 463	82
VENNING v LECKIE, 13 East, 7	58
VOLLANS v FLETCHER, 11 Jurist, 146, L J, Ex 82	53
WALE v COMMISSIONERS, 4 Ex D 270	2, 172
WALKER v ATKINSON, 6 Taunton, 11	59
WALKER v GILES, 18 L J, C P 328, 6 C. B 662, 13 Jurist, 589	3
WALKER v ROSTRON, 9 M & W 411	58
WALTHAM v ELSEE, 1 Carrington & Kirwan, 35	79
WARRINGTON v FURBER, 8 East, 242, 6 Espinasse, 89	58
WARWICK v BROWN, 2 M & S 205	60
WASHBURNE v BURROWS, 1 Ex R 107	60
WATSON v SPRATTLEY, 10 Ex R 222	61
WEBB v SMITH, 30 Ch D 192	77
WELSH'S TRUSTEES v FORBES, 12 Rettie, 4th Series, 851	56, 188
WEST MIDDLESEX WATERWORKS COMPANY v SUWERKROP, 4 C & P 87, Moody & Malkin, 478	60

	PAGE
WHITE v NORTH, 3 Ex. R 689, 16 L J. Ex 316	56
WHITE v SOUTH LONDON TRAMWAYS COMPANY, *Times* 13th December, 1889	56, 188
WHITING v LOAMES, 17 Ch D. 10, 14 Ch D. 823	210, 212
WHITROW v BROWN, 8 *Times* L. R. 75, 56 J P. 874	294
WIGRAM v. JOYCE, 13 L. R., Ir 164	103
WILLEY v. PARRATT, 18 L. J, Ex. 82	53
WILLIAMS v. STOUGHTON, 2 St 292	36, 55
WILLIS v. PALMER, 7 C B., N S 358	203
WILLS v NOOT, 4 Tyrwhitt, 726	76
WILSON v ZULUETA, 19 L. J, Q B 49, 14 Q B 405, 14 Jurist, 356	57
WINCHESTER CORN EXCHANGE COMPANY v. GILLINGHAM, 12 L. J, Q. B 159, 4 A & E, N S 475	87
WOLSELEY v COX, 2 Q B 321	3
WORTHINGTON v FRANCIS, 5 Espinasse, 182	19
WORTHINGTON v. WARRINGTON, 5 C B 635, 17 L J, C P 117	3, 148
WRIGHT v COMMISSIONERS, 11 Ex. R. 458; 25 L J., Ex 49	1, 34
WROUGHTON v TURTLE, 11 M. & W 561, 1 Dowling & Lowndes, 473	4, 170
YATES v. EVANS, 66 L T. R. 532	79
YELLAND v. VINCENT, 47 J P 230	298
YELLAND v WINTER, 50 J P 38	16, 298
YEO v DAWE, 53 L T R 125; 33 W. R 739	79
YOUNG v. COOK, 41 J. P 824, 3 Ex Div 101	304

Abbreviations of References to Reports.

A & E	- -	Adolphus & Ellis.
B & Ad	- -	Barnewell & Adolphus
B & Ald	- -	Barnewell & Alderson.
B & B	- -	Broderip & Bingham
B & C	- -	Barnewell & Creswell
C B	- -	Common Bench Reports
C & M	- -	Carrington & Marshman
C M & R	- -	Crompton, Meeson & Roscoe.
C P	- -	Law Reports, Common Pleas
C & P	- -	Carrington & Payne
Ch D	- -	Law Reports, Chancery Division
Crom & M	- -	Crompton & Meeson.
D & R	- -	Dowling & Rylands.
Dowl.	- -	Dowling
E & B	- -	Ellis & Blackburn
Esp	- -	Espinasse
Ex	- -	Law Reports, Exchequer
Ex D.	- -	,, ,, Exchequer Division.
Ex R	- -	Exchequer Reports
H & H	- -	Horn & Hurlston.
H & N	- -	Hurlston & Norman.
H & W	- -	Harrison & Wollaston.
J & H	- -	Johnson & Hemming
J P	- -	Justice of the Peace
L J, Ex	- -	Law Journal Reports, Exchequer.
L J, Q B	- -	,, ,, ,, Queen's Bench
L J, C P	- -	,, ,, ,, Common Pleas
L J, Ch	- -	,, ,, ,, Chancery.

L R , Ir	-	Law Reports, Ireland
L T R.	-	Law Times Reports
M. & G	-	Manning & Granger
M. G & S.	-	Manning, Granger & Scott.
M & R.	-	Manning & Rylands.
M. & S	-	Maule & Selwyn
M. & W	-	Meeson & Welsby.
Moo & Mal	-	Moody & Malkin.
Moo. & R	-	Moody & Robinson.
Mod.	-	Modern Reports.
N & M	-	Neville & Manning
Q B	-	Queen's Bench Reports
Q B D	-	Law Reports, Queen's Bench Division
R	-	The Reports
Sco. L R.	-	Scottish Law Reporter.
St and Str	-	Strange
Stark.	-	Starkie.
Taunt.	-	Taunton.
Tyr	-	Tyrwhitt.
W. R.	-	Weekly Reporter.

INTRODUCTION.

THE STAMP LAW is *positivi juris*. It imports nothing of principle or of reason, but depends entirely upon the language of the Legislature (*per* Taunton, J, in Morley v. Hall, 2 Dowl. 494). The Court will not adopt a strained construction of the law in order to avoid an incongruity or hardship: the error or mistake, if any there be, must be remedied by the Legislature (Lord Foley v Commissioners, 3 Ex 263) Acts of Parliament imposing stamp duties are to be construed according to the plain and ordinary meaning of the words used as it appears from the words themselves, and if a means can be found of carrying out a transaction without incurring liability to stamp duty, the subject is justified in adopting it (*per* Esher, M R., in Commissioners v. Angus & Co, Limited, 23 Q B. D. 579) If there is any doubt as to the meaning of the words, they ought to be construed in favour of the subject, because a tax cannot be imposed without clear and express words for that purpose (*per* Pollock, C.B., in Gurr v Scudd, 11 Ex. R. 190) The Court will intend nothing in favour of stamp duty (Phillipps v Morrison, 13 L. J., Ex. R. 212, 12 M & W 740); but, on the other hand, general words imposing a tax cannot be restrained (Mortimore v Commissioners, 22 L J, Q B. 94; 1 E & B. 54; Wright v. Commissioners, 11 Ex R. 458; 25 L. J, Ex 49).

An instrument must be stamped according to its legal effect and intention

A promissory note stamped as an agreement, and not with the stamp appropriated to a promissory note, cannot be given in evidence, even though bearing the adjudication stamp through the erroneous assessment of the Commissioners (Vallance v Forbes, 6 Rettie, 1099). An instrument purporting to convey real estate, inoperative as a conveyance because not under seal, was held in an old case (Rex v. Ridgwell, 6 B. & C. 666) not to be liable to conveyance duty.

A misdescription of the instrument by the framers thereof does not affect the stamp duty.

(Limmer Asphalte Company v Commissioners, 7 Ex. 211; 41 L. J., Ex. 106.) In Mortgage Insurance Corporation, Limited v Commissioners (21 Q. B. D. 352; 57 L J, Q B. 630) an instrument described as a policy was held to be chargeable under the head "Agreement." In some cases the description will turn the scale, as in British India Steam Navigation Co v Commissioners (7 Q B D 165, 50 L. J., Q B 517), where it was unsuccessfully contended that an instrument entitled "Debenture" was chargeable with lower duty as a promissory note. In Commissioners v. Angus & Co., Limited (23 Q B D. 579), no importance was attached, either in the argument or the judgment, to a clause that the instrument was intended to operate as an agreement only, and not as an assignment.

An instrument must be stamped according to its tenor, if capable of legal operation, though it may fail from some cause *aliunde*.

An instrument purporting to operate as a settlement of £10,000 would be liable to ad valorem duty, whether the money were forthcoming or not.

In determining the liability to duty, regard must be had to the substance of the transaction rather than the form of the instrument.

(Christie v Commissioners, 2 Ex. 46; 36 L. J, Ex. 11, Limmer Asphalte Company v. Commissioners, 7 Ex. 211; 41 L. J, Ex 106, Mortgage Insurance Corporation v Commissioners, *ubi supra*, Belch v Commissioners, 4 Rettie, 4th Series, 592, Wale v Commissioners, 4 Ex Div. 270, Commissioners v Glasgow & South Western Railway Company, 5 App Cases, 315.)

An instrument must be stamped for its leading and principal object (Limmer Asphalte Company v. Commissioners, *ubi supra*), and unless so stamped it cannot be given in evidence for any subordinate object.

In Corder v. Drakeford (3 Taunt. 382) a lease containing also a contract for the sale of fixtures, and stamped with an agreement stamp only, which was then an appropriated stamp, was not allowed to be given in evidence to prove the sale of the fixtures because not stamped as a lease, and in Doe dem. Wyatt v. Stagg (9 L J, O P 73, 3 Jur 1981) an unstamped instrument, which operated as a surrender as well as a disclaimer, was rejected when offered in evidence as a disclaimer (for which no duty would have been chargeable) because it was not stamped as a surrender.

If an instrument is duly stamped for its leading object, the stamp covers everything accessory to that object.

Per Martin, B, in Limmer Asphalte Co v. Commissioners, *ubi supra*, as to a conveyance on sale containing a covenant for payment of the purchase money by instalments; and see Price v. Thomas (2 B & Ad. 218), a lease, a surety joining in the covenant for the payment of the rent, Worthington v. Warrington (5 C B 635), a lease with option of purchase of the property demised, Wolseley v. Cox (2 Q B 321), transfer of shares in a joint stock company, containing a covenant of transferee with the trustees of the deed of settlement to observe all regulations affecting purchasers, Doe dem Croft v Tidbury (14 C. B. 304), conveyance with reservation to grantor of the right of occupation for life of the property conveyed; conveyance with covenant for production of title deeds or assignment of a term in trust to attend (Dart, Ven. & Pur, 6th ed 645); for examples of cases where accessory matter attracts no further duty

An instrument exempt from duty as to its leading object is not rendered liable to duty by anything accessory to that object

Curry v. Edensor (3 T.-R. 524), an agreement for the sale of goods to a broker containing a guarantee against loss on the transaction, Heron v Grainger (5 Esp. 269), an agreement for the sale of goods, containing an indemnity against the possible claim of a third person; Walker v Giles (18 L J,

C P 328; 6 C B 662; 13 Jur 589), a mortgage of leaseholds, exempt under The Building Societies Act, 1836, containing an attornment of the mortgagor to the mortgagee (under seal).

The expression in an instrument of that which the law allows does not render a further stamp necessary

Per Parke, B , in Wroughton *v* Turtle (1 Dow & L 473), where a mortgage redeemable on payment, besides the principal sum advanced, of the fine and cost of renewing a lease for lives, was held to be sufficiently stamped under the old law with duty on the principal sum; and see Lawrence *v.* Boston (21 L J., Ex 49, 7 Ex R 28), Hill *v.* Ransom (12 L J , C P 275), where an agreement that, in consideration of withdrawing a distress at the request of the tenant, the landlord should be at liberty to re-enter and distrain, was held not to be liable to agreement duty.

TABLE OF STAMP ACTS.

The Stamp Act, 1891 (54 & 55 Vict., Ch 39).

The Stamp Duties Management Act, 1891 (54 & 55 Vict, Ch. 38).

The Customs and Inland Revenue Act, 1893 (56 Vict., Ch. 7, Sections 3 and 4)

The Finance Act, 1894 (57 & 58 Vict., Ch. 30, Sections 39 and 40)

THE STAMP ACT, 1891.

(54 & 55 VICT., CHAPTER 39.)

ARRANGEMENT OF SECTIONS

PART I.

REGULATIONS APPLICABLE TO INSTRUMENTS GENERALLY

Charge of Duty upon Instruments.

Section		Page
1.	Charge of Duties in Schedule	15
2	All duties to be paid according to regulations of Act	16
3	How instruments are to be written and stamped	17
4.	Instruments to be separately charged with duty in certain cases	17
5.	Facts and circumstances affecting duty to be set forth in instruments	20
6.	Mode of calculating ad valorem duty in certain cases	21

Use of Adhesive Stamps

7.	Certain adhesive stamps to be applicable to instruments and postal purposes	22
8	General direction as to the cancellation of adhesive stamps	23
9.	Penalty for frauds in relation to adhesive stamps	25

Appropriated Stamps and Denoting Stamps

| 10. | Appropriated stamps | 26 |
| 11 | Denoting stamps | 26 |

Adjudication Stamps

| 12 | Assessment of duty by Commissioners | 27 |
| 13 | Persons dissatisfied may appeal | 30 |

Production of Instruments in Evidence

| 14 | Terms upon which instruments not duly stamped may be received in evidence | 32 |

Sec	*Stamping of Instruments after Execution*	Page
15	Penalty upon stamping instruments after execution	38

Entries upon Rolls, Books, &c.

| 16 | Rolls, books, &c., to be open to inspection | 43 |
| 17 | Penalty for enrolling, &c., instrument not duly stamped | 43 |

PART II.

REGULATIONS APPLICABLE TO PARTICULAR INSTRUMENTS

Admissions.

| 18 | Mode of denoting duty | 48 |
| 19 | Penalty on officers for neglect to make duly stamped documents or entries | 49 |

Admissions to the Degree of a Barrister-at-Law in Ireland, and of Students to the Society of King's Inns, in Dublin

| 20 | Distinct accounts to be kept of certain sums payable to King's Inns, Dublin | 49 |
| 21 | Admission of member of Inn of Court as student of King's Inns | 49 |

Agreements.

| 22 | Duty may be denoted by adhesive stamp | 53 |
| 23 | Certain mortgages of stock to be chargeable as agreements | 61 |

Appraisements

| 24 | Appraisements to be written out | 65 |

Instruments of Apprenticeship

| 25 | Meaning of "instrument of apprenticeship" | 66 |

Articles of Clerkship.

26	Articles in Scotland not to be charged with more than one duty of £60	67
27	Terms upon which articles may be stamped after execution	68
28	Distinct account to be kept of £14 payable to King's Inns	69

Bank Notes, Bills of Exchange, and Promissory Notes.

Sec.		Page
29.	Meaning of "banker" and "bank note"	70
30.	Bank notes may be re-issued	71
31.	Penalties for issuing or receiving an unstamped bank note	71
32.	Meaning of "bill of exchange"	75
33.	Meaning of "promissory note"	78
34.	Provisions for use of adhesive stamps on bills and notes	80
35.	Provisions as to stamping foreign bills and notes	81
36.	As to bills and notes purporting to be drawn abroad	82
37.	Terms upon which bills and notes may be stamped after execution	83
38.	Penalty for issuing, &c., any unstamped bill or note	83
39.	One bill only of a set need be stamped	84

Bills of Lading.

40.	Bills of lading	84

Bills of Sale.

41.	Bills of sale	85

Bonds given in Relation to the Duties of Excise.

42.	Bonds not to include goods, &c., belonging to more than one person	89

Certificates of Solicitors and others

43.	Penalty for practising without certificate, or making false statement on application for certificate	91
44.	Penalty on unqualified persons preparing instruments	92
45.	One certificate only required	93
46.	Solicitors' certificates in England and Ireland	93
47.	Other certificates	94
48.	Date and duration of certain certificates	94

Charter-parties.

49.	Provisions as to duty on charter-party	96
50.	Charter-parties executed abroad	96
51.	Terms upon which charter-parties may be stamped after execution	96

Contract Notes.

Sec		Page
52	Provisions as to contract notes	98
53	Penalty for not making a stamped note	99

Conveyances on Sale

54.	Meaning of "conveyance on sale"	101
55	How ad valorem duty to be calculated in respect of stock and securities	108
56	How consideration consisting of periodical payments to be charged	109
57.	How conveyance in consideration of a debt, &c., to be charged	110
58.	Direction as to duty in certain cases	114
59	Certain contracts to be chargeable as conveyances on sale	116
60	As to sale of an annuity or right not before in existence	121
61	Principal instrument, how to be ascertained	121

Conveyances on any Occasion except Sale or Mortgage.

62	What is to be deemed a conveyance on any occasion, not being a sale or mortgage	122

Attested Copies and Extracts

63	Stamping of certain copies and extracts after attestation	124

Certified Copies and Extracts from Registers of Births, &c

64	Duty may be denoted by adhesive stamp	125

Copyhold and Customary Estates.

65	Provisions as to payment of duty	126
66	Facts affecting duty to be stated in note	127
67	Steward to make out duly stamped copies	128
68.	Steward may refuse to proceed except on payment of his fees and duty	128

Delivery Orders

69	Provisions as to duty on delivery order	132
70.	Penalty for use of unstamped or untrue order	133
71	By whom duty on delivery order to be paid	133

Duplicates and Counterparts

72	Provisions as to duplicates and counterparts	135

Sec	*Exchange and Partition or Division*	Page
73.	As to exchange, &c.	136

Grants of Honours and Dignities.

| 74. | Duty to be charged in respect of highest rank | 139 |

Leases

75	Agreements for not more than thirty-five years to be charged as leases	144
76.	Leases, how to be charged in respect of produce, &c	145
77.	Directions as to duty in certain cases	146
78.	Duty in certain cases may be denoted by adhesive stamp	147

Letters of Allotment or Renunciation, Scrip Certificates, and Scrip.

| 79. | Provisions as to letters of allotment, &c. | 149 |

Letters or Powers of Attorney and Voting Papers

| 80 | Provisions as to proxies and voting papers | 152 |
| 81 | Power relating to Government stocks, how to be charged | 153 |

Marketable Securities

82.	Meaning of "marketable securities" for charge of duty	159
83	Penalty on issuing, &c., foreign, &c., security not duly stamped	161
84	Foreign or colonial securities may be stamped without penalty	162
85.	*Repealed*	162

Mortgages, &c

86	Meaning of "mortgage"	167
87	Direction as to duty in certain cases	172
88	Security for future advances, how to be charged	173
89	Exemption from stamp duty in favour of benefit building societies restricted	175

Notarial Acts.

| 90 | Duty may be denoted by adhesive stamp | 176 |

Policies of Insurance.

| 91 | Meaning of "policy of insurance" | 177 |

ARRANGEMENT OF SECTIONS

Policies of Sea Insurance.

Sec		Page
92.	Meaning of "policy of sea insurance"	177
93.	Contract to be in writing	178
94.	Policy for voyage and time chargeable with two duties	179
95	No policy valid unless duly stamped	179
96	Legal alterations in policies may be made under certain restrictions	180
97.	Penalty on assuring unless policy duly stamped	180

Policies of Insurance except Policies of Sea Insurance.

98	Meaning of "policy of life insurance" and "policy of insurance against accident"	183
99	Duty on certain policies may be denoted by adhesive stamp	184
100	Penalty for not making out policy, or making, &c., any policy not duly stamped	184

Receipts.

101	Provisions as to duty upon receipts	187
102	Terms upon which receipts may be stamped after execution	189
103	Penalty for offences in reference to receipts	190

Settlements

104.	As to settlement of policy or security	194
105	Settlements, when not to be charged as securities	196
106	Where several instruments, one only to be charged with ad valorem duty	197

Share Warrants.

107	Penalty for issuing share warrant not duly stamped	198

Stock Certificates to Bearer.

108	Meaning of "stock certificate to bearer"	198
109	Penalty for issuing stock certificate unstamped	199

Transfers of Shares in Cost Book Mines.

110	Duty may be denoted by adhesive stamp	200

Warrants for Goods.

111.	Provisions as to warrants for goods	201

PART III.

SUPPLEMENTAL.

Duty on Capital of Companies.

Sec		Page
112	Charge of duty on capital of limited liability companies	204
113.	Charge of duty on capital of companies with limited liability otherwise than under the Companies Acts	204

Composition for certain Stamp Duties.

114	Composition for stamp duty on transfers of Canadian and colonial stock	205
115.	Composition for stamp duty by county councils, &c.	207
116.	Composition for stamp duty on policies of insurance against accident	209

Miscellaneous.

117.	Conditions and agreements as to stamp duty void	210
118.	Assignment of policy of life assurance to be stamped before payment of money assured	210
119	Instruments relating to Crown property	212
120	As to instruments charged with duty of thirty-five shillings	212
121.	Recovery of penalties	212
122.	Definitions	213

Repeal, Commencement, Short Title.

123.	Repeal	214
124.	Commencement	214
125.	Short Title	214

THE CUSTOMS AND INLAND REVENUE ACT, 1898.
(56 Vict, Chapter 7.)

Sec		Page
3.	As to stamp duty on contract notes	99
4.	Repeal of annual duties in respect of maketable securities, and foreign or colonial share certificates	158

THE FINANCE ACT, 1894
(57 & 58 Vict, Chapter 30.)

Sec.		Page
39	Composition for certain stamp duties (Extension of 54 & 55 Vict c 39, sec 114)	206
40	Exemption of coupons from stamp duty	74

NOTE.

The references in *Italics* after the Sections of The Stamp Act, 1891, as, for instance, after Section 1—

(33 & 34 Vict , Ch 97, Sec 3)

indicate the repealed enactment from which the existing Section is derived.

THE STAMP ACT, 1891.

(54 & 55 Vict., Chapter 39.)

An Act to Consolidate the Enactments granting and relating to the Stamp Duties upon Instruments and certain other Enactments relating to Stamp Duties. [21st July, 1891.

BE IT ENACTED by the Queen's Most Excellent Majesty, by and with the advice and consent of the Lords Spiritual and Temporal, and Commons, in this present Parliament assembled, and by the authority of the same, as follows:

PART I.

Regulations Applicable to Instruments Generally.

Charge of Duty upon Instruments.

1. From and after the commencement of this Act the stamp duties to be charged for the use of Her Majesty upon the several instruments specified in the First Schedule to this Act shall be the several duties in the said Schedule specified, which duties shall be in substitution for the duties theretofore chargeable under the enactments repealed by this Act, and shall be subject to the exemptions contained in this Act and in any other Act for the time being in force. [Charge of duties in Schedule.]

(33 & 34 Vict., Ch 97, Sec 3)

Acts relating to a particular branch of revenue are *in pari materiâ*, and are to be construed as one code See, as to legacy duty, *in re* Cholmondeley (1 C. & M. 149); as to excise, Reg. v Ingham (21 Q B. D 47).

A liberal interpretation is given to exemptions, especially to those intended to promote the interests of trade and commerce; see Agreement, *post*, p 55 An instrument exempt from duty by reference to its primary object is not made chargeable by reason of any provision accessory to that object (*Introduction*, p 3), but if the additional matter is separate and distinct, the instrument is chargeable with duty as if it were made for that matter only. (Skrine v Elmore, 2 Campbell, 457, South v Finch, 3 Bing, N. C 506; Mayfield v Robinson, 14 L J, Q B 205, 7 A & E, N. S 486; Horsfall v. Hey, 17 L J, Ex 266.) Thus an agreement under hand for the sale of stock-in-trade, goodwill, and book debts is chargeable with duty upon the price of the goodwill and book debts under Section 59, and exempt as regards the stock-in-trade

If exemption from duty is claimed, the burden of proof lies upon the person claiming the benefit of the exemption. (Pinner v. Arnold, 2 C. M. & R 613; Tyr. & G. 1; Yelland v Winter, 50 J. P. 38)

An exemption in a statute not relating to stamp duties is construed by relation to the scope and purposes of the statute, rather than the generality of the words of the exemption (Royal Liver Friendly Society v Commissioners, 5 Ex 78; Attorney-General v. Gilpin, 6 Ex. 193)

The exemptions in the following Acts have been repealed —

Public Works Loans Act (3 Geo. IV, Ch 86, and Acts therein recited), by The Public Works Loans Act, 1875 (38 & 39 Vict, Ch 89).

Public Health Act, 1848 (11 & 12 Vict, Ch 63), by The Public Health Act, 1872 (35 & 36 Vict, Ch. 79, Sec 42)

Industrial and Provident Societies Act, 1867 (30 & 31 Vict., Ch 117, Sec. 3), by The Industrial and Provident Societies Act, 1876 (39 & 40 Vict, Ch. 45).

All duties to be paid according to regulations of Act

2. All stamp duties for the time being chargeable by law upon any instruments are to be paid and denoted according to the regulations in this Act contained, and, except where express provision is made to the contrary are to be denoted by impressed stamps only.

(33 & 34 Vict, Ch. 96, Secs 6 and 23)

The general regulations in Part I of this Act govern all instruments chargeable with duty, except where express provision to the contrary is made by the regulations applicable to particular instruments in Part II; while the latter are applicable only to the particular instruments to which they relate, or with which they are connected by cross references.

As to the instruments for which adhesive stamps may be used, see note to Sections 7 and 8

3. (1) Every instrument written upon stamped material is to be written in such manner, and every instrument partly or wholly written before being stamped is to be so stamped, that the stamp may appear on the face of the instrument, and cannot be used for or applied to any other instrument written upon the same piece of material.

(2) If more than one instrument be written upon the same piece of material, every one of the instruments is to be separately and distinctly stamped with the duty with which it is chargeable.

(33 & 34 Vict., Ch 97, Sec 7.)

How instruments are to be written and stamped

This Sub-section applies only to separate instruments, not to one instrument relating to several distinct matters, for which see the next Section.

A memorandum endorsed upon an instrument is liable to a separate duty, unless it is merely declaratory, and not of itself chargeable as a deed or memorandum of agreement Under the old law a memorandum, endorsed on an arbitration bond, that the parties had met on a later day than that named in the bond, and proceeded with the arbitration by consent, was held in Stephens v Lowe (2 Moore & Scott, 44) to be liable to separate duty; and the same was held of an endorsement whereby parties to a contract for sale agreed to postpone completion for a few days (Bacon v Simpson, 3 M. & W 78), also of an endorsement on a deed for securing an annuity, that at the time of the execution of the deed it was agreed that the annuity should be redeemable at six months' notice (Schumann v Weatherhead, 1 East, 537); also of a memorandum endorsed on a mortgage deed that part of the money secured had been advanced by another (Doe dem. Downe v Govier, 5 L. T R 37) An endorsement controlling an instrument which *ex facie* is a promissory note renders the two liable to one stamp as an agreement. (Leeds v. Lancashire, 2 Camp 205; Harley v. Wilkinson, 4 Camp 127, 4 M & S 25, Cholmeley v. Darley, 14 L. J, Ex. 328, 14 M & W. 344) A memorandum explanatory of an ambiguity in an instrument is not liable to duty, unless under seal, when it should be stamped as a deed.

4. Except where express provision to the contrary is made by this or any other Act—

Instruments to be separately

charged with duty in certain cases

(a) An instrument containing or relating to several distinct matters is to be separately and distinctly charged, as if it were a separate instrument, with duty in respect of each of the matters;

(b) An instrument made for any consideration in respect whereof it is chargeable with ad valorem duty, and also for any further or other valuable consideration or considerations, is to be separately and distinctly charged, as if it were a separate instrument, with duty in respect of each of the considerations

(33 & 34 Vict., Ch. 97, Sec. 8.)

An instrument which contains two or more operative parts, each falling under a specific head of charge, must be stamped with the appropriate duty for each operation e g, an instrument containing an appointment of new trustees and a conveyance of the trust property, 10s and 10s (Hadgett v Commissioners, 3 Ex Div 46, 37 L T R. 612), an instrument containing a conveyance not specially charged (Section 62) and a covenant for the payment of a sum of money, 10s and ad valorem covenant duty (Limmer Asphalte Co v Commissioners, 7 Ex 211, 41 L J, Ex. 106). A conveyance on sale operating also as a mortgage is liable to both duties (2 Dart, Ven & Pur 6th ed 798; and Section 87 [6])

If an instrument chargeable with a specific duty has an operation not accessory to the effectuation of the object in respect of which it is primarily chargeable, such operation not attracting another ad valorem duty, it must be stamped with a further duty of 10s as a deed if under seal, or 6d if under hand only Examples Lease with contract for sale of fixtures, liable to lease duty and 10s (Corder v Drakeford, 3 Taunt 382; Clayton v Burdenshaw, 5 B & C 41), lease with option of purchase of property other than that demised, lease duty and 10s. (Lovelock v Frankland, 19 L J, Q B 182, 8 A & E. 371), settlement of definite sums of money and proceeds of sale of real estate yet unsold, settlement duty and 10s (Stucley v Commissioners, 5 Ex 85)

Where an instrument operates as several conveyances or leases, separate duties, whether ad valorem or fixed, are required In Freeman v Commissioners (6 Ex 101) a conveyance by executors to four residuary legatees of shares in companies "to hold to them respectively" was held liable to four stamps. See also "Conveyance," p. 100, and "Lease," p. 140, and Index, under "INSTRUMENT Several Matters."

An instrument which includes several contracts with different persons requires separate stamps, as in Worthington v Francis (5 Esp 182), a contract by A B with parties whose names were subscribed for purchase of quantities, &c., set opposite their names, and Doe dem Copley v Day (13 East, 241), an agreement for letting lands in a similar form.

Upon a sale by auction in separate lots a distinct contract arises upon the sale of each lot and separate stamps are required if the same person purchases two or more lots (Emmerson v. Heelis, 2 Taunt 38; James v. Shore, 1 Stark 426; Roots v Lord Dormer, 4 B & Ad 77, 1 N & M 667.) But these separate contracts may be combined in one written contract (Baldey v Parker, 2 B. & C 37), which would then be liable to one stamp only.

An instrument to which several persons are parties is, however, liable to one duty only if it is entered into for a common object, or if there is a community of interest in the subject matter, as in Bowen v Ashley (1 New Reports, 274), several bond of several musicians in the penalty of £100 to attend the meetings of a harmonic society; Davis v. Williams (13 East, 232), agreement of several persons to subscribe for constructing a dock, Goodson v Forbes (1 Marsh, 525) and Allen v Morrison (8 B. & C. 565), agreement of underwriters to policies in relation to subject matter of policies, Ramsbottom v Davies (4 M & W 584; 7 Dowl 175, H & H. 464), agreement by four persons severally in consideration of the discharge of a debt by another to indemnify him to the extent of £50 apiece. In all these cases one stamp was deemed sufficient, for no one of the parties would have entered into these engagements if the others had not agreed also (per cur. Ramsbottom v Davies, supra). In Doe dem Croft v Tidbury (14 C B 304), conveyance by several persons, encroachers upon a waste, of all their encroachments to the lord of the manor, with liberty of occupation during life, for the common object of extinguishing their rights after death, was held liable to one stamp only.

In Boulton v Commissioners (5 Ex 82), a lease made in consideration of a rent and the covenant of the lessee to complete buildings in course of erection, the covenant of the lessee was held to be a further valuable consideration within 17 & 18 Vict., Ch 83, Sec 16, the terms of which were substantially the same as those of the present law, and the deed stamp was charged in addition to the ad valorem duty. The case was set aside as to leases by 33 & 34 Vict, Ch 14, repeated with verbal alterations by Section 98 (2) of The Stamp Act, 1870, and Section 77 (2) of this Act, but it illustrates the principle

Assessments of common occurrence in practice are—

Lease for a definite rent and an indefinite royalty, or conveyance for a definite sum and an indefinite royalty ad valorem duty and 10s

Conveyance (as of a beer-house) for a definite sum, and a covenant to pay a further definite sum upon a contingency (as upon obtaining a spirit licence) ad valorem conveyance duty on the former sum, and ad valorem covenant duty upon the latter.

Conveyance in consideration of a ground rent certainly payable, and a further ground rent payable in the event of the premises being used for trade, &c ad valorem conveyance duty under Section 56 upon the certain rent and 10s, unless the ad valorem conveyance duty calculated upon the aggregate of both rents amounts to a less sum, in which case such ad valorem duty is charged

For other examples see Index, under "INSTRUMENT."

Note that ad valorem duty is always chargeable where the consideration, although not expressed on the face of the instrument, is ascertainable (Parry v Deere, 5 A. & E 551, 2 H & W 395, Ulverston or Furness Railway Company v Commissioners, 2 H. & C. 855, 33 L J, Ex 173, 10 L T.R 161)

Facts and circumstances affecting duty to be set forth in instruments

5. All the facts and circumstances affecting the liability of any instrument to duty, or the amount of the duty with which any instrument is chargeable, are to be fully and truly set forth in the instrument; and every person who, with intent to defraud Her Majesty—

(a) Executes any instrument in which all the said facts and circumstances are not fully and truly set forth; or

(b) Being employed or concerned in or about the preparation of any instrument, neglects or omits fully and truly to set forth therein all the said facts and circumstances,

shall incur a fine of ten pounds

(33 & 34 Vict., Ch 97, Sec 10)

The penalty is not enforceable if the duty actually paid is that which would have been payable if all the facts,

&c, had been set forth in the instrument, for the far more stringent provisions of the old law (48 Geo III, Ch 149, Secs 22 to 26) were considered by Pollock, C B, in The Furness Railway Company v Commissioners (33 L. J., Ex. 173), where the consideration was ascertainable by reference to another instrument, to be directory rather than obligatory. *See* also Parry *v.* Deere (5 A. & E 551, 2 H & W. 395). The point is of everyday occurrence in assessing the duty upon settlements; and *see* Section 12 (2)

6. (1) Where an instrument is chargeable with ad valorem duty in respect of— Mode of calculating ad valorem duty in certain cases

(*a*) Any money in any foreign or colonial currency, or

(*b*) Any stock or marketable security,

the duty shall be calculated on the value, on the day of the date of the instrument, of the money in British currency according to the current rate of exchange, or of the stock or security according to the average price thereof.

"Stock" includes "Shares" *See* Sec. 122, *post*, p. 213

(2) Where an instrument contains a statement of current rate of exchange, or average price, as the case may require, and is stamped in accordance with that statement, it is, so far as regards the subject matter of the statement, to be deemed duly stamped, unless or until it is shown that the statement is untrue, and that the instrument is in fact insufficiently stamped

(33 & 34 Vict., Ch 97, Secs. 11, 12, and 13)

The value of shares or marketable securities that are not quoted or sold in any stock market should be based upon the average of the latest private transactions, which can generally be ascertained from the secretary or other proper officer of the particular company or corporation. If there have been no dealings, the value is to be taken at par

The correctness of a statement of current rate of exchange or average price is, of course, always tested upon adjudication by reference to published lists

In Foster (John) & Sons, Limited, v Commissioners (1894, 1 Q B 516) duty was assessed by the Commissioners upon the value of property conveyed—not the nominal value of shares and debentures, which was a much greater amount   See post, p 103

Use of Adhesive Stamps.

Certain adhesive stamps to be applicable to instruments and postal purposes

7. Any stamp duties of an amount not exceeding two shillings and sixpence upon instruments which are permitted by law to be denoted by adhesive stamps not appropriated by any word or words on the face of them to any particular description of instrument, and any postage duties of the like amount, may be denoted by the same adhesive stamps

(45 & 46 Vict, Ch 72, Sec 13)

Adhesive stamps are to be used for the following instruments—

Bills of exchange or promissory notes drawn or made out of the United Kingdom. (Sec 34 [2])

Contract notes liable to the duty of one shilling (Sec 52 [3])

The following instruments may be stamped either with an adhesive stamp or an impressed stamp—

Agreements under hand only liable to the fixed duty of sixpence (Sec 22)

Bills of exchange (including cheques) for the payment of money on demand (Sec 34 [1])

Certified copies of or extracts from registers of births, &c. (Sec 64)

Charter-parties (Sec 49 [2].)

Contract notes liable to the duty of one penny (Sec. 52 [3])

Delivery orders. (Sec. 69 [3])

Lease or tack or agreement for a lease or tack, and duplicate or counterpart thereof

    For any definite term, not exceeding a year, of a dwelling house, or part of a dwelling house, at a rent not exceeding the rate of £10 a year

    For any definite term less than a year of a furnished dwelling house or apartments (Sec 73 [1].)

Letters of renunciation (Sec 79 [2])

Notarial's (Sec. 90.)
Policies of insurance (not life or sea). (Sec. 99.)
Protests of bills of exchange or promissory notes (Sec. 90.)
Proxies liable to the duty of one penny only. (Sec. 80 [2].)
Receipts (Sec. 101 [2].)
Transfers of shares in cost-book mines (Sec 110.)
Voting papers. (Sec. 80 [2].)
Warrants for goods (Sec 111 [2].)

8. (1) An instrument, the duty upon which is required or permitted by law to be denoted by an adhesive stamp, is not to be deemed duly stamped with an adhesive stamp unless the person required by law to cancel the adhesive stamp cancels the same by writing on or across the stamp his name or initials, or the name or initials of his firm, together with the true date of his so writing, or otherwise effectively cancels the stamp and renders the same incapable of being used for any other instrument, or for any postal purpose, or unless it is otherwise proved that the stamp appearing on the instrument was affixed thereto at the proper time.

General direction as to the cancellation of adhesive stamps.

(2) Where two or more adhesive stamps are used to denote the stamp duty upon an instrument, each or every stamp is to be cancelled in the manner aforesaid.

(3) Every person who, being required by law to cancel an adhesive stamp, neglects or refuses duly and effectually to do so in the manner aforesaid, shall incur a fine of ten pounds.

(33 & 34 Vict., Ch 97, Sec 24, 45 & 46 Vict., Ch 72, Sec 14.)

"Duly stamped" (1) has not the same meaning here as in Section 33, and this Section does not apply to the adhesive stamps used for foreign bills of exchange and promissory notes. (Bradlaugh v De Rin, 18 L T R., C P. 904; Marc v. Rony, 31 L T R., Q B. 872.)

An adhesive stamp cannot legally be affixed to an instrument after signature and delivery, except to a charter-party under the provisions of Section 50, and a bill of exchange payable on demand under Section 38 (2).

As to the defacement of adhesive stamps, *see* Section 20 of The Stamp Duties Management Act, 1891, *post*, p 235 —

"Every person who by any writing in any manner defaces any adhesive stamp before it is used shall incur a fine of five pounds Provided that any person may with the express sanction of the Commissioners, and in conformity with the conditions which they may prescribe, write upon or otherwise appropriate an adhesive stamp before it is used for the purpose of identification thereof."

Adhesive stamps are to be cancelled as follows —

Agreement by the person by whom the agreement is first executed. (Sec 22)

Bill of exchange payable on demand by the person by whom the bill is signed before he delivers it out of his hands, custody, or power. (Sec 34 [1])

Foreign bills and notes by the person into whose hands the bill or note comes before it is stamped (Sec 35 [1])

Charter party by the person by whom it is last executed, or by whose execution it is completed as a binding contract (Sec 49 [2])

Contract note by the person by whom the note is executed (Sec 52 [4])

Certified copies and extracts from registers of births, &c by the person by whom the copy is signed before he delivers the same out of his hands, custody, or power (Sec 64)

Delivery order by the person by whom the instrument is made, executed, or issued. (Sec 69 [3])

Lease of a dwelling house at rent not exceeding £10 per annum, or furnished dwelling house or apartments, and duplicate or counterpart thereof by the person by whom the instrument is first executed. (Sec 78)

Letter of renunciation by the person by whom the letter of renunciation is executed (Sec. 79 [2])

Notarial act, protest of a bill or note by the notary (Sec 90)

Policy other than sea or life by the person by whom the policy is first executed (Sec 99)

Proxy or voting paper liable to the duty of one penny by the person by whom the instrument is executed. (Sec. 80 [2])

Receipt by the person by whom the receipt is given before he delivers it out of his hands (Sec 101 [2])

Transfer of shares in cost book mines by the person by whom the request, authority, or notice is written or executed. (Sec 110 [1])

Warrant for goods by the person by whom the instrument is made, executed, or issued. (Sec. 111 [2])

9. (1) If any person—

(a) Fraudulently removes or causes to be removed from any instrument any adhesive stamp, or affixes to any other instrument or uses for any postal purpose any adhesive stamp which has been so removed, with intent that the stamp may be used again; or

(b) Sells or offers for sale, or utters, any adhesive stamp which has been so removed, or utters any instrument having thereon any adhesive stamp which has to his knowledge been so removed as aforesaid;

he shall, in addition to any other fine or penalty to which he may be liable, incur a fine of fifty pounds.

Penalty for frauds in relation to adhesive stamps

(2) The expression "instrument" in this Section includes any post letter as defined by The Post Office Protection Act, 1884, and the cover of any post letter.

47 & 48 Vic. c. 76.

(33 & 34 Vict, Ch 97, Sec 25; 45 & 46 Vict, Ch 72, Sec 15)

The definition in The Post Office Protection Act, 1884 (Section 19 [1]), is as follows:—

The expression "post letter" shall mean a postal packet, as defined by this Act, from the time of its being delivered to a post office to the time of its being delivered to the person to whom it is addressed, and a delivery of a postal packet of any description to a letter carrier or other person authorised to receive postal packets of that description for the post shall be a delivery to the post office; and a delivery at the house or office of the person to whom the postal packet is addressed, or to him or to his servant or agent, or other person considered to be authorised to receive the postal packet according to the usual manner of delivering that person's postal packets, shall be a delivery to the person addressed.

Appropriated Stamps and Denoting Stamps

Appropriated stamps

10. (1) A stamp which by any word or words on the face of it is appropriated to any particular description of instrument is not to be used, or, if used, is not to be available, for an instrument of any other description.

(2) An instrument falling under the particular description to which any stamp is so appropriated as aforesaid is not to be deemed duly stamped unless it is stamped with the stamp so appropriated

(33 & 34 *Vict*, *Ch.* 97, *Sec.* 9.)

In Ashling v Boon (64 L T R 193, 39 W R) an instrument liable to duty as a promissory note, stamped with a penny "Postage and Inland Revenue" stamp only, was not allowed to be given in evidence to prove payment of the sum in dispute.

The appropriated stamps are :—
Impressed—
    Bill or Note —For bills of exchange (payable otherwise than on demand or at sight or on presentation) and promissory notes purporting to be drawn or made in the United Kingdom.

Adhesive—
    Bill or Note.—For bills of exchange (payable otherwise than on demand or at sight or on presentation) and promissory notes purporting to be drawn or made out of the United Kingdom

    Contract Note.—One Shilling duty.

For the special terms on which bills or notes written on material bearing an *impressed* stamp of sufficient amount but improper denomination may be stamped, *see* Section 37, *post*, p 83

Denoting stamps

11. Where the duty with which an instrument is chargeable depends in any manner upon the duty paid upon another instrument, the payment of the last-mentioned duty shall, upon application to the Commissioners and production of both the instruments, be denoted upon the first-mentioned instrument in such manner as the Commissioners think fit

(33 & 34 *Vict*, *Ch* 97, *Sec* 14.)

The denoting stamps used are—

(1) Duplicate denoting stamp ("Duplicate or Counterpart Original stamped with £—"), required upon duplicates and counterparts (stamped with five shillings) of instrument liable to a higher duty than five shillings. If the duty on the original does not exceed five shillings, the duplicate or counterpart must be stamped with the same amount of duty, and does not require a denoting stamp, being stamped as an original instrument (Sec 72, *post*, p 135)

(2) Duty paid denoting stamp ("Duty Paid, ad valorem, £—"), required upon collateral, &c, securities stamped with sixpence per £100 under the head "Mortgage," &c (2), securities by way of further charge under Section 87 (3), substituted security to bearer, lease stamped with sixpence, made in conformity with an agreement stamped with ad valorem lease duty (Sec 75); conveyances made in pursuance of a contract upon which ad valorem conveyance duty has been paid under Section 59.

(3) Substituted security ("Original Security Duly Stamped") and ("Original Security stamped 10s per cent"), used instead of (2) when substituted securities are stamped in large batches, and only given upon substituted securities which are to be issued to the identical holders of the primary securities

In order to obtain the denoting stamps (1) and (2) the instruments bearing the higher duty, as well as those to be denoted, must be sent to the chief office through the local distributor of stamps, or produced at the Solicitor's Department, Somerset House, between the hours of ten and two (one on Saturdays)

The denoting stamp does not afford the protection against objections relating to duty given by the adjudication stamp under Section 12 (5), but it is not granted (except in very doubtful cases) unless the officials are satisfied that the original or primary instrument is stamped with the proper duty.

Adjudication Stamps

12. (1) Subject to such regulations as the Commissioners may think fit to make, the Commissioners may be required by any person to express their opinion with reference to any executed instrument upon the following questions—

(a) Whether it is chargeable with any duty;
(b) With what amount of duty it is chargeable

Assessment of duty by Commissioners

(2) The Commissioners may require to be furnished with an abstract of the instrument, and also with such evidence as they may deem necessary, in order to show to their satisfaction whether all the facts and circumstances affecting the liability of the instrument to duty, or the amount of the duty chargeable thereon, are fully and truly set forth therein

(3) If the Commissioners are of opinion that the instrument is not chargeable with any duty, it may be stamped with a particular stamp denoting that it is not chargeable with any duty.

(4) If the Commissioners are of opinion that the instrument is chargeable with duty, they shall assess the duty with which it is in their opinion chargeable, and when the instrument is stamped in accordance with the assessment it may be stamped with a particular stamp denoting that it is duly stamped.

(5) Every instrument stamped with the particular stamp denoting either that it is not chargeable with any duty, or is duly stamped, shall be admissible in evidence, and available for all purposes notwithstanding any objection relating to duty.

(6) Provided as follows :—

(*a*) An instrument upon which the duty has been assessed by the Commissioners shall not, if it is unstamped or insufficiently stamped, be stamped otherwise than in accordance with the assessment·

(*b*) Nothing in this Section shall extend to any instrument chargeable with ad valorem duty, and made as a security for money or stock without limit, or shall authorise the stamping after the execution thereof of any instrument which by law cannot be stamped after execution

(*c*) A statutory declaration made for the purpose of this Section shall not be used against any person making the same in any proceeding whatever, except in an inquiry as to the duty with which the instrument to which it relates is chargeable; and every person by whom any such declaration is made shall, on payment of the duty chargeable upon the instrument to which it relates, be relieved from any fine or disability to which he may be liable by reason of the omission to state truly in the instrument any fact or circumstance required by this Act to be stated therein.

(33 & 34 Vict., Ch. 97, Secs. 18 and 20.)

An instrument falling under (b) of Sub-section 6 would not be protected by the adjudication stamp—the "particular stamp" mentioned in Sub-sections (4) and (5)—against an objection relating to duty. In Vallance v. Forbes (6 Rettie, 4th Series, 1099) the Commissioners had adjudged an instrument as being chargeable with the duty of sixpence as an agreement, but the Court of Session held it to be a promissory note, and refused to allow it to be given in evidence, although stamped with the adjudication stamp. Again, *in re* The Belfort (L. R., 9 Probate, 215), the adjudication of the Commissioners upon a charter-party was questioned upon the ground that the stamping of the instrument was prohibited by Section 68 of The Stamp Act, 1870, the terms of which are identical with Section 51 of this Act. In Morgan v Pike (14 C. B 473), a security without limit, stamped with the adjudication stamp, was put in evidence, and the Court, treating the adjudication stamp as a nullity, held that the security was good only for the amount it was stamped to cover

For the new provision for increasing the duty upon a security without limit *see* Section 88 (3)

An instrument stamped with the adjudication stamp is admissible in evidence, though the assessment of duty is incorrect in amount (Prudential Assurance Society v. Curzon, 22 L. J, Ex. 85, 8 Ex R 97.)

The Commissioners require the instrument, together with a full abstract thereof, to be produced at the office of the Solicitor of Inland Revenue between 10 a.m and 4 p m, accompanied by a warrant (provided by them) stating the date and description of the instrument, the names and addresses of the parties thereto, the date of the application for adjudication, the name and address of the applicant, and the amount of duty, if any, with which the instrument is stamped The abstract should contain a full abstract of the recitals and operative parts of the instrument, but mere common form may be disregarded; and if the instrument is a short one, it is better to furnish a copy than an abstract.

The abstract of a settlement should be accompanied by a valuation of the stocks and securities settled The valuation may be made by a stockbroker, or by the applicant himself from prices quoted in the *Times* or any authorised stock and share list, or, where there is no quotation, in the manner indicated in the note to Section 6, *ante*, p 21 If a reversionary interest in a trust fund is settled, particulars should be given of the investment of the fund at the date of the settlement and the settlor's interest therein; and if the settlement contains a covenant to settle other and after-acquired property, a statement should be made whether the covenantor is entitled in possession or reversion, or, in default of the exercise of any power of appointment, to any property bound by the covenant.

The abstract of an instrument of dissolution of partnership should be accompanied by a copy of the balance-sheet, or statement of account between the partners, showing the amount of the liabilities and the share of the outgoing partner in the partnership; the abstract of a conveyance on sale of property subject to a mortgage, by a statement of the amount owing for principal (and interest, if any and the purchaser undertakes payment thereof) at the date of the conveyance, the abstract of an instrument chargeable under Section 59, by an apportionment of the purchase-money among the different heads of property included in the contract, showing especially the price of goodwill, patents, trade-marks, book debts, and benefit of contracts *See* the table on p. 120, *post*

Adjudication cannot be conducted by correspondence, and the personal attendance of the applicant, or a solicitor or agent, or a law stationer skilled in such matters, is required in all cases

Persons dissatisfied may appeal

13. (1) Any person who is dissatisfied with the assessment of the Commissioners may, within twenty-one days after the date of the assessment, and on payment of duty in conformity therewith, appeal against the assessment to the High Court of the part of the United Kingdom in which the case has arisen, and may for that purposes require the Commissioners to state and sign a case, setting forth the question upon which their opinion was required, and the assessment made by them

(2) The Commissioners shall thereupon state and sign a case and deliver the same to the person by whom it is required, and the case may, within seven days thereafter, be set down by him for hearing.

(3) Upon the hearing of the case the Court shall determine the question submitted, and, if the instrument in question is in the opinion of the Court chargeable with any duty, shall assess the duty with which it is chargeable.

(4) If it is decided by the Court that the assessment of the Commissioners is erroneous, any excess of duty which may have been paid in conformity with the erroneous assessment, together with any fine or penalty which may have been paid in consequence thereof, shall be ordered by the Court to be repaid to the appellant, with or without costs as the Court may determine

(5) If the assessment of the Commissioners is confirmed, the Court may make an order for payment to the Commissioners of the costs incurred by them in relation to the appeal.

(33 & 34 Vict, Ch 97, Sec 19)

The limitation to seven days of the time within which a case may be set down for hearing after it has been delivered to the appellants is new. Under the old law there was no limit

After the case has been set down for hearing, points for argument must be exchanged between the parties, and should disclose all the points intended to be raised If a point not so disclosed should be raised in the argument, the Court would probably adjourn the case

The power now given to the Court to refuse costs to a successful appellant is new.

Upon the hearing of the case the appellant has the right to begin, upon the hypothesis that he has tendered a sum as sufficient stamp duty and the Commissioners have declined to accept it, and to reply The Crown has the right to a general reply (Marquis of Chandos v Commissioners, 6 Ex

R. 464, Potter v Commissioners, 10 Ex R. 147, 23 L J, Ex. 345; Conservators of River Thames v Commissioners, 18 Q B D 279, 56 L J, Q B 181) In the Divisional Court one counsel only is heard on each side Since the passing of The Appellate Jurisdiction Act, 1876, appeals have been made against the decisions of the Divisional Court to the Court of Appeal in Commissioners v. Mortgage Insurance Corporation, Limited (21 Q B D 352); Commissioners v. Angus & Company, Limited (23 Q. B. D. 579); Onslow v Commissioners ([1891] 1 Q B 239); Great Western Railway Company v Commissioners ([1894], 1 Q B 507), and Foster (John) & Sons, Limited, v Commissioners ([1894], 1 Q B 516), and from the Court of Session to the House of Lords in Commissioners v Glasgow & South Western Railway Company (12 App. Ca. 315).

A decision of the Queen's Bench Division upon a case stated by the Commissioners under the corresponding section (19) of The Stamp Act, 1870, was held in Onslow v. Commissioners (25 Q B D 465; 38 W. R. 728) to be a "judgment," not an order, and an appeal from such a decision must be brought within twenty-one days (R S C 1883, Order LVIII. 9 to 15) But under the special circumstances of that case the time for appeal was extended

Production of Instruments in Evidence.

Terms upon which instruments not duly stamped may be received in evidence

14. (1) Upon the production of an instrument chargeable with any duty as evidence in any Court of Civil Judicature in any part of the United Kingdom, or before any arbitrator or referee, notice shall be taken by the judge, arbitrator, or referee of any omission or insufficiency of the stamp thereon, and if the instrument is one which may legally be stamped after the execution thereof, it may, on payment to the officer of the Court whose duty it is to read the instrument, or to the arbitrator or referee, of the amount of the unpaid duty, and the penalty payable on stamping the same, and of a further sum of one pound, be received in evidence, saving all just exceptions on other grounds.

(2) The officer, or arbitrator, or referee receiving the duty and penalty shall give a receipt for the same, and make an entry in a book kept for that

purpose of the payment and of the amount thereof, and shall communicate to the Commissioners the name or title of the proceeding in which, and of the party from whom, he received the duty and penalty, and the date and description of the instrument, and shall pay over to such person as the Commissioners may appoint the money received by him for the duty and penalty.

(3) On production to the Commissioners of any instrument in respect of which any duty or penalty has been paid, together with the receipt, the payment of the duty and penalty shall be denoted on the instrument

(4) Save as aforesaid, an instrument executed in any part of the United Kingdom, or relating, wheresoever executed, to any property situate, or to any matter or thing done or to be done, in any part of the United Kingdom, shall not, except in criminal proceedings, be given in evidence, or be available for any purpose whatever, unless it is duly stamped in accordance with the law in force at the time when it was first executed.

(33 & 34 Vict., Ch 97, Secs 16 and 17, 44 Vict., Ch. 12, Sec. 44)

RULES OF THE SUPREME COURT, 1883   ORDER XXXIX. 8

"A new trial shall not be granted by reason of the ruling of any judge that the stamp upon any document is sufficient, or that the document does not require a stamp."

The rule is taken from Section 31 of The Common Law Procedure Act, 1854 (17 & 18 Vict, Ch. 125). By Sections 28 and 29 of that Act a document insufficiently stamped could not be received in evidence until the deficiency of the stamp duty, together with the statutory penalty and the additional penalty of one pound, had been paid to the officer of the Court who was expressly charged with the duty of calling the attention of the judge to any omission or insufficiency of the stamp These sections are now replaced by Section 14 (1), (2), (3)

The ruling of the judge is final only when he decides that the instrument is admissible in evidence (Sharples v. Rickard,

2 H & N 57; 26 L J, Ex. 302; *in re* The Belfort, L R., 9 Probate, 215) If the judge rules that the stamp upon a document is sufficient, no appeal lies against his ruling, even though it should appear to be incorrect (Blewitt *v* Tritton, C A, *Law Times* 9th July, 1892, p. 221, as to a promissory note for £216 stamped with a penny stamp which had been admitted in evidence in the Divisional Court). If the judge rules that the instrument is not admissible, it is the duty of counsel to tender it formally and require that a note be taken of the tender otherwise the objection to its admission will prevail (Campbell *v.* Loader, 34 L J, Ex. 50).

It is the duty of the judge to reject an unstamped or insufficiently stamped document tendered in evidence, whether counsel take objection to its admissibility or not In Bowker *v* Williamson (5 Times L R 382), the Divisional Court rejected an unstamped bill of sale which the County Court judge had admitted "The judge ought not to have admitted it in evidence, and had no right to do so The Act of Parliament has expressly made it the duty of any judge to reject any document which requires a stamp and is not stamped, and whether or not counsel object to its admission." —*Per* Coleridge, L C J "The objection could not in any way be got rid of, even by consent of the parties."—*Per* Hawkins, J

Sub-section 5. This Sub-section practically supplies the test by which the scope of the operation of the stamp law is determined

"Duly stamped" means stamped in accordance with the law in force when the instrument was first executed, without regard to the nominal date. (Clarke *v.* Roche, 3 Q B D 170, 37 L T R 633)

A conveyance of land in Australia executed in this country was held in Wright *v* Commissioners (11 Ex. R 458; 25 L J, Ex 49) to be liable to ad valorem conveyance duty It is to be observed that a mere contract for the sale of property locally situate out of the United Kingdom is excepted from the liability to ad valorem conveyance duty imposed by Section 59

The words "any matter or thing done or to be done in any part of the United Kingdom" do not apply to the mere production of an instrument in evidence, and accordingly in Gilchrist *v* Herbert (26 L, T R 381) Lord Romilly held that a contract relating to property abroad, executed abroad, need not be stamped

A power of attorney executed in England to receive debts in Newfoundland was held to be chargeable in Stonelake *v* Babb (5 Burr, 2673).

No notice is taken by the Court of the revenue laws of a foreign State, unless the absence of a stamp would render the instrument void in the country where it was executed (James v. Catherwood, 2 Esp. 528; 7 T. R. 241.) In Bristowe v. Sequeville (19 L. J., Ex. 289, 5 Ex. R. 275), in which all the cases were reviewed, unstamped receipts given at Cologne were admitted in evidence to prove payments. Such instruments, however, would now fall under the general provisions in Section 15 (3) relating to instruments executed abroad. Powers of attorney executed abroad, as well as the notarial acts usually attached to them, are liable to British stamp duty if acted upon here.

"*Available for any purpose whatsoever.*"—The words in the corresponding 17th Section of The Stamp Act, 1870, were—"admitted to be good, useful, or available in law or equity," and it remains to be seen whether this change of language does or does not override the cases relating to the admissibility in evidence of unstamped or insufficiently stamped instruments for a collateral purpose. The rule was that an unstamped or insufficiently stamped instrument might be given in evidence to prove a fact collateral, provided no attempt was made to set up the instrument itself. The leading case upon this point was Matheson v. Ross (2 H. L. C. 286), where an unstamped receipt at the foot of a debtor and creditor account, signed by the party who received the balance, was admitted as evidence against him of the state of the account, the fact of payment not being disputed. This decision was followed in Rutty v. Benthall (3 C. P. 488), where an unstamped document which contained an assent to a deed of composition and also an authority to execute the deed for a creditor was admitted to prove the written assent to what had been done. It was not required in evidence as a letter of attorney. *See* also Evans v. Prothero (20 L. J., Ch. 448, and 21 L. J., Ch. 772), Ponsford v. Walton (3 C. P. 167), and *ex parte* Squire (4 Ch. D. 47). In commenting upon Matheson v. Ross, Palles, C. J., observed, in Adams v. Morgan (12 Ir. L. R., Ex. 1), "I think the decision of the House of Lords amounts to this, that when an instrument is capable of being viewed in two aspects, in one of which it is liable to a stamp and in the other is free from duty, such instrument, though unstamped, may be offered in evidence if used in the aspect in which it is not liable to duty." Some of the old cases went beyond this. In Grey v. Smith (1 Camp. 388) a receipt given upon a receipt stamp was held not to be invalidated by the addition of matter which required an agreement stamp. Lord Ellenborough said that if what followed had in any way controlled what went before, he should have rejected the instrument *in toto;* but as it contained a simple acknowledgment that money had been paid, the receipt stamp made it legal evidence, notwithstanding that something else was inscribed upon it

In the recent case of Durie's Executrix v. Fielding (30 Sco L R 371), a bill of exchange insufficiently stamped, which was relied upon by reason of its obligatory character as the basis of the defence, was not allowed to be read for the collateral purpose of proving a donation "If an unstamped instrument contains evidence of a fact foreign to the purpose for which it was executed," said Lord Kinnear, "it may be admitted in evidence notwithstanding the terms of the Stamp Act"

In Powell v London and Provincial Bank ([1893] 1 Ch. 610; L T. R 421), the holder of a sum of stock of a company, regulated by the Companies Clauses Consolidation Act, 1845, deposited with a bank as security for an advance, first, the stock certificate which showed that he was entitled as an executor, secondly, a loan note, undertaking to execute a proper assignment of the stock when required, thirdly, a blank transfer, signed and sealed by him, purporting to transfer, in consideration of five shillings, £1,000 stock of the company The transfer was not dated nor stamped, and did not contain the name of any transferee. The bank subsequently executed the transfer, and became registered as the holder of the stock In giving judgment, Wright, J., said, "The Companies Clauses Consolidation Act, 1845, requires a transfer by deed duly stamped, in which the consideration is truly stated. I am inclined to think that the transfer was invalid, on the ground that the consideration was not truly stated nor the transfer duly stamped"

An instrument, even though coming from the hands of the opposite party, cannot be read until the penalty and duty are paid by the party calling for its production. (Doe dem St John v Hore, 2 Esp 724, Williams v. Stoughton, 2 St 292)

The known want of a stamp upon an instrument lost or destroyed cannot be remedied. (Rippener v Wright, 2 B & Ald 478) In London and County Banking Corporation v Ratcliffe (6 App Ca. 730) an objection was taken to the reception in evidence in the Court of Appeal of a copy, stamped as an original, of an unstamped instrument which had been destroyed; but the point was not argued out As regards the stamps on instruments that have been lost or destroyed, there is a presumption that an instrument was duly stamped unless some evidence is given to the contrary, and the onus of proving it to have been unstamped lies on the party taking the objection to its production, but if evidence be given that an executed instrument was unstamped at a particular time, the onus of proof is shifted, and the party who relies upon the instrument must prove it to have been duly stamped (Marine Investment Co v Haviside, 5 L R, H L 624, 42 L J, Ch 173) The same rule applies to instruments retained by the opposite party after notice to produce (Crisp v Anderson, 1 Stark, 35, Crowther v. Solomons, 6 C B 758) Obliterated stamps are assumed to have been of the right amount (Doe dem. Fryer v. Coombes, 12 L. J, Q B 36, 3 A & E 687; 6 Jur 930)

If an examined copy of an unstamped instrument is produced as secondary evidence of the contents of the instrument it may be read, the theory being that it is used merely to refresh the memory of the witness (Braythwaite v Hitchcock, 10 M. & W. 494), and this is often done to avoid the consequences of the known want of a stamp, but in Nixon v Albion Marine Insurance Co. (2 Ex 338), an action upon a contract of insurance, no stamped policy being in existence, the agreement between the parties to a special case that the case should be argued as if a stamped policy existed as set aside by the Court "If we were to hear the case we should be neglecting the duty imposed upon us to protect the revenue" *per* Kelly, C B And in the Court of Session (Cowan v Stewart, 10 Rettie, 4th Series, 785) the consent of parties to hold the copy of an agreement in suit to be the true copy, the original not being alleged to be lost or destroyed, was not allowed without payment of the penalty and stamp duty on the copy as if it had really been the original

Instruments tendered in evidence to prove fraud are considered to be used for a collateral purpose, and are admissible unstamped "A stamp is unnecessary where the instrument shows no contract in law between the parties and cannot be enforced" *per* Alderson, B, in Holmes v. Sixsmith (7 Ex R 802, 21 L. J, Ex 312, 16 Jur 619), where unstamped articles of agreement for a trotting match were admitted to show that one horse had been substituted for another, and see the cases there reviewed.

An instrument made for an illegal consideration is admissible unstamped, see Coppock v Bower (4 M & W. 361, H & H 340), where an unstamped agreement in consideration of a bribe not to proceed with an election petition was admitted "A paper containing evidence of an illegal contract need not be stamped" *per* Abinger, B. *A fortiori*, a forged instrument is admissible unstamped (R. v. Hawkesworth, 1 Leach, C C. 811, 2 East, P. C. 955)

The exception as to criminal proceedings includes proceedings for the recovery of penalties, the rules of evidence being substantially the same (Miller v Denham, 5 Q. B. D. 467, and *per* Field, J., in Reg v Lee, 9 Q. B. D. 394, and Bowen, L. J., in Reg v Tyler, 56 J. P. 118.)

When by reason of an alteration an executed instrument becomes a new instrument, or has a new operation, a further stamp is required, or an objection lies as if the instrument were unstamped. In London, Brighton, and South Coast Railway Company v Fairclough (2 M. & G. 675, 3 Scott, N. R. 68), the substitution, after execution by the vendor, of the name of a sub-purchaser for that of the original purchaser in a transfer of shares was held to require a fresh stamp. An alteration made whilst an instrument is *in fieri* is permissible, as in Jones v Jones (1 Crompt. & Mees 74), where the only conveying party to a deed had executed it, and upon the objection of another party a clause was struck out and the deed re-executed, and it was held that if upon all the facts the fair conclusion is that the execution was *in fieri* only, no fresh stamp is required. If the alteration was made before the instrument had had operation, it is incumbent on the party relying on the instrument to prove the facts, as the Court will not presume that the alteration was properly made (Johnson v Duke of Marlborough, 2 Stark. 313). Where a date has been altered, and the question of penalty upon stamping arises, the Commissioners require evidence, by statutory declaration or otherwise, that the alteration was properly made.

Stamping of Instruments after Execution.

Penalty upon stamping instruments after execution.

15. (1) Save where other express provision is in this Act made, any unstamped or insufficiently stamped instrument may be stamped after the execution thereof, on payment of the unpaid duty and a penalty of ten pounds, and also by way of further penalty, where the unpaid duty exceeds ten pounds, of interest on such duty, at the rate of five pounds per centum per annum, from the day upon which the instrument was first executed up to the time when the amount of interest is equal to the unpaid duty.

(2) In the case of such instruments hereinafter

mentioned as are chargeable with ad valorem duty, the following provisions shall have effect:—

(a) The instrument, unless it is written upon duly stamped material, shall be duly stamped with the proper ad valorem duty before the expiration of thirty days after it is first executed, or after it has been first received in the United Kingdom in case it is first executed at any place out of the United Kingdom, unless the opinion of the Commissioners with respect to the amount of duty with which the instrument is chargeable has, before such expiration, been required under the provisions of this Act.

(b) If the opinion of the Commissioners with respect to any such instrument has been required, the instrument shall be stamped in accordance with the assessment of the Commissioners within fourteen days after notice of the assessment:

(c) If any such instrument executed after the sixteenth day of May, one thousand eight hundred and eighty-eight, has not been or is not duly stamped in conformity with the foregoing provisions of this Sub-section, the person in that behalf hereinafter specified shall incur a fine of ten pounds, and in addition to the penalty payable on stamping the instrument there shall be paid a further penalty equivalent to the stamp duty thereon, unless a reasonable excuse for the delay in stamping, or the omission to stamp, or the insufficiency of stamp, be afforded to the satisfaction of the Commissioners, or of the Court, judge, arbitrator, or referee before whom it is produced:

(*d*) The instruments and persons to which the provisions of this Sub-section are to apply are as follows.—

Title of Instrument as described in the First Schedule to this Act	Person Liable to Penalty.
Bond, covenant, or instrument of any kind whatsoever	The obligee, covenantee, or other person taking the security
Conveyance on sale - - - -	The vendee or transferee
Lease or tack - - - -	The lessee.
Mortgage, bond, debenture, covenant, and warrant of attorney to confess and enter up judgment.	The mortgagee or obligee; in the case of a transfer or reconveyance, the transferee, assignee, or disponee, or the person redeeming the security.
Settlement - - - -	The settlor.

(3) Provided that save where other express provision is made by this Act in relation to any particular instrument·

(*a*) Any unstamped or insufficiently stamped instrument which has been first executed at any place out of the United Kingdom may be stamped, at any time within thirty days after it has been first received in the United Kingdom, on payment of the unpaid duty only: and

(*b*) The Commissioners may, if they think fit, at any time within three months after the first execution of any instrument, mitigate or remit any penalty payable on stamping

(4) The payment of any penalty payable on stamping is to be denoted on the instrument by a particular stamp

(33 & 34 *Vict*, *Ch* 97, *Sec* 15, 51 *Vict*, *Ch* 8, *Sec* 18.)

It is the theory of the stamp law that every instrument not subject to special regulations first executed in the United Kingdom should be written on stamped paper or be stamped before execution, and that the permission given by the Commissioners to stamp instruments without penalty within a stated period is an indulgence Section 18 of 51 Vict., Ch. 8, to which Sub-section 2 corresponds, first allowed as of right a period of thirty days for stamping the instruments specified in Sub section (d) It is to be observed that the penalties imposed by Sub-section 2 are additional to those under Sub-section 1, and an application to the Commissioners for mitigation or return of penalty should be accompanied by a separate memorial showing cause why proceedings should not be instituted for recovery of the personal penalty. If an instrument specified in Sub-section 2 (d) is presented for stamping after the expiration of three months, payment of the "further penalty" under Sub section 2 (c) may be required, as well as that under Sub-section 1; but in practice the Commissioners do not enforce it. It seems clear, however, that a "Court, judge, arbitrator, or referee" would have no alternative, in the absence of a "reasonable excuse," &c , but to require payment of both penalties

"Equivalent to the stamp duty thereon" means the unpaid stamp duty.

Unless an instrument is expressly taken out of this Section by an express provision, the Commissioners have power to stamp under it. (*Per* Butt, J , *re* The Belfort, L R , 9 Probate, 215, *post*, p 97)

In Fitzgerald's Trustees v Mellersh (*Law Times* 16th Jan , 1892) it was held, confirming the common practice of the Commissioners, that they had power, under the corresponding section of The Stamp Act, 1870, to impress additional duty upon an instrument made as a security without limit, the amount which it was originally stamped to cover having been exceeded by the addition of interest. See now Section 88 (2), *post*, p. 174.

The Section does not apply to the following instruments, which are subject to "other express provision"—

Bills of Exchange and Promissory Notes. (Secs. 34 [2] and 37 [2])

Bills of Lading (Sec 40 [1])

Charter-parties (except those wholly executed out of the United Kingdom). (Secs 50 and 51)

Contract Notes liable to the duty of one shilling. (Sec 52 [3] and 56 Vict , Ch 7, Sec 3.)

Proxies and Voting Papers liable to the duty of one penny (except those executed abroad) (Sec 80 [2])

Policies of Sea Insurance. (Sec 95)

Receipts (except those executed abroad). (Sec 102.)

The issue or execution, unstamped, of the following instruments being prohibited by penal sections, the Commissioners usually decline to stamp them after execution without inflicting a penalty.—

> Contract Notes liable to the duty of one penny.
> Delivery Orders
> Leases or Agreements for Leases for a definite term less than a year, specified in Section 78, and counterparts or duplicates thereof
> Letters of Allotment and Renunciation
> Policies of Insurance other than Sea Insurance
> Scrip Certificates and Scrip
> Share Warrants
> Warrants for Goods
> Appraisements and Valuations not stamped within fourteen days of the making   (Sec. 24.)

By Section 63, attested copies and extracts may be stamped within fourteen days after the date of the attestation or authentication without penalty.

By the regulations of the Commissioners, agreements under hand only, liable to the fixed duty of sixpence, may be stamped without penalty within fourteen days from the date of execution, and all instruments not specified above within thirty days, except articles of clerkship, which are not allowed to be stamped without penalty after execution (Sec 27, *post*, p. 68) The date of the instrument is accepted as *primâ facie* evidence of the date of execution, but any alteration or erasure of the date must be explained by a statutory declaration

As to instruments executed abroad, the date of receipt in the United Kingdom should be verified by the production of the envelope, or, unless the date of the instrument shows that the instrument must have been received within thirty days, by statutory declaration   The period within which an instrument may be stamped without penalty is calculated exclusively of the date of execution or receipt from abroad. Thus, if a deed is executed or received from abroad on the 1st January, the last day for stamping without penalty is the 31st

An escrow is not an executed instrument for the purposes of the stamp laws   The date of delivery is taken as the date of execution; but evidence is required to show that the delivery did not take place before the date alleged

The Commissioners have no power to *remit or mitigate* penalties after three months. After three months the full penalty must be paid on stamping, and a memorial for *return* thereof, accompanied by a statutory declaration as to facts, may be presented to them

If a penalty is payable upon stamping an instrument, there

should also be a stamp to show that it has been paid, but it is scarcely probable, as regards impressed stamps, that an objection to the admission of the instrument in evidence upon the ground of the absence of the penalty stamp could be maintained. (See Rex v. Preston, 5 B & A 1028.)

Entries upon Rolls, Books, &c.

16. Every public officer having in his custody any rolls, books, records, papers, documents, or proceedings, the inspection whereof may tend to secure any duty, or to prove or lead to the discovery of any fraud or omission in relation to any duty, shall at all reasonable times permit any person thereto authorised by the Commissioners to inspect the rolls, books, records, papers, documents, and proceedings, and to take such notes and extracts as he may deem necessary, without fee or reward, and in case of refusal shall for every offence incur a fine of ten pounds. *(Rolls, books, &c., to be open to inspection.)*

(33 & 34 Vict., Ch. 97, Sec. 21.)

"Every public officer" appears to include officers of incorporated companies against whom a prerogative writ of mandamus would lie for the performance of a duty. (Norris v Irish Land Company, 8 E & B 512, also per Fry, J., in Glover v. Giles, 18 Ch. D. 180.)

17. If any person whose office it is to enrol, register, or enter in or upon any rolls, books, or records any instrument chargeable with duty, enrols, registers, or enters any such instrument not being duly stamped, he shall incur a fine of ten pounds. *(Penalty for enrolling, &c., instrument not duly stamped.)*

(33 & 34 Vict., Ch. 97, Sec 22.)

This Section is of great importance to the secretaries of public companies, stewards of manors, and others, and it is the Section upon which the Registrar of Joint Stock Companies relies in refusing to file a contract which he does not consider to be sufficiently stamped. A mandamus will not lie to compel him (Reg. v Registrar of Joint Stock Companies, 21 Q B D 131.) The proper course, if there is any doubt as to duty, is to present the instrument for adjudication under Section 12.

PART II.

Schedule of Duties
and
Regulations applicable to Particular Instruments

ADMISSION in England of any person—   £   s.   d.
  To the degree of barrister-at-law.
    If he has been previously duly admitted to the said degree in Ireland 10   0   0
    In any other case . .. 50   0   0

Exemption.

Admission of any person who has been previously duly admitted as an advocate in Scotland.
And *see* Sections 18, 19, and 20.

ADMISSION in Ireland of any person—
  To the degree of barrister-at-law
    If he has been previously duly admitted to the said degree in England, or as an advocate in Scotland 10   0   0
    In any other case 50   0   0
  And *see* Sections 18, 19, and 20

ADMISSION in Scotland of any person—
  As an advocate
    If he has been previously duly admitted to the degree of barrister-at-law in Ireland .. 10   0   0
    In any other case 50   0   0

Exemption. £ s d.

Admission of any person who has been previously duly admitted to the degree of barrister-at-law in England

(37 & 38 *Vict*, *Ch* 19, *Sec.* 1)

And *see* Sections 18, 19, and 20.

ADMISSION of any person—
To be a member of either of the four Inns of Court in England, or a student of the Society of King's Inns in Dublin 25 0 0

Exemptions.

(1) Admission of any person who has been previously duly admitted a member of one of the Inns of Court in England, to be a member of any other of the said Inns.

(2) Admission of any person who has been previously duly admitted a student of the Society of King's Inns in Dublin, to be a member of any of the Inns of Court in England.

And *see* Sections 18, 19, 20, and 21

ADMISSION of any person—
As a solicitor of the Supreme Court in England, or of the Court of Judicature in Ireland 25 0 0

(36 & 37 *Vict*, *Ch.* 66, *Sec* 87; 40 & 41 *Vict*, *Ch* 57, *Sec.* 78.)

And *see* Sections 18 and 19

ADMISSION in Scotland of any person— £ s d
(1) As a law agent to practise before the Court of Session or as a writer to the signet:
    If he has previously paid the sum of £60 for duty upon his articles of clerkship .. 25 0 0
    If he has been previously duly admitted as a law agent to practise before a sheriff court 30 0 0
    In any other case 85 0 0

(2) As a law agent to practise before a sheriff court.
    If he has previously paid the sum of 2s. 6d for duty on his articles of clerkship 54 17 6
    In any other case 55 0 0

(36 & 37 Vict., Ch. 63.)

Exemption.

Admission of any person who has been previously duly admitted as a law agent to practise before the Court of Session or as a writer to the signet to act in the other of those capacities.
And *see* Sections 18 and 19.

ADMISSION to act as a notary public.

See **Faculty.**

ADMISSION of any person—
As a Fellow of the College of Physicians in England, Scotland, or Ireland... 25 0 0
And *see* Sections 18 and 19.

ADMISSIONS 47

ADMISSION of any person to the degree of doctor of medicine in either of the universities in Scotland. . . £10 0 0
    And *see* Sections 18 and 19.

ADMISSION in England or Ireland of any person—
  As a burgess, or into any corporation or company, in any city, borough, or town corporate—
    In respect of birth, apprenticeship, or marriage, or, in Ireland, in respect of being engaged in any trade, mystery, or handicraft £1 0 0
    Upon any other ground . . £3 0 0

Exemptions.

(1) Admission of any person to the freedom of the City of London by redemption
(2) Admission of any person to the freedom of the company of watermen and lightermen of the River Thames

    (36 *Vict.*, *Ch.* 18, *Sec* 5.)

And *see* Sections 18 and 19.

ADMISSION in Scotland of any person—
  As a burgess, or into any corporation or company, in any burgh... .. £0 5 0

Exemption.

Admission of a craftsman or other person into any corporation within any royal burgh, burgh of royalty, or burgh of barony incorporated by the magistrates and council of such burgh, provided such craftsman or other person has been previously duly admitted a freeman or burgess of the burgh

And *see* Sections 18 and 19 *

Admissions.

Mode of denoting duty

18. The duty payable upon an admission is to be denoted on the instrument of admission delivered to the person admitted, if there be any such instrument, or, if not, on the register, entry, or memorandum of the admission in the rolls, books, or records of the court, inn, college, borough, burgh, company, corporation, guild, or society in which the admission is made, and in cases in which no instrument of admission is delivered, and no register, entry, or memorandum is made, on the rescript or warrant for admission.

(33 & 34 *Vict*, Ch 97, Sec 29)

---

* The duties on appointments and admissions to ecclesiastical benefices and offices or employments contained in The Stamp Act, 1870, have been repealed, and they are therefore exempt from any duty. The charges were as follows —

Appointment, whether by way of donation, presentation, or nomination, and admission, collation, or institution to and licence to hold—
   Any ecclesiastical benefice, dignity, or promotion, or any perpetual curacy :
      In England—ad valorem duty according to the net yearly value
      In Scotland—the fixed duty of £2
(Charge of duty repealed by 40 Vict., Ch. 13, Sec 13)
An appointment, &c, not falling under the above description is liable to ten shillings if under seal *e.g.*, the appointment by a nobleman of a private chaplain

Admission and appointment or grant by any writing—
   To or of any office or employment where the annual salary, fees, or emoluments appertaining to such office or employment do not exceed £100   £2
And so on ad valorem.
(Charge of duty repealed by 38 Vict, Ch. 23, Sec. 14)

As to the effect of the repeal of a specific charge of duty, *see* Attorney-General *v* Lamplough (3 Ex D, C A. 214)
This charge extended only to admissions, &c., to offices or employments to which annual salary, fees, or emoluments were attached (Roberts *v* Elliott, 11 M & W 527) An admission and appointment or grant under seal to an honorary office was and is still liable to the deed duty (10s.), or if, being under hand, it operates as a "letter of attorney," it is liable to the duty of ten shillings under that head

19. If any person whose office it is to prepare or deliver out any instrument of admission chargeable with duty, or to register, enter, or make any memorandum of any admission in respect of which no instrument of admission is delivered to the person admitted, neglects or refuses, within one month after the admission, to prepare a duly stamped instrument of admission, or to make a duly stamped register, entry, or memorandum of the admission, as the case may require, he shall incur a fine of ten pounds.

(33 & 34 Vict., Ch. 97, Sec 30.)

Penalty on officers for neglect to make duly stamped documents or entries.

Admissions to the Degree of a Barrister-at-Law in Ireland, and of Students to the Society of King's Inns, in Dublin.

20. Distinct accounts are to be kept of the sums following; that is to say—
(a) Ten pounds, part of the duty of fifty pounds payable on the admission to the degree of a barrister-at-law in Ireland of a person not previously admitted to that degree in England, or as an advocate in Scotland
(b) Ten pounds, payable for duty on the like admission of a person who has been previously admitted to the said degree in England, or as an advocate in Scotland.
(c) Ten pounds, part of the duty payable on the admission of a person as a student of the Society of King's Inns, in Dublin

And the said sums are respectively to be paid over by the Commissioners to the treasurer of the Society of King's Inns, in Dublin, to be applied by him according to the directions of the Society.

(33 & 34 Vict., Ch 97, Sec 31, 37 & 38 Vict., Ch 19, Sec 2.)

Distinct accounts to be kept of certain sums payable to King's Inns, Dublin

21. If any person who has been duly admitted a member of one of the Inns of Court in England is afterwards duly admitted a student of the Society

Admission of Member of Inn of Court as

student of King's Inns

of King's Inns, in Dublin, the duty paid by him in respect of his former admission is, on application made within six months after the last admission, to be allowed and returned to him.

(33 & 34 Vict., Ch. 97, Sec. 32.)

AFFIDAVIT and STATUTORY DECLARATION ... £ s d.
.. 0 2 6

Exemptions.

(1) Affidavit made for the immediate purpose of being filed, read, or used in any Court, or before any judge, master, or officer of any Court.

(2) Affidavit or declaration made upon a requisition of the commissioners of any public board of revenue, or any of the officers acting under them, or required by law, and made before a justice of the peace

"Required by law" extends to private Acts. If an affidavit or declaration "required by law" is made before any person other than a justice of the peace, it is not within this exemption

Section 21 of The Interpretation Act, 1889 (52 & 53 Vict., Ch. 63), enacts that in all Acts, past and future, the expression "Statutory Declaration" shall, unless the contrary intention appears, mean a declaration made by virtue of The Statutory Declarations Act, 1835

A declaration made upon the transmission of an interest in the shares of a company which exceeds the purposes of Section 18 of The Companies Clauses Consolidation Act, 1845, is not within this exemption If it contains a statement of the identity of the person deceased with the registered holder of the shares, it is chargeable with duty, such a statement not being "required" by Section 18; and this appears from the specific mention of a declaration of identity in Section 19 of the same Act when the transmission of interest occurs by reason of the marriage of a female shareholder.

A declaration voluntarily presented to the Commissioners of Inland Revenue not covered by their regulations or requisitions is liable to duty, but the duty, in administration, is not enforced.

> (3) Affidavit or declaration which may be required at the Bank of England or the Bank of Ireland to prove the death of any proprietor of any stock transferable there, or to identify the person of any such proprietor, or to remove any other impediment to the transfer of any such stock

"Proprietor" does not include "trustee," and this exemption does not extend to an affidavit or declaration required to be made upon the occasion of a transfer of stock consequent upon the death of a trustee.

> (4) Affidavit or declaration relating to the loss, mutilation, or defacement of any bank note or bank post bill.
>
> (5) Declaration required to be made pursuant to any Act relating to marriages in order to a marriage without licence.
>
> (6) Declaration forming part of an application for a patent in conformity with The Patents, Designs, and Trade Marks Act, 1883.

(As to (6), 47 & 48 Vict, Ch. 62, Sec 9.)

AGREEMENT or CONTRACT accompanied with a deposit

See **Mortgage**, &c, and Sections 23 and 86.

AGREEMENT for a lease or tack or for any letting

See **Lease or Tack**, and Section 75.

AGREEMENT for sale of property.
See **Conveyance on Sale**, and Section 59.

AGREEMENT or CONTRACT made or entered into pursuant to the Highway Acts for or relating to the making, maintaining, or repairing of highways

£ s. d.

0 0 6

The principal Highway Acts are 5 & 6 Will. IV., Ch. 50; 25 & 26 Vict., Ch 61; 27 & 28 Vict., Ch 101, 41 & 42 Vict., Ch 77. By The Public Health Act, 1875 (38 & 39 Vict., Ch. 55), the urban authority had the same powers, &c., as those given to highway boards by 5 & 6 Will. IV, Ch 50, and *see* now The Local Government Act, 1888 (51 & 52 Vict, Ch 41), whereby powers relating to highways are vested in the county councils. An agreement relating to highways under the seal of a county council is therefore chargeable with the duty of sixpence only, but it must be an agreement entered into pursuant to the Highway Acts, not, for example, an agreement relating to the repair of county bridges, which if under the seal of the county council, is chargeable with deed duty of ten shillings as a deed.

AGREEMENT or any MEMORANDUM of an AGREEMENT, made in England or Ireland under hand only, or made in Scotland without any clause of registration, and not otherwise specifically charged with any duty, whether the same be only evidence of a contract, or obligatory upon the parties from its being a written instrument

£ s d.

0 0 6

Exemptions.

(1) Agreement or memorandum the matter whereof is not of the value of £5.

(2) Agreement or memorandum for the hire of any labourer, artificer, manufacturer, or menial servant

(3) Agreement, letter, or memorandum made for or relating to the sale of any goods, wares, or merchandise.

(4) Agreement or memorandum made between the master and mariners of any ship or vessel for wages on any voyage coastwise from port to port in the United Kingdom

(5) Agreement entered into between a landlord and tenant pursuant to Sub-section 6 of Section 8, or Sub-section 2 of Section 20 of The Land Law (Ireland) Act, 1881.

And *see* Sections 22 and 23.

(45 & 46 *Vict.*, *Ch* 73, *Sec* 10)

Agreements.

22. The duty of sixpence upon an agreement may be denoted by an adhesive stamp, which is to be cancelled by the person by whom the agreement is first executed.

Duty may be denoted by adhesive stamp.

(33 & 34 *Vict*, *Ch* 97, *Sec* 36.)

The instrument to be chargeable with duty as an agreement must relate to a contract If there is no contract, there is no liability to duty. Thus in Vollans v. Fletcher (11 Jur. 416; L. J, Ex 82) a letter purporting to allot a greater number of shares than had been applied for, and on terms differing from those of the application, was admitted in evidence unstamped, for the letter and the application not being *ad idem* no contract had been made. *See* also Willey v. Parratt (18 L J, Ex 82), and Moore v. Garwood (19 L. J, Ex. Ch 15, 4 Ex R. 681).

It is immaterial whether the instrument be signed or not, if it embodies the binding terms of the contract (Walker v. Rostron, 9 M & W. 411), for the words "under hand only" are to be read as "not under seal" (Chadwick v. Clark, 9 Jur. 539, 14 L J, C P 233, 1 C B. 700).

A memorandum of agreement presupposes an antecedent parol contract A mere offer in writing, though accepted by parol, does not require a stamp (Chaplin v Clark, 4 Ex. R. on p. 407) In Hudspeth ı Yarnold (14 Jur 578, 19 L. J.,

C. P 321, 9 C. B. 625) letters offering terms to an actor were admitted unstamped, on the ground that the contract would consist of the letters and matter *extrinsic* of the writing and see Drant v. Brown (3 B & C 665), Doe dem. Bingham v. Cartwright (3 B & Ald. 326). A writing made with the intention of containing within itself the terms of agreement between the parties is within the charge (Knight v. Barber, 10 Jur 929; 16 L J, Ex. 18, 16 M & W 66), where a note, "Bought of Knight 50 shares at £10 per share," signed by Barber, was held to be chargeable In Hegarty v. Milne (18 Jur. 496; 23 L J, C P 151, 14 C B 627) an instrument written by one of the parties and signed by the other, and in Bowen v. Fox (2 M. & R 167) a memorandum, signed by the depositor, of the terms upon which a certificate of a ship's registry had been deposited, were held to be chargeable

It is not a necessary element of liability to duty that an instrument should contain all the particulars of the contract. The memorandum or note of agreement required by Section 4 of the Statute of Frauds is liable in all cases (unless it falls under Exemption 1), being obligatory upon the parties from its being a written instrument (*See* Hughes v. Budd, 4 Jur 654, Benjamin on Sales, 3rd ed, p 107.) In Beeching v. Westbrook (10 L. J, Ex 464, 8 M & W 411) Maule, J, observed that the words from "*whether*" to the end of the charge were "put in to exclude the argument that the agreement of which some memorandum is given in evidence need not have been made in writing, which would in every case not within the Statute of Frauds enable a party to give in evidence a written contract without its being stamped" But a memorandum or note which does not satisfy the Statute of Frauds is liable if it contains a material part of the agreement Thus in Ramsbottom v Wortley (2 M & S 445) the signed note of an auctioneer was held to be chargeable, although the name of the vendor was omitted, and in Glover v. Halkett (3 Jur, N S 1083, 26 L. J, Ex. 416; 2 Hurl & N, Ex. 490) a guarantee under Section 3 of The Mercantile Law Amendment Act, 1856 (19 & 20 Vict, Ch. 97) was held to be chargeable, although the consideration for the contract was not expressed. And in Vaughten v Brine (1 M & G. 359, 1 Scott, N. R. 258) Tindal, C J, expressed the opinion that the charge extends to all cases in which recourse is had to a writing as evidence of a *contract*

The independent memorandum of one party made for his own use is not within the charge, nor is the unsigned note of an auctioneer (Ramsbottom v Tonbridge, 2 M & S. 434.)

An agreement consisting of several letters may be proved under one stamp, the letters being those written while the contract is being made (Beeching v Westbrook, 8 M. & W. 411; 1 Dowl, N. S 18.) The stamp may be upon any letter of the series, but it should be upon an original document, not a copy In Peate v. Dicken (1 C., M. & R 422, 5 Tyr. 116) this principle was extended to two separate instruments relating to the same subject matter, and made one in consideration of the other See also in re Albert Average Association (L R. 13 Eq. 529)

The agreement stamp has been held to be unnecessary where the writing amounts merely to—(a) An acknowledgment of a fact, as that A holds goods belonging to B. (Blackwell v. M'Naughten, 1 A. & E, N S 127, 1 Q B. 127), (b) An acknowledgment or admission of the existence of a previous contract, the acknowledgment not being itself an agreement or memorandum of agreement (Fraser v Bunn, 8 C. & P 704; Marshall v Powell, 11 Jur. 61, 16 L. J. Q. B 5; Beeching v Westbrook, 8 M & W 411; 1 Dowl, N S 18); (c) A licence or authority under hand to do that which would otherwise be a trespass or breach of contract, as a licence to demise, an authority to a landlord, on withdrawing a distress, to resume possession if rent is not paid (Hill v Ransom, 12 L J, C P. 275; Fishwick v. Milnes, 4 Ex R. 824, 19 L J, Ex 153; Barry v. Goodman, 2 M & W. 768); (d) An undertaking to perform a duty which the law implies, as of a solicitor to recover the value of bills deposited in his hands by a client (Langdon v Wilson, 7 B & C 640, note; 2 M & R. 10); and see Muller v Hutchinson (3 G. & P. 92, 7 B. & C 639, 1 M & R. 522), De Parquet v. Page (20 L J, Q B 28; 15 Jur. 148, 15 Q. B. 1073)

A document, as a prospectus, the terms of which are adopted by parol, is not thereby rendered liable to the agreement duty (Edgar v Blick, 1 Stark 464; Clay v. Crofts, 20 L J, Ex. 361). A prospectus relied upon as containing the terms of a contract must be stamped, and an unstamped facsimile will not be admitted. (Williams v Stoughton, 2 St. 292) An instrument liable to any duty, referred to as the basis of a contract, cannot be produced in evidence unless stamped with its appropriate duty (Turner v Power, 1 Moo & M 113, 7 B. & C 625.)

An I O U is not liable to any stamp duty (Fisher v. Leslie, 1 Esp 426, Israel v Israel, 1 Camp 499, Childers v. Boulnois, 1 Dow & R. 8), even with the words "for value received" (Gould v Coombs, 9 Jur 494, 14 L J, C P. 175, 1 M G & S 543); nor is a mere acknowledgment of a debt, unless so worded as to bring it within the definition of a receipt in Section 101 (see "Receipt," post), but the addition of special matter may render an I O U or other acknowledgment of debt, or a receipt, liable either as an agreement or a promissory note e.g.—

"I, A, owe B £6, which is to be paid by instalments, for rent" an agreement. (Moffatt v Edwards, 1 Carr & M. 16.)

"I O U £45, which I borrowed of Mrs M, and to pay her five per cent till paid" an agreement. (Melanotte v Teesdale, 13 L. J., Ex 358, 13 M & W 216.)

"Received of A £170, for which I promise to pay five per cent from date" an agreement. (Taylor v Steele, 11 Jur. 806, 16 L J, Ex 177, 16 M & W 665.)

"Borrowed of A B £200, to account for at two months' notice if required": an agreement. (White v North, 3 Ex R. 689, 16 L J., Ex. 316.)

An unstamped instrument worded "Received from A B. on loan £400" was admitted in evidence, after much discussion, in the Court of Session, upon payment of duty as an agreement, and penalty. (Welsh's Trustees v Forbes, 12 Rettie, 4th Series, 851.)

A receipt for £70 "in settlement of all claims," stamped as a receipt, was held by Huddleston, B, to be liable to duty as an agreement. (White v South London Tramways Company, *Times* 13th December, 1889.)

An attornment under hand is not liable to duty (Doe dem Linsey v Edwards, 5 A & E 95, Doe dem Wright v Smith, 8 A & E 255, 2 Jur 854, Doe dem Frankis v Frankis, 11 A & E 792, 3 P. & D. 565), but if it contain special terms, as to hold upon such conditions as might be subsequently agreed upon (Cornish v Searell, 8 B & C 471), or "the rent to be paid quarterly" (Doe dem Frankis v Frankis, *ubi supra*), it is liable to duty as an agreement.

A cognovit is not liable to duty (Ames v Hill, 2 B & P. 150), even though containing a stipulation that time shall be given for payment (Jay v Warren, 1 C & P 532; Morley v Hall, 2 Dowl 494), or that plaintiff may sign judgment in default of payment by a day named (Bray v Hanson, 8 M & W 668), but if it contain special terms, as a provision for payment of a debt by instalments, it is liable to duty as an agreement. (Reardon v. Swabey, 4 East, 188.)

An acknowledgment of the right to production of documents, or an undertaking for safe custody under Section 9 of The Conveyancing Act, 1881 (44 & 45 Vict, Ch 41), is liable to duty as an agreement.

Exemption 1

Under the statutes in force before the passing of The Stamp Act, 1870, value was an essential condition of the *charge*, an agreement being liable to duty only when "the matter thereof" was of the value of £20 or upwards under 55 Geo III, Ch. 184, and 13 & 14 Vict, Ch 97, or £5 or upwards under 23 Vict., Ch. 15. "The value must be measurable and capable of being ascertained at the date of the contract," per Parke, B, in Liddiard v. Gale (19 L J., Ex 160, 4 Ex R. 416), where a contract to do an uncertain quantity of brickwork at £1 14s per rod was held not to be within the charge; and *see* also Semple v. Steinan (22 L. J., Ex. 224, 8 Ex R. 622), where the same was held respecting an agreement to pay interest at the rate of one shilling in the pound per month upon a bill for £100 if not honoured at maturity, although in both cases the amount owing, for which the action was actually brought, exceeded £20. The *ratio decidendi* of these cases is not applicable to the present law, for *value* is now made an essential condition of *exemption*, and to bring an agreement within the exemption it is submitted that the value of the subject matter must be measurable, and it must be shown that at the date of the agreement such value was less than £5

Exemption 2.

This exemption is not applicable to an agreement for the hire of a clerk (Dakin v. Watson, 2 Cr & Dix, Cir. Rep 225) Firemen and stokers employed on board ship are "labourers" within the meaning of the exemption, and so also are persons engaged in similar capacities on engines, fixed or moveable, on land. (Wilson v Zulueta, 19 L J, Q B 49, 14 Q B 405; 14 Jur 356) A farm bailiff who took charge of glebe lands at a salary and a share of profits was held to be a "labourer" in Reg v Wortley (21 L J Mag. 44, 15 Jur 1137).

The Truck Act, 1 & 2 Will. IV, Ch 37, contains a wide definition (for the purpose of that Act) of "artificer," upon which was decided Sharman v Sanders (12 C. B 166) A foreman contractor who employed others under him was held not to be an "artificer," although he superintended the work, and from time to time laboured personally therein; and a contractor for making a railway cutting is not a "workman or labourer" under the Truck Act, although he does a portion of the work himself. (Riley v. Warden, 2 Ex R 59) A person who possessed a knowledge of mechanics, and assisted as a practical working mechanic in developing ideas, was held by Smith,

J, to be an artificer in Jackson v. Hill (*Justice of the Peace* 5 January 1884)

No general rules can be laid down as to who do or who do not come within the category of "menial servants"; but in the following cases persons employed in the capacities named were held to be entitled to a month's notice within the rule relating to menial or domestic servants —

Johnson v Blenkinsopp (5 Jur 870), a person hired to keep the gardens and assist in the stable

Nowland v Ablett (2 C M & R 54; L. J, Ex. 155), a head-gardener, though residing in an adjacent cottage.

Nicoll v Greaves (33 L J, C P 259, 17 C. B., N. S. 27), a huntsman living in an adjacent cottage

A governess is not a menial servant (Todd v Kerrage, 8 Ex R 151; 22 L J., Ex 1)

Exemption 3

A liberal interpretation has usually been given to this exemption, on the ground that it was enacted in the interest of trade, and it has been extended to agreements connected with the sale of goods which were not strictly agreements for sale In the following cases it has been allowed —

> Agreement by a vendor of goods to indemnify the purchaser, a broker, against loss (Curry v. Edensor, 3 T. R. 524.)
>
> Guarantee for payment of goods supplied to another. (Warrington v. Furber, 8 East, 242; 6 Esp. 89; Sadler v Johnson, 16 M. & W 775, Chatfield v Cox, 18 Q B. 321, 21 L J, Q. B 279)
>
> Indemnity against the claim of a third person to goods sold (Heron v Grainger, 5 Esp. 269.)
>
> Agreement to share in profit or loss upon goods already purchased. (Venning v Leckie, 13 East, 7)
>
> Warranty upon sale of a horse (Skrine v Elmore, 2 Camp 457)

An agreement for the sale of goods together with other property is not within the exemption, as in South v Finch (3 Bing N C 506), an agreement for the sale of cabs and goodwill; Horsfall v Hey (17 L J, Ex. 266), an agreement for the sale of goods and fixtures

If the sale of goods is not the primary object of the transaction, the agreement is not within the exemption, as in Smith v Cator (2 B & Ald 733), where the primary object was to obtain advances upon goods in the hands of a factor, who might recoup himself out of the proceeds of sale; and *see* Southgate v Bohn (16 M. & W. 34); Attenborough v. Commissioners of Inland Revenue (11 Ex. R 461; 25 L J, Ex. 22).

The words "goods, wares, or merchandise" include all tangible movable property. (Blackburn on Sales, 9.) They occur in Section 17 of the Statute of Frauds, and all contracts governed by that section, as amended by Section 8 of Lord Tenterden's Act (9 Geo IV., Ch. 14), are within the exemption. After a series of apparently conflicting decisions, the question whether executory contracts for the sale of goods not yet in existence, or not manufactured or completed, were contracts for the sale of goods within the statute, or contracts for work, labour, or materials, was settled in Lee v Griffin (30 L. J, Q B 252; 1 B. & S 272), an action for the price of a set of artificial teeth, and the rule deduced in Benjamin on Sales (3rd ed, p. 99) is that if the contract is intended to result in transferring for a price from B. to A. a chattel in which A. had no previous property, it is a contract for the sale of a chattel. The cases of this class under the Principal Act in which the exemption has been allowed are —

Garbutt v. Watson (5 B and Ald. 613), contract for the sale of flour to be made out of wheat yet unground, Walker v Atkinson (6 Taunt. 11), contract for the sale of oil not yet expressed from seed; Pinner v Arnold (2 C M & R 613, Tyr. & G. 1; 1 Gale, 271), contract for making a press and supplying it within six months, Gurr v Scudd (11 Ex R. 190), contract to take at a fixed price all the manure to be made in two years

But a contract for making a chattel and fixing it to the freehold is not within the exemption Chanter v. Dickenson (12 L J, C P 147, 5 M & G. 253, 2 Dowl, N. R 83, 6 Scott, N. R. 182), in which the contract was for supplying and fitting up a patent furnace And for cases decided on the Statute of Frauds, *see* Cotterell v Apsley (6 Taunt. 322), Tripp v. Armitage (1 M. & W. 687), Clark v. Bulmer (11 M. & W 242), and Anglo Egyptian Navigation Company v Rennie (10 L R., C P 271)

An agreement for work and labour is not within this exemption Fielder v Ray (4 C & P 63), Hughes v Budd (8 Dowl 478), and *see*, as to Section 17 of the Statute of Frauds, Clay v Yates, a contract for printing and publishing a book (25 L J, Ex. 237, 1 H. & N. 73).

A contract for the supply of water by a water company is
exempt (West Middlesex Water Works Company v.
Suwerkrop, 4 C & P 87, Moo. & Mal 478)

A contract on the hire-purchase system containing a clause
that until the payment of the last instalment the
property in the goods let remains in the lender was
formerly considered chargeable with duty, but in
Helby v Matthews ([1894] 2 Q B, C. A 262, 70
L T R 887), following Lee v Butler ([1893] 2 Q B
318), a contract on the hire-purchase system containing
a condition that until payment of the last instalment
the goods let should continue to be the sole property
of the person letting was held to be an agreement
to "purchase" within Section 9 of the Factory Act,
1889 A contract similar to that in Helby v. Matthews
would be considered to be within the exemption.
Hire purchase contracts differ greatly in form. If the
ultimate object is a sale, the exemption applies, if
merely a letting, duty is payable

A contract for the sale of an interest in land (Section 4 of
the Statute of Frauds) is chargeable, and with regard
to growing crops the rules are —

 A crop which is to be severed before the property
in it passes is not an interest in land, and a
contract for sale thereof is exempt; timber sold
at a price per foot, to be cut down by vendor
(Smith v Surman, 9 B & C. 561), potatoes in
the ground, at a price per sack (Parker v
Staniland, 11 East, 362, Sainsbury v Matthews,
4 M & W 343), crop of growing grass, to be
mown and delivered to purchaser (Washburne v
Burrows, 1 Ex R 107), standing timber, to be cut
down by the purchaser and removed as soon as
possible (Marshall v Green, 1 C. P 35).

 If the property in the crop is transferred before
severance, the agreement for sale is exempt if the
crop is *fructus industriales*—i e, a crop produced
by the annual industry of man· liable as an agreement for the sale of an interest in land, if the
crop is *fructus naturales* Examples —

 Fructus Industriales —A plot of growing potatoes to
be turned up by the seller when ripe (Evans v.
Roberts, 5 B & C 836), or by the purchaser
(Warwick v. Brown, 2 M & S 205), the price in
both cases being a gross sum, growing corn and
potatoes, the corn to be harvested, &c., by the
purchaser (Jones v Flint, 9 P & D 594).

Fructus Naturales.—" All the crop of the fruit trees, &c., in the garden" (Rodwell v Phillips, 9 M & W 501, 11 L J., Ex 217), growing grass at £5 per acre, half the price to be paid before the crop was cut (Carrington v Roots, 2 M & W 248; Crosby v Wadsworth, 6 East, 602), standing underwood (Scovell v. Boxall, 1 G. & J 396), growing poles (Teal v. Anty, 2 B & B 99, 4 Moore, 542)

The following are not "goods, wares, or merchandise" —

Shares in a railway company (Bowlby v Bell, 3 M G. & S 284, Tempest v. Kilne, 3 C B. 249), in a joint stock bank (Humble v. Mitchell, 11 A. & E 205); in a cost-book mine (Watson v. Sprattley, 10 Ex. R. 222).

Foreign stock (Heseltine v Siggers, 1 Ex. R. 856.)

Scrip certificates (Knight v. Barber, 16 L J, Ex 18; 16 M & W 66)

An adventure in a ship. (Leigh v. Banner, 1 Esp 403)

Fixtures not severed from the freehold (Horsfall v Hey, 17 L J, Ex. 266; Lee v Gaskell, 19 Q B D 701.)

A house sold as old building materials to be pulled down and taken away by purchaser (Lavery v. Pursell, 39 Ch. D 508)

Crops and labour on a farm taken by an incoming tenant at a valuation. (Earl of Falmouth v Thomas, 1 Crom & M 89; Mayfield v Wadsley, 3 B & C. 266.)

23. (1) Every instrument under hand only (not being a promissory note or bill of exchange) given upon the occasion of the deposit of any share warrant or stock certificate to bearer, or foreign or colonial share certificate, or any security for money transferable by delivery, by way of security for any loan, shall be deemed to be an agreement, and shall be charged with duty accordingly

(2) Every instrument under hand only (not being a promissory note or bill of exchange) making redeemable or qualifying a duly stamped transfer, intended as a security, of any registered stock or marketable security, shall be deemed to be an agreement, and shall be charged with duty accordingly.

Certain mortgages of stock to be chargeable as agreements.

(3) A release or discharge of any such instrument shall not be chargeable with any ad valorem duty.

(51 & 52 Vict., Ch. 8, Sec 14.)

The instrument must be under hand, if under seal, it is chargeable with ad valorem mortgage duty under Section 86 (1) (d) and (g), p 168

The transfer mentioned in Sub-section 2 is "duly stamped" if stamped with the maximum duty of ten shillings, or ad valorem mortgage duty upon the amount secured if such duty is less than ten shillings Sub-section 2 contemplates a transaction carried out by two instruments—the duly stamped transfer, and the instrument under hand making redeemable or qualifying the transfer If no transfer is executed, and the transaction is effected by the deposit of share certificates, or scrip, or bills, or notes, with a covering memorandum under hand that the deposit has been made as a security for a loan, the memorandum is liable to the duty of sixpence as an agreement

ALLOTMENT. *See* Letter of Allotment.

ANNUITY, conveyance in consideration of:

 See **Conveyance on Sale,** and Section 56

Purchase of:

 See **Conveyance on Sale,** and Section 60

Creation of, by way of security

 See **Mortgage,** &c, and Section 87.

Instruments relating to, upon any other occasion

 See **Bond, Covenant,** &c

	£ s d.
APPOINTMENT of a new trustee, and APPOINTMENT in execution of a power of any property, or of any use, share, or interest in any property, by any instrument not being a will	0 10 0

And *see* Section 62

"Appointment of a new trustee" means the appointment of a trustee in succession or addition to a trustee or trustees previously appointed to perform the same trust The appointment of a trustee for a specific purpose by an order of Court, as for the purposes of the Settled Land Acts, the

Trustee Acts, &c., is not considered to be an appointment of a new trustee and is not chargeable with any duty. An appointment under hand of an original trustee—*e.g.*, a trustee of moneys payable under a policy effected in pursuance of Section 11 of The Married Women's Property Act, 1882—is not chargeable with any duty: if under seal, however, such an appointment would be chargeable with the duty of ten shillings as a "deed."

Two or more persons may be appointed new trustees of one will or settlement under one stamp, but an appointment by one instrument to the performance of several trusts is chargeable with several duties.

If the instrument of new appointment contains a conveyance of any of the trust property, or a covenant to surrender copyholds, or a declaration under Section 34 of The Conveyancing Act, 1881, vesting the trust property in the new trustee, it is liable to the further duty of ten shillings as a conveyance (Hadgett *v* Commissioners, 3 Ex Div. 46; 37 L. T. R. 612)

A declaration that trust property when transferred is to be held upon the trusts declared by a previous instrument, or a direction that the trust property shall be transferred so as to vest in the new trustee, or a release to the outgoing trustee, does not attract further duty, these being regarded as incidental to the new appointment; but a release in a deed of new appointment in respect of a breach of trust renders the deed liable to the further duty of ten shillings.

A record upon minutes of the election or appointment of a trustee by resolution at a meeting is not chargeable with duty.

The deed of discharge of a trustee retiring under Section 32 of The Conveyancing Act, 1881, containing also the consent to the vesting of the trust property in the continuing trustees, is considered liable to one stamp of ten shillings only; but if it operates to vest the property in the continuing trustees, it is considered liable to two stamps of ten shillings each, upon the authority of Hadgett *v* Commissioners, *ubi supra*.

APPOINTMENT of a gamekeeper.
See Deputation.

APPRAISEMENT or VALUATION of
any property, or of any interest therein, or of the annual value thereof, or of any dilapidations, or of any repairs wanted, or of the materials and labour used or

to be used in any building, or of any artificer's work whatsoever—

	£	s	d.
Where the amount of the appraisement or valuation does not exceed £5	0	0	3
Exceeds £5 and does not exceed £10	0	0	6
,, £10 ,, £20	0	1	0
,, £20 ,, £30	0	1	6
,, £30 ,, £40	0	2	0
,, £40 ,, £50	0	2	6
,, £50 ,, £100	0	5	0
,, £100 ,, £200	0	10	0
,, £200 ,, £500	0	15	0
,, £500	1	0	0

Exemptions

(1) Appraisement or valuation made for, and for the information of, one party only, and not being in any manner obligatory as between parties either by agreement or operation of law

This exemption is based on Atkinson v Fell (5 M & S 240), in which Lord Ellenborough held that a valuation not obligatory upon the parties interested, nor in itself intrinsically evidence between them, was not a valuation requiring the maker thereof to hold a licence, and this now governs stamp duty. An appraisement or valuation made upon a dissolution of partnership, or for the purpose of ascertaining the price at which property is to be estimated upon the conversion of a commercial firm into a company, or for production to the Commissioners of Inland Revenue to verify an apportionment of purchase money, is not within the exemption

A valuation that is originally within this exemption does not become liable to duty by reason of being subsequently used or adopted for a dutiable purpose. (Jackson v Stophurd, 4 Tyr. 330)

(2) Appraisement or valuation made in pursuance of the order of any Court of Admiralty, or of any Court of Appeal, from a judgment of any Court of Admiralty

(3) Appraisement or valuation of property of a deceased person made for the information of an executor or other person required to deliver, in England or Ireland, an affidavit, or to record in any commissary court in Scotland an inventory of the estate of such deceased person.

(4) Appraisement or valuation of any property made for the purpose of ascertaining the legacy or succession or account duty payable in respect thereof.

And *see* Section 24.

Appraisements made for the purpose of estate duty are within these Exemptions (57 & 58 Vict, Ch 30, Sec 8)

An appraisement or valuation made for the purpose of obtaining a return of duty is not within Exemption 4

Appraisements

24. (1) Every appraiser, by whom an appraisement or valuation chargeable with stamp duty is made, shall, within fourteen days after the making thereof, write out the same, in words and figures showing the full amount thereof, upon duly stamped material, and if he neglects or omits so to do, or in any other manner discloses the amount of the appraisement or valuation, he shall incur a fine of fifty pounds.

Appraisements to be written out.

(2) Every person who receives from any appraiser, or pays for the making of, any such appraisement or valuation, shall, unless the same be written out and stamped as aforesaid, incur a fine of twenty pounds.

(33 & 34 *Vict*, *Ch.* 97, *Sec.* 38.)

"Appraiser" is defined by 46 Geo. III, Ch. 43, Sec. 4, to be a person who values or appraises any estate or property, real or personal, or any interest, whether in possession or not, in any estate or property, or any goods, merchandise, or effects, for or in expectation of any hire, gain, fee, or reward

Valuations of separate properties must be separately stamped, though written on the same paper *See* Section 4 (*a*).

F

By 31 & 32 Vict., Ch 89, Sec 2, it is enacted that in all cases of exchange, partition, or division of intermixed land proposed to be effected under the Acts for the Commutation of Tithes, the Copyhold Acts, and the Acts for the Inclosure, Exchange, and Improvement of Land, the valuations required to be furnished to the Copyhold Commissioners shall be duly stamped, and, as a general rule, appraisements made for the information of the Commissioners of Inland Revenue for any purpose not covered by the exemptions are liable to duty

	£	s.	d
APPRENTICESHIP, instrument of.	0	2	6

Exemptions

(1) Instrument relating to any poor child apprenticed by or at the sole charge of any parish or township, or by or at the sole charge of any public charity, or pursuant to any Act for the regulation of parish apprentices.

A sectarian charity is not considered to be a "public charity", but a charity restricted to the members of a particular trade, or confined to the inhabitants of a particular locality, is a public charity, and instruments of apprenticeship relating to persons apprenticed at the sole cost of such a charity are exempt. *See* Hall *v.* Urban Sanitary Authority, &c, of Derby (16 Q B D 163), and as to a local charity *see* Rex *v.* Halesworth (3 B & Ad. 717)

(2) Instrument of apprenticeship in Ireland, where the value of the premium or consideration does not exceed £10

And *see* Section 25.

(53 & 54 Vict., Ch 8, Sec 19)

Instruments of Apprenticeship.

Meaning of instrument of apprenticeship.

25. Every writing relating to the service or tuition of any apprentice, clerk, or servant placed with any master to learn any profession, trade, or employment (except articles of clerkship to a solicitor or law agent or writer to the signet), is to be deemed an instrument of apprenticeship

(33 & 34 Vict., Ch 97, Sec 39)

ARTICLES OF CLERKSHIP whereby any person first becomes bound to serve as a clerk in order to his admission—

	£	s	d
(1) As a solicitor of the Supreme Court in England or of the Court of Judicature in Ireland	80	0	0
(2) As a law agent to practise before the Court of Session or as writer to the signet Scotland	60	0	0
(3) As a law agent to practise before a sheriff court in Scotland	0	2	6

And *see* Sections 26, 27, and 28

(36 & 37 *Vict*, *Ch.* 63, 36 & 37 *Vict*, *Ch.* 66, *Sec* 87, 40 & 41 *Vict.*, *Ch.* 57, *Sec.* 78)

Articles of Clerkship

26. (1) Where the same articles are a qualification for the admission of any person as a law agent to practise before the Court of Session, and also as a law agent to practise before a sheriff court in Scotland, the articles are not to be charged with any further duty than sixty pounds. *(Articles in Scotland not to be charged with more than one duty of £60)*

(2) Where any person has become bound by duly stamped articles in order to his admission as a law agent to practise before a sheriff court in Scotland, the articles shall, on payment of such further amount of duty as, together with the amount previously paid thereon, will make up the sum of sixty pounds, be impressed with a stamp denoting the payment of the further duty, and shall thereupon be considered to be sufficiently stamped for entitling the person to admission as a law agent to practise before the Court of Session

(33 & 34 *Vict*, *Ch* 97, *Sec* 42)

ARTICLES OF CLERKSHIP

Terms upon which articles may be stamped after execution.

27. Save as hereinbefore provided, articles of clerkship are not to be stamped at any time after the date thereof, except upon payment of penalties, as follows :—

(a) If brought to be stamped within one year after date, ten pounds.

(b) If so brought after one year, and within five years after date—
For every complete year, and also for any additional part of a year elapsed since the date, ten pounds

(c) In every other case, fifty pounds

(33 & 34 Vict., Ch. 97, Sec. 43.)

Distinct account to be kept of £14 payable to King's Inns

28. The sum of fourteen pounds, part of the duty payable on articles of clerkship in Ireland, shall be carried to a separate account, and paid over by the Commissioners to the treasurer of the Society of King's Inns in Dublin, to be applied by him according to the directions of the said society.

(33 & 34 Vict., Ch. 97, Sec 44.)

Articles of clerkship are not allowed to be stamped after execution without penalty.

Unstamped articles of clerkship cannot be enrolled, and service under them is not computed, but the Court will on application allow service for the period during which they were unstamped to be computed if a satisfactory reason be given for not paying the duty at the proper time, and it is shown that the applicant was prevented from doing so by causes over which he had no control. (In re Sayer, 10 C. P. 569.)

ARTICLES OF CLERKSHIP whereby any person, having been bound by previous duly stamped articles to serve as a clerk in order to his admission in any of the courts aforesaid, and not having completed his service so as to be

entitled to such admission, becomes
bound afresh for the same purpose—

	£	s.	d.
Where the duty upon the previous articles was 2s 6d.	0	2	6
In any other case	0	10	0

ASSIGNMENT or ASSIGNATION—
By way of security, or of any security
See **Mortgage**, &c

Upon a sale or otherwise See **Conveyance**.

ASSURANCE. See **Policy.**

ATTESTED COPY. See **Copy.**

ATTORNEY, LETTER or POWER of.
See **Letter of Attorney.**

ATTORNEY, WARRANT of. See **Warrant of Attorney.**

AWARD in England or Ireland, and AWARD or DECREET ARBITRAL in Scotland

In any case in which an amount or value is the matter in dispute—

	£	s.	d.
Where no amount is awarded or the amount or value awarded does not exceed £5	0	0	3

Where the amount or value awarded—

			£	s.	d.
Exceeds £5	and does not exceed	£10	0	0	6
,, £10	,,	£20	0	1	0
,, £20	,,	£30	0	1	6
,, £30	,,	£40	0	2	0
,, £40	,,	£50	0	2	6
,, £50	,,	£100	0	5	0
,, £100	,,	£200	0	10	0
,, £200	,,	£500	0	15	0
,, £500	,,	£750	1	0	0
,, £750	,,	£1,000	1	5	0
,, £1,000			1	15	0
In any other case			1	15	0

BANK NOTE

The duties on awards and appraisements are the same up to £500. Beyond that limit, awards are liable to a higher duty. The test to be applied for ascertaining whether an instrument is an award or an appraisement is set out in Carus-Wilson v Greene (18 Q B. D 7) "To make a decision an award, there must be a dispute on foot between the parties" The decision of an umpire called in between two valuers who could not agree is not an award, the umpire being called in to prevent a dispute, not to settle one See also Leeds v Burrows (12 East, 1)

If the award is not measured by a money value, the duty is one pound fifteen shillings The highest duty upon any award is one pound fifteen shillings therefore, if it is partly measurable in money value, and relates in other part to matters not so measurable, ad valorem duty is not chargeable in addition to the one pound fifteen shillings

Arbitrations made under the provisions of The Common Law Procedure Act, 1854, Secs 3 to 17, are exempted from duty by Section 30 of the Act

BACK BOND or BACK LETTER. See Mortgage, &c, and Sections 23 and 86.

BANK NOTE—

	£	s	d
For money not exceeding £1	0	0	5
Exceeding £1 and not exceeding £2	0	0	10
,, £2 ,, £5	0	1	3
,, £5 ,, £10	0	1	9
,, £10 ,, £20	0	2	0
,, £20 ,, £30	0	3	0
,, £30 ,, £50	0	5	0
,, £50 ,, £100	0	8	6

And see Sections 29 30, and 31

Bank Notes, Bills of Exchange, and Promissory Notes

Meaning of banker and bank note

29. For the purposes of this Act the expression "banker" means any person carrying on the business of banking in the United Kingdom, and the expression "bank note" includes—

(a) Any bill of exchange or promissory note issued by any banker, other than the Bank of England, for the payment of money not exceeding one hundred pounds to the bearer on demand; and

(b) Any bill of exchange or promissory note so issued which entitles or is intended to entitle the bearer or holder thereof, without indorsement, or without any further or other indorsement than may be thereon at the time of the issuing thereof, to the payment of money not exceeding one hundred pounds on demand, whether the same be so expressed or not, and in whatever form, and by whomsoever the bill or note is drawn or made

30. A bank note issued duly stamped, or issued unstamped by a banker duly licensed or otherwise authorised to issue unstamped bank notes, may be from time to time re-issued without being liable to any stamp duty by reason of the re-issuing *Bank notes may be re-issued.*

31. (1) If any banker, not being duly licensed or otherwise authorised to issue unstamped bank notes, issues or permits to be issued any bank note not being duly stamped, he shall incur a fine of fifty pounds *Penalties for issuing or receiving an unstamped bank note.*

(2) If any person receives or takes in payment or as a security any bank note issued unstamped contrary to law, knowing the same to have been so issued, he shall incur a fine of twenty pounds

(33 & 34 Vict., Ch. 97, Secs 45, 46, and 47.)

BILL OF EXCHANGE—   £ s. d.
    Payable on demand or at sight or on presentation 0 0 1
    And *see* Sections 32, 34, and 38
        (34 & 35 Vict., Ch 74, Sec 2)

BILL OF EXCHANGE of any other kind whatsoever (*except a Bank Note*) and **PROMISSORY NOTE** of any kind whatsoever (*except a Bank Note*)—

drawn, or expressed to be payable, or actually paid, or endorsed, or in any manner negotiated in the United Kingdom—

	£	s	d
Where the amount or value of the money for which the bill or note is drawn or made does not exceed £5	0	0	1
Exceeds £5 and does not exceed £10	0	0	2
,, £10 ,, £25	0	0	3
,, £25 ,, £50	0	0	6
,, £50 ,, £75	0	0	9
,, £75 ,, £100	0	1	0
,, £100— for every £100, and also for any fractional part of £100, of such amount or value	0	1	0

Exemptions

(1) Bill or note issued by the Bank of England or the Bank of Ireland

(2) Draft or order drawn by any banker in the United Kingdom upon any other banker in the United Kingdom, not payable to bearer or to order, and used solely for the purpose of settling or clearing any account between such bankers

(3) Letter written by a banker in the United Kingdom, to any other banker in the United Kingdom, directing the payment of any sum of money, the same not being payable to bearer or to order, and such letter not being sent or delivered to the person to whom payment is to be made or to any person on his behalf

(4) Letter of credit granted in the United Kingdom, authorising drafts to be drawn out of the United Kingdom payable in the United Kingdom.

(5) Draft or order drawn by the Paymaster-General on behalf of the Court of Chancery in England or by the Accountant-General of the Supreme Court of Judicature in Ireland.

(6) Warrant or order for the payment of any annuity granted by the National Debt Commissioners or for the payment of any dividend or interest on any share in the Government or Parliamentary stocks or funds

(7) Bill drawn by any person under the authority of the Admiralty, upon and payable by the Accountant-General of the Navy.

(35 & 36 Vict., Ch. 20, Sec 7.)

(8) Bill drawn (according to a form prescribed by Her Majesty's orders by any person duly authorised to draw the same) upon and payable out of any public account for any pay or allowance of the army or auxiliary forces or for any other expenditure connected therewith

(57 Geo III., Ch 41, Sec 8.)

(9) Draft or order drawn upon any banker in the United Kingdom by an officer of a public department of the State for the payment of money out of a public account

(45 & 46 Vict., Ch 72, Sec 9.)

(10) Bill drawn in the United Kingdom for the sole purpose of remitting money to be placed to any account of public revenue

(53 & 54 Vict, Ch 8, Sec. 21)

This exemption is considered to be confined to the remittance of money which is money standing to a Revenue account prior to remittance Official Circular, 9th August, 1894

(11) Coupon or warrant for interest attached to and issued with any security, or with an agreement or memorandum for the renewal or extension of time for payment of a security.

(33 & 34 Vict, Ch 97, Sch, and 52 & 53 Vict Ch 42, Sec 16.)

The coupon exempted by the first part of this exemption must be attached to and issued with the security, not to interim scrip certificate or scrip, neither of which is a security for the purposes of the Stamp Law

THE FINANCE ACT, 1894 (57 & 58 VICT, CH. 30).

Exemption of Coupons from Stamp Duty

Exemption of coupons

40. A coupon for interest on a marketable security as defined by The Stamp Act, 1891, being one of a set of coupons whether issued with the security or subsequently issued in a sheet, shall not be chargeable with any stamp duty.

This exemption was enacted in consequence of the decision of the Queen's Bench Division, in the case of Rothschild & Sons v Commissioners ([1894] 2 Q B 142), that one of a set of coupons (for interest on a foreign bond) not issued with the security, but "subsequently issued in a sheet" attached to a "talon," was not within any of the exemptions provided by The Stamp Act, 1870, and Section 16 of The Revenue Act, 1889 (52 & 53 Vict Ch 42), in force at the time the coupons were issued See also Australasian Mortgage &c Company v Commissioners (16 Court Sess Cas, 4th series, Rettie, 64, 26 Sco L R 47)

To these exemptions may be added cheques drawn by Registrars of County Courts upon their public banking accounts, which are not considered liable to duty

And *see* Sections 32, 33, 34, 35, 36, 37, 38, and 39

32. For the purposes of this Act the expression "bill of exchange" includes draft, order, cheque, and letter of credit, and any document or writing (except a bank note) entitling or purporting to entitle any person, whether named therein or not, to payment by any other person of, or to draw upon any other person for, any sum of money; and the expression "bill of exchange payable on demand" includes— Meaning of "bill of exchange."

(a) An order for the payment of any sum of money by a bill of exchange or promissory note, or for the delivery of any bill of exchange or promissory note in satisfaction of any sum of money, or for the payment of any sum of money out of any particular fund which may or may not be available, or upon any condition or contingency which may or may not be performed or happen; and

(b) An order for the payment of any sum of money weekly, monthly, or at any other stated periods, and also an order for the payment by any person at any time after the date thereof of any sum of money, and sent or delivered by the person making the same to the person by whom the payment is to be made, and not to the person to whom the payment is to be made, or to any person on his behalf

(32 & 33 Vict., Ch 97, Sec 48)

To "Bill of Exchange" are referred in the Schedule—
Cheque
Draft for money
Letter of credit
Order for the payment of money

A coupon is a bill of exchange for the purpose of this Section (Rothschild & Sons v Commissioners, [1894] 2 Q B 142, Australasian Mortgage &c Company v Commissioners, 16 Rettie, 4th series, 64, 26 Sco L R. 47)

Instruments falling within the definition of "bill of exchange" in The Bills of Exchange Act, 1882 (45 & 46 Vict, Ch 61, Sec 3), are liable to duty as bills of exchange

The definition is as follows —

3. (1) A bill of exchange is an unconditional order in writing, addressed by one person to another, signed by the person giving it, requiring the person to whom it is addressed to pay on demand or at a fixed or determinable future time a sum certain in money to, or to the order of, a specified person, or to bearer

An order to pay out of a particular fund is not unconditional within the meaning of this section, but an unqualified order to pay, coupled with (a) an indication of a particular fund out of which the drawee is to reimburse himself or a particular account to be debited with the amount, or (b) a statement of the transaction which gives rise to the bill, is unconditional

The sum payable must be a sum certain for the purposes of the Stamp Act (Jones v Simpson, 2 B & C 818, 3 D & R. 545 &c), as well as the Bills of Exchange Act, Sec 9 of which applies to notes as well as bills, and is as follows.—

9. (1) The sum payable by a bill is a sum certain within the meaning of this Act, although it is required to be paid—

(a) With interest·
(b) By stated instalments
(c) By stated instalments, with a provision that upon default in payment of any instalment the whole shall become due
(d) According to an indicated rate of exchange, or according to a rate of exchange to be ascertained as directed by the bill.

A bill or note for the payment of money "with interest" or interest at a given rate is chargeable with duty only for the principal sum (Preussing v Ing 4 B & Ald 204), though the interest be payable from a date antecedent to the date of the instrument (Wills v Noot, 4 Tyr 726)

But if any sum by way of interest be added to the principal sum the stamp must cover the aggregate See Durie's Executrix v Fielding (30 Sco L R 371), where a bill for £205, £200 of which represented a loan, and £5 the first half-year's interest, was held to be insufficiently stamped with duty on £200

The Bills of Exchange Act, 1882, is not (Sec. 97 [3]) to affect the provisions of the Stamp Acts; and Section 32 of The Stamp Act, 1891, which repeats previous enactments, brings within the charge of duty instruments which are not bills of exchange in law

An *order for the payment of money* presupposes moneys of the drawer in the hands of the party to whom the order is addressed, held on the terms of applying such moneys as directed by the order of the party entitled to them No such obligation arises out of the ordinary contract of sale *per* Cockburn, C J, in Buck v Robson (3 Q B D. 687, 39 L T R., Q. B. 325) The document in that case was as follows "Dear Sir—I hereby assign to Messrs R. & Co. the sum of £40, or any other sum now due or that may hereafter become due in respect of the steam launch which I am building for you." The document was addressed to the debtor and given to the payee, and upon an objection taken that it was an order for payment of money not capable of being stamped after execution, the Court held that it was in effect an assignment and not an order, and that it was admissible on payment of stamp duty and penalty. The same had been held in the nearly contemporaneous case of Brice v Bannister (3 Q B. D 569, 38 L T 739), where the document given, under similar circumstances, in the form, "I do hereby order, authorise, and request you to pay," &c, was held to be an assignment of a debt, or chose in action, within Section 25 of The Judicature Act, 1873 *Ex parte* Shellard, *re* Adams (L. R 17 Eq 109), was thus overruled See also Adams v Morgan (12 L R., Ir. Ex. 1), Fisher v Calvert (27 W R 301), and Webb v Smith (30 Ch. D. 192) The result of the cases seems to be that an order or authority for payment, sent to the person to whom the payment is to be made, of a debt owing by a third person who is not under the obligation indicated in the judgment of Cockburn, C J., is an assignment liable to the duty of ten shillings as a "conveyance not hereinbefore charged," or ad valorem conveyance duty if on sale, or in consideration *pro tanto* of any debt under Section 57.

By Section 73 of The Bills of Exchange Act, 1882, a cheque is defined as a bill of exchange drawn on a banker payable on demand A post-dated cheque is liable to stamp duty as a bill of exchange payable on demand, whether to order or bearer (Bull v O'Sullivan, 6 Q B 209, Gatty v Fry. 2 Ex. D 265) In the latter case the Court observed "In considering whether the stamp is sufficient, we must look at the face of the instrument itself alone, because upon the face of the instrument the stamp was sufficient, since the cheque when presented in evidence at the time of the trial was payable on demand " (See also Misa v Currie, 1 App Cas 554, and Tottenham v. Royal Bank of Scotland, 9 R. 223.)

A stamp is *functus officio* as regards a bill of exchange for value when the bill has been paid or satisfied by the acceptor (Callow v Lawrence, 3 M & S 95, Hubbard v Jackson, 4 Bing 390, 3 C & P 134), as regards an accommodation bill, when the bill has been paid or satisfied by the drawer (Lazarus v Cowie, 11 L J, Q B 310, 3 A & E, N. S 459)

Meaning of "promissory note"

33. (1) For the purposes of this Act the expression "promissory note" includes any document or writing (except a bank note) containing a promise to pay any sum of money

(2) A note promising the payment of any sum of money out of any particular fund which may or may not be available, or upon any condition or contingency which may or may not be performed or happen, is to be deemed a promissory note for that sum of money.

(33 & 34 Vict, Ch. 97, Sec 49.)

Instruments falling within the definition of "promissory note" in The Bills of Exchange Act, 1882 (45 & 46 Vict, Ch 61, Sec. 83), are liable to duty as promissory notes

The definition is as follows :—

83. (1) A promissory note is an unconditional promise in writing made by one person to another, signed by the maker, engaging to pay, on demand or at a fixed or determinate future time, a sum certain in money to, or to the order of, a specified person, or to bearer

(2) An instrument in the form of a note payable to maker's order is not a note within the meaning of this section unless and until it is indorsed by the maker.

(3) A note is not invalid by reason only that it contains also a pledge of collateral security with authority to sell or dispose thereof

(4) A note which is, or on the face of it purports to be, both made and payable within the British Islands, is an inland note   Any other note is a foreign note

The sum payable must be a sum certain   see note to Section 32, and Section 9 of The Bills of Exchange Act, 1882, *ante*, p 76

The Bills of Exchange Act, 1882, is not (Section 97 [3]) to

affect the provisions of the Stamp Acts, and Section 33 of The Stamp Act, 1891, brings within the charge of duty instruments which are not promissory notes in law, especially those included in Sub-section 2.

The provision in The Stamp Act, 1870, Section 49 (1), corresponding to Section 33 (1) above, was considered in Yeo v Dawe (53 L T R. 125; 33 W. R. 739) and Mortgage Insurance Corporation v. Commissioners (20 Q B D. 352; 57 L J, Q. B 174), and on appeal (21 Q B. D. 352; 57 L J, Q B. 630; 36 W R 833). In Yeo v. Dawe the Court of Appeal was divided in opinion whether a document, "I, J Dawe, promise to pay J Yeo, on his signing a lease of the Castle Hotel, £150," was a promissory note within that provision, the view taken by the majority being that it was not, inasmuch as it was a record of the result of the negotiations between the parties, and was not intended as a promissory note. In Mortgage Insurance Corporation v. Commissioners, a document containing a promise to pay as part of a contract containing other stipulations was held to be chargeable with duty as an agreement, not as a promissory note. In order that an instrument may fall within the charge, it must contain substantially a promise to pay, and nothing the contents of which are not substantially such a promise; and the intention of the parties is to be taken into account in deciding what is the nature of the document. This judgment accords with Sibree v Tripp (15 L. J., Ex. 318), where it was said that the document must be something which the parties intended to be a promissory note, for it was not the intention of the Legislature to prevent parties from making written contracts for the payment of money, other than bills or notes.

In Yates v. Evans (66 L. T R. 532) a joint and several promissory note made by a principal and his surety for £5 to be paid by weekly instalments, with a provision that "time may be given to either without the consent of the other and without prejudice to the rights of holders to proceed against either party notwithstanding time given to the other," was held to be sufficiently stamped with a promissory note stamp.

The following have been held to be promissory notes:—

"Received of A B £150, which I promise to pay on demand, with interest" (Ashby v Ashby, Moore & P. 186; Green v Davis, 1 C & P. 451.)

"I acknowledge myself to be indebted to B in £50, to be paid on demand, for value received." (Cashbourne v. Dutton, Selwyn, N P 371.)

"I O U £20 to be paid on the 22nd instant." (Brooks v. Elkins, 2 Gale, 200; 2 M. & W 74, Waltham v Elsee, 1 Car. & K. 35.)

"I promise to pay or cause to be paid," &c (Lovell v. Hill, 6 C & P 238)

"I promise to account with T S or his order for £50 for value received" (Morris v Lee, 1 Str 629, 5 Mod 362)

An instrument is not the less a promissory note from the fact of having coupons attached. (British India Steam Navigation Company v Commissioners, 7 Q B. D. 165; 50 L J, Q. B. 517, 44 L T R 378)

Many of the old cases relating to the stamp duty on promissory notes were decided by reference to the exemption from promissory note duty in 55 Geo III, Ch. 85, in favour of "other instruments bearing in any degree or form the style of promissory notes, but which in law shall be deemed special agreements." The exemption was repealed by 33 & 34 Vict., Ch 99, and not re-enacted

Provisions for use of adhesive stamps on bills and notes.

34. (1) The fixed duty of one penny on a bill of exchange payable on demand or at sight or on presentation may be denoted by an adhesive stamp, which, where the bill is drawn in the United Kingdom, is to be cancelled by the person by whom the bill is signed before he delivers it out of his hands, custody, or power.

(2) The ad valorem duties upon bills of exchange and promissory notes drawn or made out of the United Kingdom are to be denoted by adhesive stamps

(33 & 34 Vict, Ch 97, Secs 50 & 51; 34 & 35 Vict., Ch. 74, Sec 2)

Bills of Exchange Act, 1882 (45 & 46 Vict., Ch 61, Sec. 10)
A bill of exchange is payable on demand—

(a) Which is expressed to be payable on demand, or at sight, or on presentation, or

(b) In which no time for payment is expressed

In addition, the instruments specified in Section 32 (a) and (b) fall under this section

The duty on a bill on demand which purports to be drawn abroad (Sec 36) should be denoted by the penny "Postage and Inland Revenue" adhesive stamp, not by the penny adhesive "Foreign Bill or Note" stamp, which is an appropriated stamp, and may be used for ad valorem duty only

36. (1) Every person into whose hands any bill of exchange or promissory note drawn or made out of the United Kingdom comes in the United Kingdom before it is stamped shall, before he presents for payment, or indorses, transfers, or in any manner negotiates, or pays the bill or note, affix thereto a proper adhesive stamp or proper adhesive stamps of sufficient amount, and cancel every stamp so affixed thereto.

Provisions as to stamping foreign bills and notes

(2) Provided as follows .

(a) If at the time when any such bill or note comes into the hands of any *bonâ fide* holder there is affixed thereto an adhesive stamp effectually cancelled, the stamp shall, so far as relates to the holder, be deemed to be duly cancelled, although it may not appear to have been affixed or cancelled by the proper person;

(b) If at the time when any such bill or note comes into the hands of any *bonâ fide* holder there is affixed thereto an adhesive stamp not duly cancelled, it shall be competent for the holder to cancel the stamp as if he were the person by whom it was affixed, and upon his so doing the bill or note shall be deemed duly stamped, and as valid and available as if the stamp had been cancelled by the person by whom it was affixed.

(3) But neither of the foregoing provisoes is to relieve any person from any fine or penalty incurred by him for not cancelling an adhesive stamp

(33 & 34 Vict., Ch. 97, Sec 51)

The adhesive stamps for ad valorem duties on foreign bills and notes are appropriated stamps

"Presents for payment" (1) means presentment according to the custom of merchants, not a mere demand unaccompanied by the presentation of the bill (Griffin v Weatherby, 3 Q B. 753, 18 L T. R., Ex 881)

"Negotiate" does not include presentment for acceptance A bill drawn on London at Quebec, and endorsed there to a holder in London, and presented for acceptance and refused, was held, in Sharples v. Rickard (2 H. & N., Ex. 57, 26 L J , Ex 382), not to require a stamp It follows that a foreign bill may be accepted in this country without becoming liable to duty merely by reason of the acceptance

The cancellation of the stamp may be effected at any time. It is sufficient if it appears on the stamp at the trial (Bradlaugh v De Rin, 3 C P 286, 18 L. T. R., C. P. 904), and in Veale v Mitchell (30 L. T. R 433) defective cancellation was allowed to be completed in court before the verdict was given. In Marc v Rony (31 L T R , Q B. 372) a foreign bill bearing a stamp which had not been cancelled was admitted upon the evidence of the holder that the proper stamp was affixed to the bill when it came into his possession, the onus of proving the contrary being thereby thrown upon the party objecting to the admission of the bill.

A bill on demand which purports to be drawn abroad falls under Section 38 (2), not Section 35. (In re Boase, Crofton v Crofton, 56 L J , Ch 135, decided upon the corresponding Sections of The Stamp Act, 1870)

As to bills and notes purporting to be drawn abroad

36. A bill of exchange or promissory note which purports to be drawn or made out of the United Kingdom is, for the purpose of determining the mode in which the stamp duty thereon is to be denoted, to be deemed to have been so drawn or made, although it may in fact have been drawn or made within the United Kingdom.

(33 & 34 Vict , Ch 97, Sec 52)

The difference between this definition and the definitions of inland and foreign bills and notes in The Bills of Exchange Act, 1882, should be noted. By that Act (Sec. 4) "an inland bill is a bill which is, or on the face of it purports to be, (a) both drawn and payable within the British Islands, or (b) drawn within the British Islands upon some person, resident therein Any other bill is a foreign bill" And by Section 83 (4), "a note which is, or on the face of it purports to be, both made and payable within the British Islands, is an inland note Any other note is a foreign note."

"British Islands," for the purposes of The Bills of Exchange Act, 1882, includes the Channel Islands and the Isle of Man (Sec 4) The Channel Islands and the Isle of Man, having their own revenue laws, are not within the United Kingdom for the purposes of The Stamp Act, 1891 (See Griffin v Weatherby, 3 Q B. 753 ; 18 L T R , Ex. 881)

BILLS OF EXCHANGE 83

37. (1) Where a bill of exchange or promissory note has been written on material bearing an impressed stamp of sufficient amount but of improper denomination, it may be stamped with the proper stamp on payment of the duty, and a penalty of forty shillings if the bill or note be not then payable according to its tenor, or of ten pounds if the same be so payable

Terms upon which bills and notes may be stamped after execution.

(2) Except as aforesaid, no bill of exchange or promissory note shall be stamped with an impressed stamp after the execution thereof.

(33 & 34 Vict., Ch 97, Sec. 53)

38. (1) Every person who issues, indorses, transfers, negotiates, presents for payment, or pays any bill of exchange or promissory note liable to duty and not being duly stamped shall incur a fine of ten pounds, and the person who takes or receives from any other person any such bill or note either in payment or as a security, or by purchase or otherwise, shall not be entitled to recover thereon, or to make the same available for any purpose whatever.

Penalty for issuing, &c., any unstamped bill or note.

(2) Provided that if any bill of exchange payable on demand or at sight or on presentation is presented for payment unstamped, the person to whom it is presented may affix thereto an adhesive stamp of one penny, and cancel the same, as if he had been the drawer of the bill, and may thereupon pay the sum in the bill mentioned, and charge the duty in account against the person by whom the bill was drawn, or deduct the duty from the said sum, and the bill is, so far as respects the duty, to be deemed valid and available

(3) But the foregoing proviso is not to relieve any person from any fine or penalty incurred by him in relation to such bill

(33 & 34 Vict, Ch. 97, Sec. 54, 34 & 35 Vict., Ch. 74, Sec 2)

This section applies to foreign as well as inland bills and notes

(1) The penalty does not extend to the acceptance or presentation for acceptance of a bill.

"Duly stamped" has not the same meaning here as in Section 8. If so, the proviso in Section 35 (2) would have no effect. Section 38 means, with reference to foreign bills, that a holder cannot recover unless a proper adhesive stamp has been affixed (Marc v. Rouy, 31 L. T. R., Q. B 372.)

(2) The drawer and the banker are the only persons who can affix and cancel the stamp in the manner permitted by this Sub section. A cheque drawn on unstamped paper, to which an intermediate holder had affixed an adhesive stamp and cancelled it, was held by Huddleston, B, to be invalid, in Hobbs v Cathie, 6 *Times* L R 292.

A bill on demand which purports to be drawn abroad falls under (2). (*In re* Boase, Crofton v. Crofton, 50 6 L J, Ch 135.)

<small>One bill only of a set need be stamped</small>

39. When a bill of exchange is drawn in a set according to the custom of merchants, and one of the set is duly stamped, the other or others of the set shall, unless issued or in some manner negotiated apart from the stamped bill, be exempt from duty; and upon proof of the loss or destruction of a duly stamped bill forming one of a set, any other bill of the set which has not been issued or in any manner negotiated apart from the lost or destroyed bill may, although unstamped, be admitted in evidence to prove the contents of the lost or destroyed bill

(33 & 34 *Vict.*, Ch. 97, Sec 55.)

BILL OF LADING of or for any goods, merchandise, or effects to be exported or carried coastwise .. .. £ s d 0 0 6

And *see* Section 40

Bills of Lading.

<small>Bills of lading</small>

40. (1) A bill of lading is not to be stamped after the execution thereof

(2) Every person who makes or executes any bill of lading not duly stamped shall incur a fine of fifty pounds.

(33 & 34 *Vict*, Ch 97, Sec 56.)

A bill of lading for goods imported into the United Kingdom is not liable to duty.

"A bill of lading is a well-known mercantile instrument signed by the master of a vessel passing along the high seas or along some estuary or navigable river between port and port." (Bryans *v* Nix, 4 M & W 775) It does not apply to inland navigation, and documents relating thereto are chargeable under the head "Agreement."

BILL OF SALE—
 Absolute *See* **Conveyance on Sale.**
 By way of security *See* **Mortgage,** &c.
 And *see* Section 41.

Bills of Sale.

41. A bill of sale is not to be registered under any Act for the time being in force relating to the registration of bills of sale unless the original, duly stamped, is produced to the proper officer.

  (*33 & 34 Vict., Ch. 97, Sec. 57.*)

Bills sale.

BOND for securing the payment or repayment of money or the transfer or retransfer of stock
 See **Mortgage,** &c., and **Marketable Security.**

BOND in relation to any annuity upon the original creation and sale thereof.
 See **Conveyance on Sale,** and Section 60.

BOND, COVENANT, or INSTRUMENT of any kind whatsoever—
(1) Being the only or principal or primary security for any annuity (*except upon the original creation thereof by way of sale or security, and except a superannuation annuity*), or for any sum or sums of money at stated periods, not being interest for any principal sum secured by a duly stamped instrument, nor rent reserved by a lease or tack.

For a definite and certain period, so that the total amount to be ultimately payable can be ascertained. { The same ad valorem duty as a bond or covenant for such total amount.

For the term of life or any other indefinite period.

For every £5, and also for any fractional part of £5, of the annuity or sum periodically payable ... ...

£ s. d.

0 2 6

(2) Being a collateral or auxiliary or additional or substituted security for any of the above-mentioned purposes where the principal or primary instrument is duly stamped.

Where the total amount to be ultimately payable can be ascertained { The same ad valorem duty as a bond or covenant of the same kind for such total amount.

In any other case—

For every £5, and also for any fractional part of £5, of the annuity or sum periodically payable ...

£ s. d.

0 0 6

(3) Being a grant or contract for payment of a superannuation annuity, that is to say a deferred life annuity granted or secured to any person in consideration of annual premiums payable until he attains a specified age, and so as to commence on his attaining that age.

For every £5, and also for any fractional part of £5 of the annuity 0 0 6

(*As to* (3), 45 & 46 *Vict*, *Ch.* 72, *Sec.* 8)

It is immaterial with respect to this charge whether the instrument be under hand or seal

The charge extends to all instruments creating a personal obligation to pay an annuity or periodical sums for an executed consideration which are not chargeable with ad valorem duty under the head "Conveyance" (Sec 60), or "Lease," or "Mortgage," &c. Of these, familiar examples are:—

 Licence to fix and maintain bookstalls, or automatic machines, or telephone poles.

 Licence to advertise on tramcars or hoardings, where no interest in the land on which the hoardings are erected passes to the licensee

 Licence to use a patented invention, where there is no grant of an interest in property (*see* p. 105, and Limmer Asphalte Company v. Commissioners, 7 Ex. 211, 41 L. J, Ex. 106).

 Instrument containing a personal undertaking only for repayment of a loan by instalments, or for payment of interest alone where no stamped security for repayment of the principal sum exists In the latter case duty is payable at the rate of two shillings and sixpence for every £5 of the annual interest, unless the loan is for a definite period, so that the total amount of interest can be ascertained.

Under this head are charged covenants contained in settlements for the payment of annuities, so far as such covenants are not exempt from duty under Section 105, and covenants in deeds of separation for the payment of annuities.

A bond, &c., for the payment of a weekly sum for life or any other indefinite period is chargeable with ad valorem duty at the rate of two shillings and sixpence for every £5 and part of £5 of the amount payable in the course of a year.

A bond, &c., for the payment of an annuity during joint lives, and a diminished annuity during the life of the survivor, is chargeable with ad valorem duty on the original annuity If the original annuity, according to the terms of the instrument, is susceptible of increase, and the amount of increase is definite, ad valorem duty is chargeable upon the amount of the increased annuity.

If two annuities may, under any circumstances, become payable concurrently, the bond, &c, for securing the payment thereof must be stamped with ad valorem duty upon both.

If a bond, &c., is given for making up the annual income of a particular fund, or the rents of property, to a greater sum named, ad valorem duty must be paid upon the difference between that sum and the present amount of such income or rents

This charge does not extend to a grant of an annuity or

limitation of a rent-charge out of real estate which contains no covenant to pay, nor to a declaration of trust of property vested in trustees upon trust out of the rents or income thereof to pay an annuity, there being no covenant to pay; nor to a bond, &c., for payment of an annuity or instalment of purchase-money where ad valorem conveyance duty has been paid under Section 56 (4); nor to a contract for payment of an annual sum in consideration of a grant or licence revocable at the will of the grantor (Conservators of River Thames v. Commissioners, 18 Q B D 279, 56 L J, Q B 181), nor to a contract for payment of salary for services to be rendered (Mounsey v Stephenson, 7 B & C 403)

Under the old law a bond for payment of rent reserved by a duly stamped lease was held to be liable to the deed stamp only, not to ad valorem duty under the head of charge corresponding to this (Winchester Corn Exchange Company v Gillingham, 12 L J, Q. B 159; 4 A & E., N S 475.)

The provision relating to a security without limit, which is a special regulation under the head "Mortgage," &c, does not apply to this charge

Superannuation Annuity.—A grant of an annuity in consideration of a single payment is liable to conveyance duty under Section 60.

BOND given pursuant to the directions

of any Act, or of the Commissioners or the Commissioners of Customs, or any of their officers, for or in respect of any of the duties of excise or customs, or for preventing frauds or evasions thereof, or for any other matter or thing relating thereto—

{ The same ad valorem duty as a bond for the amount of the penalty.

Where the penalty of the bond does not exceed £150.

£ s d

In any other case . . 0 5 0

Exemption

Bond given as aforesaid upon, or in relation to, the receiving or obtaining, or for entitling any person to receive or obtain, any drawback of any duty of excise or customs, for or in respect of any goods, wares, or merchandise exported or shipped to be exported from the United Kingdom to any parts beyond the seas, or upon or in relation to the obtaining of any debenture or certificate for entitling any person to receive any such drawback as aforesaid.

And *see* Section 42.

Bonds given in Relation to the Duties of Excise.

42. If any person required by any Act for the time being in force, or by the Commissioners, or any of their officers, to give or enter into any bond for or in respect of any duty of excise, or for preventing any fraud or evasion in relation to any such duty, or for any matter or thing relating thereto, includes in one and the same bond any goods or things belonging to more persons than one, not being partners or joint tenants, or tenants in common, he shall for every offence incur a fine of fifty pounds. *[Bonds not to include goods, &c., belonging to more than one person.]*

(33 & 34 Vict, Ch. 97, Sec 58; 34 & 35 Vict, Ch 103, Sec.18.)

	£	s.	d.
BOND on obtaining letters of administration in England or Ireland, or a confirmation of testament in Scotland	0	5	0

Exemptions

(1) Bond given by the widow, child, father, mother, brother or sister, of any common seaman, marine or soldier, dying in the service of Her Majesty.

(2) Bond given by any person where the estate to be administered does not exceed £100 in value

BOND of any kind whatsoever not specifically charged with any duty—
Where the amount limited to be recoverable does not exceed £300 — { The same ad valorem duty as a bond for the amount limited.

In any other case — — — — — 0 10 0

Under this head are charged fidelity bonds, bonds for due performance of office, and other bonds the condition of which is other than the payment of an annuity or money.

BOND, accompanied with a deposit of title deeds, for making a mortgage, wadset, or other security on any estate or property therein comprised

See **Mortgage**, &c., and Section 86.

BOND, DECLARATION, or other DEED or WRITING for making redeemable any disposition, assignation, or tack, apparently absolute, but intended only as a security

See **Mortgage**, &c., and Sections 23 and 86.

CERTIFICATE to be taken out yearly—
(1) By every person admitted or enrolled in England or Ireland as a solicitor, or in Scotland as a law agent or writer to the signet, or in any part of the United Kingdom as a notary public

(2) By every other legally qualified person who carries on business in England or Ireland as a conveyancer, special pleader, or draftsman in equity, and is obliged by law to take out such a certificate

CERTIFICATES   91

If such person practises or carries on his business	If he has been admitted or inrolled, or has carried on business for three years or upwards.	If he has not been so long admitted or inrolled, or has not so long carried on business
	£ s. d	£ s. d
In England, within ten miles from the General Post Office in the City of London		
In Scotland, within the city or shire of Edinburgh	9 0 0	4 10 0
In Ireland, in the city of Dublin, or within three miles therefrom		
In England, Scotland, or Ireland, beyond the above-mentioned limits	6 0 0	3 0 0
And *see* Sections 43, 44, 45, 46, 47, and 48.		

For a solicitor, &c., the three years are calculated from the date of his admission, whether he then began to practise or not

Certificates of Solicitors and others

43. (1) Every person who in any part of the United Kingdom— *Penalty for practising without certificate, or making false statement on application for certificate.*

(a) Directly or indirectly acts or practises as a solicitor or law agent in any court, or as a notary public, without having in force at the time a duly stamped certificate; or

(b) On applying for his certificate does not truly specify the facts and circumstances upon which the amount of duty chargeable upon the certificate depends

shall incur a fine of fifty pounds, and shall be incapable of maintaining any action or suit for the recovery of any fee, reward, or disbursement on account of or in relation to any act or proceeding done or taken by him in any such capacity.

(2) Every person in whose name, either alone or together with any other person, any proceeding is taken in any court, shall, unless the proceeding is set aside by the court as irregular, or unless the contrary is otherwise satisfactorily proved, be deemed to have acted in the proceeding.

(3) Nothing in this Act shall require a stamped certificate to be taken out by a person who is by law authorised to act as solicitor of a public department without admission, or by any assistant or clerk or officer appointed to act under the direction of such solicitor.

(33 & 34 *Vict*, *Ch*. 97, *Sec*. 59; 47 & 48 *Vict*, *Ch* 62, *Sec*. 10)

Penalty on unqualified persons preparing instruments.

44. Every person who (not being a barrister, or a duly certificated solicitor, law agent, writer to the signet, notary public, conveyancer, special pleader, or draftsman in equity), either directly or indirectly, for or in expectation of any fee, gain, or reward, draws or prepares any instrument relating to real or personal estate, or any proceeding in law or equity, shall incur a fine of fifty pounds.

Provided as follows ·

(1) This Section does not extend to—
(a) Any public officer drawing or preparing instruments in the course of his duty, or
(b) Any person employed merely to engross any instrument or proceeding.

(2) The expression "instrument" in this Section does not include—
(a) A will or other testamentary instrument; or
(b) An agreement under hand only, or

(c) A letter or power of attorney; or

(d) A transfer of stock containing no trust or limitation thereof.

(33 & 34 Vict, Ch 97, Sec 60.)

An uncertificated solicitor cannot recover costs or disbursements for business done in or out of court, nor if a person employs an uncertificated solicitor can he, even though successful in a legal proceeding, recover costs or disbursements from the party otherwise liable (Fowler v. Monmouthshire Canal Company, 4 Q B D. 334; 37 & 38 Vict., Ch. 68, Sec. 12.)

A solicitor with a country certificate practising at Birmingham, who attended a taxation upon a retainer within the ten-mile radius, was held not to have acted or practised in London by reason of the single transaction within the meaning of the statute (In re Horton, 8 Q B. D. 434.)

These penalties are (Secs 43 & 44) imposed not merely for the protection of the Revenue. (Taylor v. Crowland Gas and Coke Co, 16 Jur 728) The intention of the Legislature was to confine the drawing of instruments to a class possessing a competent knowledge of the subject

45. It shall not be necessary for any person required to take out a stamped certificate to take out in England, or in Scotland, or in Ireland more than one certificate for any one year.

(33 & 34 Vict., Ch. 97, Sec 61.)

One certificate only required

46. The certificates of solicitors in England and Ireland are to be applied for, taken out, issued, dated, and stamped—

(a) In England, in accordance with the provisions in that behalf of The Solicitors Acts, 1843, 1860, 1877, and 1888;

(b) In Ireland, in accordance with the provisions in that behalf of The Attorneys and Solicitors Act, Ireland, 1866.

(33 & 34 Vict, Ch. 97, Sec. 62.)

Solicitors' certificates in England and Ireland.

If the stamp duty is paid between the 16th November and 15th December inclusive, the certificate is dated and the qualification dates from the 16th November. If the duty is paid after the 15th December, the certificate bears the date of the payment of the stamp duty, and the qualification to practise dates only from the date of the certificate If the duty is paid after the 15th December and on or before the 1st January, the solicitor's name appears in the Law List, but his qualification to practise dates only from the date of the certificate, and he cannot recover costs for any business that he may have done during the uncertificated period. The Law List, therefore, is not in all cases evidence of the qualification of a solicitor to practise for the whole of the year, inasmuch as the contrary may be shown by reference to the Secretary of Inland Revenue

The Act 37 & 38 Vict., Ch. 68, Sec 12, imposes a penalty of £10 for each offence on a person who wrongfully acts as an attorney or solicitor, and enacts that the production of a duly stamped certificate is to be evidence of qualification.

Other Certificates.

47. Every person required to take out a certificate to authorise him to practise:—

(a) In Scotland, as a law agent or writer to the signet, or

(b) In England or Ireland, as a conveyancer, special pleader, or draftsman in equity; or

(c) In any part of the United Kingdom, as a notary public;

shall in every year, before he does any act in any of the aforesaid capacities, deliver to the Commissioners, or to their proper officer, in such manner and form as they direct, a note in writing stating his full name and the place where he carries on his business, and thereupon, and upon payment of the proper duty, shall be entitled to a certificate, which is to be duly stamped and issued to him by the Commissioners.

(33 & 34 Vict., Ch. 97, Sec. 63.)

Date and duration of certain certificates

48. The certificates in this section specified are to be dated and to expire at the times hereinafter in that behalf mentioned, that is to say,

(a) The certificates of law agents, writers to the signet, and notaries public in Scotland, and of conveyancers, special pleaders, and draftsmen in equity in England, are to be dated if taken out between the thirty-first of October and the first of December, on the first of November, and if taken out at any other time, on the day on which they are issued, and are in all cases to expire on the thirty-first of October next after their date.

(b) The certificates of notaries public in England are to be dated, if taken out between the fifteenth of November and the sixteenth of December, on the sixteenth of November, and if taken out at any other time, on the day on which they are issued, and are in all cases to expire on the fifteenth of November next after their date.

(c) The certificates of conveyancers, special pleaders, draftsmen in equity, and notaries public in Ireland are to be dated on the day on which they are issued, and are to expire, as to the certificates of notaries public, on the twenty-fifth day of March next after their date, and in all other cases on the sixth day of January next after their date.

(33 & 34 Vict., Ch. 97, Sec. 64.)

	£ s. d.
CERTIFICATE of any goods, wares, or merchandise, having been duly entered inwards, which shall be entered outwards for exportation at the port of importation, or be removed from thence to any other port for the more convenient exportation thereof, where such certificate is issued for enabling a person to obtain a debenture or certificate entitling him to receive a drawback of any duty of customs - - - -	0 4 0

CHARTER of resignation, or of confir-mation, or of novodamus or upon apprising, or upon a decreet of adjudi-

		£	s	d.
cation, or sale of any lands, or other heritable subjects in Scotland	- -	0	5	0
CHARTER-PARTY - - - -		0	0	6

And *see* Sections 49, 50, and 51

Charter-parties.

<small>Provisions as to duty on charter-party</small>

49. (1) For the purposes of this Act the expression "charter-party" includes any agreement or contract for the charter of any ship or vessel, or any memorandum, letter, or other writing between the captain, master, or owner of any ship or vessel, and any other person, for or relating to the freight or conveyance of any money, goods, or effects on board of the ship or vessel.

(2) The duty upon a charter-party may be denoted by an adhesive stamp, which is to be cancelled by the person by whom the instrument is last executed, or by whose execution it is completed as a binding contract.

(33 & 34 *Vict., Ch.* 97, *Sec* 66.)

<small>Charter parties executed abroad.</small>

50. Where a charter-party is first executed out of the United Kingdom without being duly stamped, any party thereto may, within ten days after it has been first received in the United Kingdom, and before it has been executed by any person in the United Kingdom, affix thereto an adhesive stamp denoting the duty chargeable thereon, and at the same time cancel such adhesive stamp, and the instrument when so stamped shall be deemed duly stamped.

(33 & 34 *Vict., Ch.* 97, *Sec.* 67.)

<small>Terms upon which charter-parties may be stamped after execution</small>

51. A charter-party may be stamped with an impressed stamp after execution upon the following terms; that is to say,

  (1) Within seven days after the first execution thereof, on payment of the duty and a penalty of four shillings and sixpence;

(2) After seven days, but within one month after the first execution thereof, on payment of the duty and a penalty of ten pounds;

and shall not in any other case be stamped with an impressed stamp.

(33 & 34 Vict., Ch 97, Sec. 68.)

Section 51 does not apply to a charter-party wholly executed out of the United Kingdom. Such an instrument may be stamped with an impressed stamp under the regulations applicable to instruments executed out of the United Kingdom (Sec 15 [8]), as was done in re The Belfort (L. R., 9 Probate, 215).

CHEQUE. *See* **Bill of Exchange.**

CLARE CONSTAT. *See* **Precept and Writ.**

COLONIAL SECURITY. *See* **Marketable Security** and Section 82.

COMMISSION : £ s. d.
(1) To any officer in the army, or in the corps of Royal Marines ... 1 10 0
(2) To any officer in the navy . 0 5 0

Exemption.

Commission to any officer of militia, yeomanry, or volunteers.

COMMISSION OF LUNACY. 0 5 0

COMMISSION to act as a notary public in Scotland. *See* **Faculty.**

COMMISSION in the nature of a power of attorney in Scotland *See* **Letter or Power of Attorney.**

H

CONDITIONAL SURRENDER of any
   copyhold or customary estate by way
   of mortgage.
   See **Mortgage,** &c., and Sections 86
   and 87

CONGE D'ELIRE. See **Grant.**

CONSTAT of Letters Patent. See **Exemplification.**

CONTRACT. See **Agreement.**

CONTRACT NOTE for or relating to
   the sale or purchase of any stock or
   marketable security—   £ s. d
   Of the value of £5, and under the
      value of £100   .   .   ..   0 0 1
   Of the value of £100 or upwards .   0 1 0
      (56 Vict, Ch 7, Sec. 3)
   And see Sections 52 and 53.

Contract Notes.

Provisions as to contract notes.

52. (1) For the purposes of this Act the expression "contract note" means the note sent by a broker or agent to his principal (except where such principal is acting as broker or agent for a principal) advising him of the sale or purchase of any stock or marketable security.

(2) Where a note advises the sale or purchase of more than one description of stock or marketable security, the note shall be deemed to be as many contract notes as there are descriptions of stock or security sold or purchased

(3) The duty of one penny on a contract note may be denoted by an adhesive stamp, and the duty of sixpence on a contract note is to be denoted by an adhesive stamp appropriated to a contract note

(4) Every adhesive stamp on a contract note is to be cancelled by the person by whom the note is executed.

(51 & 52 Vict, Ch 8, Secs 16 & 17.)

53. (1) Any person who effects any sale or purchase of any stock or marketable security, of the value of five pounds or upwards, as a broker or agent, shall forthwith make and execute a contract note and transmit the same to his principal, and in default of so doing shall incur a fine of twenty pounds.

(2) Every person who makes or executes any contract note chargeable with duty, and not being duly stamped, shall incur a fine of twenty pounds.

(3) No broker, agent, or other person shall have any legal claim to any charge for brokerage, commission, or agency, with reference to the sale or purchase of any stock or marketable security of the value of five pounds or upwards mentioned or referred to in any contract note, unless the note is duly stamped.

(4) The duty of one shilling upon a contract note may be added to the charge for brokerage or agency.

(33 & 34 Vict., Ch. 97, Sec. 60, 51 & 52 Vict., Ch. 8, Secs 16 & 17.)

The duty of sixpence upon a contract note was increased to a shilling by Section 3 of The Customs and Revenue Act, 1893 (56 Vict., Ch. 7), which came into operation on the 12th May, 1893, and is as follows —

3. (1) In lieu of the stamp duty of sixpence now payable under The Stamp Act, 1891, upon a contract note, as defined by Section 52 of the said Act, for or relating to the sale or purchase of any stock or marketable security of the value of one hundred pounds or upwards there shall be charged the stamp duty of one shilling.

(2) The duty imposed by this section is to be denoted by an adhesive stamp appropriated to a contract note and may be added to the charge for brokerage or agency.

In Knight v Barber (16 L J, Ex. 18; 16 M. & W 66, 10 Jur. 929), decided before a special duty was imposed upon contract notes, it was held that a "bought note" was liable to duty as a memorandum of agreement; and that case now governs transactions between principals, to which contract note duty does not apply, as well as "bucket shop" transactions

In Learoyd v. Bracken ([1894] 1 Q B, C A. 114)—a case relating to carrying-over transactions by a broker who did not make or transmit any contract note when the stocks were carried over—it was held that though the broker incurred a penalty every time he failed to make a contract note duly stamped, yet no contract note being made at all, he could recover commission.

A continuation note is to be regarded as either in form or substance a contract note advising the sale or purchase of stock or marketable securities at the expiration of one account, and the purchase or sale thereof for the following account, and it follows that such a note should bear two stamps either of one shilling or one penny each in respect of each description of stock or securities to which it refers according to the value of such stock or securities (Official Circular, 1890)

CONVEYANCE or TRANSFER,

whether on sale or otherwise—

	£	s.	d.
(1) Of any stock of the Bank of England	0	7	9
(2) Of any stock of the Government of Canada inscribed in books kept in the United Kingdom, or of any colonial stock to which The Colonial Stock Act, 1877, applies— For every £100, and also for any fractional part of £100, of the nominal amount of stock transferred	0	2	6

(37 & 38 Vict., Ch. 26, Sec 2, 41 & 42 Vict, Ch 59, Sec 2)

And see Section 62.

CONVEYANCE or TRANSFER on sale,

Of any property (*except such stock as aforesaid*)—

CONVEYANCE

	£	s.	d.
Where the amount or value of the consideration for the sale does not exceed £5	0	0	6
Exceeds £5, and does not exceed £10	0	1	0
,, £10 ,, £15	0	1	6
,, £15 ,, £20	0	2	0
,, £20 ,, £25	0	2	6
,, £25 ,, £50	0	5	0
,, £50 ,, £75	0	7	6
,, £75 ,, £100	0	10	0
,, £100 ,, £125	0	12	6
,, £125 ,, £150	0	15	0
,, £150 ,, £175	0	17	6
,, £175 ,, £200	1	0	0
,, £200 ,, £225	1	2	6
,, £225 ,, £250	1	5	0
,, £250 ,, £275	1	7	6
,, £275 ,, £300	1	10	0
,, £300—			
For every £50, and also for any fractional part of £50, of such amount or value	0	5	0

And see Sections 54, 55, 56, 57, 58, 59, 60, and 61.

Conveyances on Sale

54. For the purposes of this Act the expression "conveyance on sale" includes every instrument, and every decree or order of any court or of any commissioners, whereby any property, or any estate or interest in any property, upon the sale thereof is transferred to or vested in a purchaser, or any other person on his behalf or by his direction.

(33 & 34 Vict., Ch 97, Sec 70.)

Meaning of "conveyance on sale."

For the purposes of stamp duty, it is immaterial whether a conveyance be under hand or seal.

The words "or any estate or interest in any property" are new, and the words "legally or equitably," which preceded "transferred to or vested in a purchaser" in the corresponding Section (70) of The Stamp Act, 1870, have been omitted The meaning of that Section was discussed in Commissioners v Angus & Company, Limited (23 Q B D 579), where it was held that a contract for the sale of goodwill, the effect of which was to make the purchaser the owner, and of which a Court of Equity would decree specific performance, did not fall within the definition See the judgment of Lord Esher, M.R., on p 590. The importance of the decision was greatly diminished by 52 and 53 Vict, Ch. 42, Sec. 15, re-enacted by Sec 59, *post*, p 116

To Conveyance on Sale are referred—
  Annuity, conveyance in consideration of (Sec. 56).
     „   purchase of (Sec. 60)
  Assignment or assignation upon a sale or otherwise
  Bill of sale absolute.
  Bond in relation to any annuity upon the original creation and sale thereof (Sec 60)
  Copyhold and customary estates, instruments relating thereto, upon a sale thereof.
  Covenant in relation to any annuity upon the original creation and sale thereof.
  Disposition of heritable property in Scotland to singular successors or purchasers.
  Disposition of heritable property in Scotland to a purchaser, containing a clause declaring all or any part of the purchase money a real burden upon or affecting the heritable property thereby disposed, or any part thereof
  Disposition in Scotland containing constitution of feu or annual ground right
  Feu contract in Scotland
  Grant of copyhold or customary estates
  Release or renunciation of any proportion or of any right or interest in any property
  Share warrant issued under the provisions of The Companies Act, 1867, and stock certificate to bearer.
  Transfer

An enfranchisement award under The Copyhold Act, 1894 (57 & 58 Vict, Ch 46), is chargeable (Section 58 [2]) "with the like stamp duty as is chargeable in respect of an enfranchisement deed"—i e, with an ad valorem conveyance duty on the amount paid for enfranchisement, or, if nothing is paid, ten shillings

In Great Western Railway Company v Commissioners ([1894] 1 Q B, C. A. 507; 42 W R 711), where by a special Act of Parliament, which recited that it was expedient that a certain railway company should be "amalgamated" with the G. W. R Company, it was provided that the undertaking of the former company should be "amalgamated" with and form part of the undertaking of the G W R. Company as from a certain date, that the former company should from that date be dissolved, and that the holders of shares in that company should in lieu thereof become holders of consolidated stock of the G. W R. Co in proportion to the shares held by them respectively, it was held that the transaction was a sale for the purposes of the Stamp Acts, and that ad valorem conveyance duty was chargeable upon the value, at the date of "amalgamation," of the consolidated stock of the G W R Co. issued to the shareholders of the other company

Upon the "amalgamation" under the same Act of another railway company with the G. W. R. Co., all shares and debentures in which were held by the G W R Company, except £11,600 in debentures subsequently paid off, the transaction was held to be a sale, and ad valorem conveyance duty on £11,600 to be chargeable. *See also* Furness Railway Co. *v* Commissioners (38 L. J , Ex. 173, *post*, p. 111).

In the old case of Horsfall *v*. Hey (2 Ex R. 778), a document in the following terms · "Memorandum—A. has sold to B. all the goods and fixtures in a certain shop for £50," was held to be liable to duty as a conveyance on sale. Words in the past tense were formerly in general use in conveyancing

The conveyance must be a conveyance on *sale* "Sale" is defined in "Benjamin on Sale" as "the transfer of the absolute or general property in a thing for a price in money," or (for purposes of stamp duty) stock or security There must be a sale as to both parties. In Doe dem Manifold *v* Diamond (4 B & C 243, 6 D & R 328), a conveyance by father to son in consideration of natural love and affection, and the bond of the son to augment his sisters' portions by £1,500, was held to be a deed of family arrangement, not a conveyance on sale. In Massey *v* Nanney (3 Bing. N. C 478) the covenant of the husband's uncle to pay to the trustees of the marriage settlement an annuity of £300 in consideration of the settlement of £4,000 on the wife by her father, was held not to be a sale of the annuity (*See* also Wigram *v* Joyce, 13 L. R , Ir 164.)

In Foster (John) and Sons, Limited, *v* Commissioners ([1894] 1 Q B. C. A 516, 63 L J R 173, and 69 L T R. 817), wherein upon the conversion of a partnership consisting of eight persons into a limited liability company formed of the same eight persons, all the shares and debentures of the company being allotted to them in proportion to their respective shares in the partnership, the eight partners conveyed the partnership property to the company, the transaction was held to be a sale, and the conveyance liable to ad valorem duty as a conveyance on sale. Duty was charged upon the value of the property, not upon the nominal amount of the shares and debentures

In some cases, as upon the transfer of a business from father to son, it is difficult to determine whether the transaction is a sale or a family arrangement. If it is in fact or is expressed to be a sale, ad valorem conveyance duty must be paid upon the consideration; if it is an arrangement consequent upon which estate duty would be payable upon the death of the assignor, conveyance duty is not charged, but covenants for payment of annuities and other sums must bear their proper duties under the heads "Bond," &c, and "Mortgage," &c. As to cases in which estate duty would be charged, reference may be made to Crossman v. The Queen (18 Q. B. D. 256) and The Finance Act, 1894 (57 & 58 Vict., Ch. 30)

A partition is not a sale. (*See* Henniker v. Henniker, 22 L. J., Q. B. 94; 1 E & B 54, and *see* Section 73, *post*, p. 136.)

When, as occasionally happens upon the surrender of a lease, money is paid by the surrenderor to the surrenderee, there is no sale, and the instrument is chargeable with ten shillings as a surrender or "conveyance not hereinbefore described."

The redemption of a "ground annual" or "feu duty" created by a conveyance on sale, which contained a provision that the purchaser might redeem at any time, upon giving notice, by paying a fixed number of years' purchase, has been held in the Court of Session not to be a conveyance on sale for the purpose of the Stamp Acts. (Belch v Commissioners, 4 Rettie, 4th Series, 592; Gibb v Commissioners, 8 Rettie, 120.)

The subject matter of the conveyance must be *property*. "Property is that which belongs to a person exclusive of others, and can be the subject of bargain and sale to another." (*Per* Pollock, C. B., in Potter v Commissioners, 10 Ex. R. 147, 18 Jur. 778, 23 L. J. 345.) In Limmer Asphalte Paving Company v Commissioners (7 Ex. 211; 41 J. L., Ex. 106, 28 L. T. R. 633), the grant of an exclusive right to carry on the business of asphalte paving with the company's asphalte in a limited district was considered an attempt to create a monopoly, and not a conveyance of "property." In Conservators of River Thames v. Commissioners (18 Q. B. D. 279, 56 L. J., Q. B. 181, 56 L. T. 198), a "permissive licence" to erect a jerty in the Thames, revocable at the will of the licensors, was held not to be a conveyance of property, but the *ratio decidendi* rested in part, at least, upon the special provisions of the Thames Conservancy Act.

A personal licence does not operate to convey "property," but a licence coupled with a grant, as a licence to enter upon land and take anything away, is a grant of an interest in property and is chargeable with ad valorem duty (See Newby v Harrison, 1 J & H. 393, and Heap v Hartley, 42 Ch. D. 461, 58 L J, Ch 790, *per* Fry, L J.) A licence to demise is not chargeable with any duty unless under seal, when it is chargeable as a deed with ten shillings.

A policy of marine insurance or fire insurance, no loss having occurred, is not property. (Blandy v. Herbert, 9 B & C 396)

The goodwill of a business is property for the purposes of the Stamp Act (Potter v Commissioners, *ubi supra*, the business being a papermaker's), and ad valorem duty must be paid upon the conveyance Upon the doubtful question whether personal goodwill, as of a solicitor's practice, is property, see Arundell v Bell (52 L J, Ch 587; 49 Jur., N L 345, 31 W. R 477).

Patents, licences to *use and vend* an invention protected by a patent, and trade marks, are property. An exclusive licence to *use* (only) a patented invention within a specified district was held in Heap v Hartley (42 Ch. D 461; 58 L. J., Ch. 790) not to confer any interest in property, and such a licence is not chargeable with ad valorem conveyance duty, but may be liable to ad valorem duty under the head "Bond, Covenant, or Instrument," &c., *ante*, p. 85 (as a security for the payment of sums of money at stated periods), and a deed stamp For a judicial assessment of duty on a similar instrument, see Limmer Asphalte Paving Company v Commissioners, *ubi supra*.

Under the old law the duty on conveyances was chargeable upon the consideration *expressed*, and the omission to set forth the true consideration was prohibited by severe penalties (48 Geo III, Ch. 149, Secs 22 to 26; Attorney-General v Brown, 3 Ex. R 662, 18 L J, Ex. 336, Gingell v. Perkins, 4 Ex R 720, 19 L J, Ex. 129); but an objection based upon such an omission to the admissibility of an instrument stamped in accordance with the consideration expressed was not maintainable This is now altered Section 5 (which is also a penal section) requires all the facts and circumstances affecting the liability of an instrument to duty to be fully and truly set forth, and the Commissioners are empowered upon adjudication to call for evidence to show that this direction has been complied with (Sec. 12) Unless, therefore, ad valorem conveyance duty is paid upon "the amount or value of the consideration for the sale," the instrument is *insufficiently stamped*, and not admissible in evidence, notwithstanding that the stamp duty accords with the consideration expressed. The difficulty may be surmounted by increasing the duty to the proper amount, and obtaining the protection of the adjudication stamp, without altering the deed As to the invalidity of a transfer of shares on the ground that the consideration was not truly stated nor the transfer duly stamped see *per* Wright, J, in Powell *v* London and Provincial Bank ([1893] 1 Ch 610, *ante*, p 36)

As to the consideration, duty must be paid upon the price of all property passing by the conveyance, whether specifically described or passing by operation of law As to what passes by a conveyance of land, reference should be made to Section 6 of The Conveyancing Act, 1881 (44 & 45 Vict, Ch 41) Fixtures of every kind pass without being specified by the conveyance of the property to which they are affixed, and where fixtures, standing timber, or any other part of the inheritance are taken at a valuation, the amount of the valuation must be included in the consideration, and duty paid thereon. (Dart, V & P 6th ed. pp. 606, 788.) Where land is agreed to be sold, and the vendee takes from the vendor the growing crops, the crops pass as an interest in the land by the conveyance (*per* Littledale, J, in Mayfield *v* Wadsley, 3 B & C. 366, and *see* Earl of Falmouth *v* Thomas, 3 Tyr. 26, 1 Crom & M 89) Goodwill attached to premises (as the goodwill of a public house) passes by the conveyance of the premises (*ex parte* Punnett, 16 Ch D 233, &c), and the price paid for goodwill attached to premises should be included in the consideration expressed in the conveyance and ad valorem conveyance duty paid thereon (Commissioners *v.* Angus & Co, Limited, 23 Q. B D 579, W R [1889] 60)

In the following common case—where land is conveyed from A to B. in consideration of a rentcharge, and B. subsequently conveys a portion of the land to C in consideration of money, and a rentcharge which may or may not be proportionate to the area of the land, and A is not a party to the conveyance from B to C, and there has been no apportionment of the first rentcharge—the conveyance from B to C must be stamped with ad valorem duty upon the amount of rentcharge payable to B during the next twenty years as well as the money Most deeds of this kind are stamped with duty upon the money only.

Upon a compulsory sale of property under The Lands Clauses Consolidation Acts, 1845 and 1846, the amount paid for compensation for loss of business must be included in the consideration upon which ad valorem duty is payable (Commissioners v. Glasgow and South Western Railway Company, 12 App. Ca. 315), but not, it seems, upon a sum allowed as compensation for damage for severance or injury to adjacent property (Dart, V. and P. 6th ed p 599)

An order for payment of money given or sent, and addressed to the person to whom such money is to be paid, and not to the person by whom it is to be paid, is liable to duty as a conveyance (see ante, p 77)

When in articles of partnership a premium is paid by the incoming partner to the owner of the business, ad valorem conveyance duty is payable upon the amount of the premium No duty is payable upon money brought into the business as capital the instrument in such a case is chargeable with the fixed duty of ten shillings as a deed, or sixpence as an agreement under hand, as the case may be

If the consideration for a conveyance is not ascertained, and is to be fixed by a subsequent valuation or examination of books, the amount should be inserted in the conveyance and ad valorem duty paid thereon A conveyance for a consideration that cannot be ascertained, as for a royalty to be calculated upon future trading, is liable to ten shillings whether under hand or seal; but if a minimum amount is payable by way of royalty for a definite period, the conveyance is chargeable with ad valorem duty upon the aggregate amount under Section 56, irrespective of any provision for cancelling the arrangement at an earlier period than that originally agreed upon Thus an assignment of letters patent for ten years in consideration of a yearly payment of £100 is liable to duty on £1,000 under Section 56 (1), though terminable upon the default of the assignee to pay, or by notice on either side If further indefinite sums are made payable in addition to the fixed payments, the instrument is chargeable with the further duty of ten shillings in respect of a further valuable consideration under Section 4 (2)

In administration ad valorem conveyance duty is charged only upon the consideration which, according to the terms of the instrument, is payable in any event Thus a conveyance in consideration of a sum certainly payable, and a further sum payable upon a contingency which may or may not happen, as the granting of a spirit licence to a beerseller, is charged with conveyance duty on the former sum only The further duty will be either ten shillings, or, when there is a covenant to pay the further sum, ad valorem covenant duty at the rate of two shillings and sixpence per hundred pounds, under the head "Bond, Covenant, or Instrument," ante, p 85

When a conveyance on sale of property operates also as a conveyance of any other property than the property sold, or contains any other matter or thing besides that which is incidental to the sale and conveyance of the property sold or relates to the title thereto, it is liable, in addition to the ad valorem duty, to the duty with which a separate instrument containing the other matter would be chargeable.

Where persons having separate interests in the same property join in the conveyance, only one stamp is necessary; and if the conveyance is on sale, ad valorem duty is payable upon the aggregate of the separate considerations, but upon a conveyance by several persons of separate interests in separate properties several stamps are required, and ad valorem duty must be paid upon the separate considerations (See Dart, V & P. 6th ed 794)

Where, upon the sale of property subject to a mortgage, the mortgagee joins with the mortgagor in the conveyance to the purchaser, the conveyance is sufficiently stamped with ad valorem conveyance duty on the amount of the consideration money moving from the purchaser The same rule applies when the conveyance is made by a *cestui que* trust and his trustee, or by several joint tenants or tenants in common upon the sale of the interest of one or more of them, to complete the purchaser's title But if a legal estate is outstanding in a stranger to the transaction of purchase and sale, and the person in whom it is vested joins in, the conveyance will be chargeable as an instrument relating to several distinct matters under Section 4 (*a*) *i. e*, if the outstanding estate is that of a mortgagee, with ad valorem reconveyance duty upon the greatest amount at any time secured by the discharged mortgage, in addition to the ad valorem conveyance duty on the consideration moving from the purchaser; if that of a trustee or other person, with ten shillings in addition to ad valorem duty, as a conveyance not otherwise charged, in addition to the above-mentioned ad valorem conveyance duty.

Where several properties are conveyed to several persons by one instrument several stamps are required (Freeman *v* Commissioners, 6 Ex. 101)

How ad valorem duty to be calculated in respect of stock and securities.

55. (1) Where the consideration, or any part of the consideration, for a conveyance on sale consists of any stock or marketable security, the conveyance is to be charged with ad valorem duty in respect of the value of the stock or security.

See note to Sec 6 and Foster (John) & Sons, Limited, *v* Commissio *ante*, p 103

(2) Where the consideration, or any part of the consideration, for a conveyance on sale consists of any security not being a marketable security, the conveyance is to be charged with ad valorem duty in respect of the amount due on the day of the date thereof for principal and interest upon the security.

(33 & 34 Vict., Ch 97, Sec 71.)

The value of the stock or marketable security under (1) is to be ascertained according to the directions contained in Section 6

56. (1) Where the consideration, or any part of the consideration, for a conveyance on sale consists of money payable periodically for a definite period not exceeding twenty years, so that the total amount to be paid can be previously ascertained, the conveyance is to be charged in respect of that consideration with ad valorem duty on such total amount

How consideration consisting of periodical payments to be charged.

(2) Where the consideration, or any part of the consideration, for a conveyance on sale consists of money payable periodically for a definite period exceeding twenty years or in perpetuity, or for any indefinite period not terminable with life, the conveyance is to be charged in respect of that consideration with ad valorem duty on the total amount which will or may, according to the terms of sale, be payable during the period of twenty years next after the day of the date of the instrument

(3) Where the consideration, or any part of the consideration, for a conveyance on sale consists of money payable periodically during any life or lives, the conveyance is to be charged in respect of that consideration with ad valorem duty on the amount which will or may, according to the terms of sale, be payable during the period of twelve years next after the day of the date of the instrument

(4) Provided that no conveyance on sale chargeable with ad valorem duty in respect of any periodical payments, and containing also provision for securing the payments, is to be charged with any duty in respect of such provision, and no separate instrument made in that case for securing the payments is to be charged with any higher duty than ten shillings.

(33 & 34 Vict, Ch 97, Sec. 72)

In the administration of The Stamp Act, 1870, the consideration computed at twenty years' purchase was taken in practice as a maximum, although not so according to the letter of the law. The present law confirms this practice.

A conveyance in consideration of an annuity payable during the joint lives of A and B, and a less annuity during the life of the survivor, is chargeable with duty on twelve times the sum annually payable during the joint lives.

A covenant to pay £6,000, balance of purchase money, by six half-yearly instalments of £1,000 each, is a provision for securing periodical payments, and not chargeable with further duty, even though interest be payable in addition in default of payment. (Limmer Asphalte Company v. Commissioners, 7 Ex 211, 41 L J, Ex. 106) But where purchase money is a present debt, and payment is deferred, interest being paid by the debtor, the case does not fall under (4), and a covenant for payment of purchase money and interest is chargeable with separate ad valorem duty under the head "Mortgage," &c A conveyance operating also as a mortgage is liable to both duties (Dart, V & P. 6th ed pp 796 to 799, and see Section 87 (6), post, p 173)

How conveyance in consideration of a debt, &c, to be charged

57. Where any property is conveyed to any person in consideration, wholly or in part, of any debt due to him, or subject either certainly or contingently to the payment or transfer of any money or stock, whether being or constituting a charge or incumbrance upon the property or not, the debt, money, or stock is to be deemed the whole or part, as the case may be, of the consideration in respect whereof the conveyance is chargeable with ad valorem duty.

(33 & 34 Vict., Ch 97, Sec. 73)

The cases bearing upon Section 57 are—

(1) Furness Railway Company v. Commissioners (38 L J, Ex 173). Conveyance on sale of the undertaking of one company to another in consideration of the exchange of stock in the vendor company for an equivalent amount of stock in the purchasing company, and payment by the purchasing company of the debenture debts and the ordinary debts of the vendor company. liable to ad valorem duty upon the total consideration, i e, the value of the stock, plus the amount of debentures and ordinary debts The argument that the transaction was, in effect, an amalgamation of two companies, and the creation of a partnership rather than a sale, was disregarded This case was followed in Great Western Railway Company v Commissioners ([1894] 1 Q. B., C A 507; 42 W. R. p. 211, *ante*, p 102)

(2) Mortimore v. Commissioners (2 H. & C 828; 10 L. T R 657). Conveyance on sale of a remainder contingent upon vendor surviving tenant for life, subject to a mortgage to a reversionary interest society for £38,000, payable only in the event of the vendor so surviving liable to ad valorem duty upon the price of the equity of redemption, plus £38,000.

(3) Liquidators of City of Glasgow Bank v Commissioners (8 Rettie, 4th Series, 391, 18 Sco L. R. 242) Conveyance of equity of redemption in property mortgaged for £2,400, in satisfaction of £2,350, part of a larger debt liable to ad valorem duty on £2,350, plus £2,400 = £4,750

In a conveyance of property subject to a mortgage, the amount owing upon the mortgage for principal *and interest* accruing to the date of conveyance must be included in the consideration unless interest be paid to date by the vendor

A conveyance of an equity of redemption to which the mortgagee is a party is not chargeable with any further duty by reason of containing a covenant of the grantor with the mortgagee for payment of the mortgage debt and interest. The absence of such a covenant does not affect the liability of the conveyance to ad valorem conveyance duty in respect of the mortgage debt and interest, such debt and interest being a charge or incumbrance on the property

A release of an equity of redemption to a mortgagee which contains a declaration against merger to protect the mortgagee against mesne incumbrancers is nevertheless liable to ad valorem conveyance duty in respect of the amount owing upon the mortgage.

A conveyance on sale of a moiety or other part of mortgaged property must be stamped with ad valorem duty under Section 57 in respect of the moiety or other proportionate part of the amount owing on the mortgage for principal and interest

In a conveyance of property subject to a mortgage to a building society, the amount for which the mortgage could be redeemed by immediate payment is the amount to be included in the consideration. This amount can be ascertained by application to the secretary of the society

Rentcharges and annuities charged upon property are not charges or incumbrances within Section 57, except rentcharges and annuities by way of repayment, &c, under Section 87 (2)

An order for foreclosure is not chargeable with conveyance duty, nor is a conveyance by an officer of the Court or other person appointed to convey to an equitable mortgagee in an action for foreclosure But ad valorem duty is payable if, to save the expense of litigation, the mortgagor conveys to the mortgagee before decree obtained.

Where upon the release of an equity of redemption to a mortgagee the amount owing upon the mortgage exceeds the value of the property, the Commissioners accept duty upon that value if satisfactory evidence thereof can be furnished For this practice Pooley v. Goodwin (4 A & E. 94, 1 H. & W 567) is an authority The adjudication stamp is necessary

A conveyance of an equity of redemption in consideration of natural love and affection, or by way of gift, is not liable to ad valorem duty, though the grantee indemnifies the grantor against payment of the mortgage debt and interest

The words "whether being or constituting a charge or incumbrance upon the property or not" were new in The Stamp Act, 1870, and have an important bearing upon many transactions, especially dissolutions of partnership When a retiring partner conveys or releases his share in the business or the partnership assets in consideration of a fixed sum, or an indemnity against liabilities, or both, the amount of liabilities from which, as between his partner and himself, he is relieved, must be included in the consideration upon which the duty is paid (Dart, V. and P. 6th ed 509) Thus if upon an account stated and a balance sheet between two partners in equal shares, the value of the outgoing partner's share or "capital" is found to be £5,000, and the continuing partner undertakes to pay the liabilities of the business amounting to £3,000, the conveyance of the outgoing partner's share is chargeable with duty on £6,500— e, £5,000 plus half the liabilities If the chattel property is transferred by delivery, an apportionment of the consideration must be made to show upon what amount duty is chargeable in respect of the property transferred by conveyance, and the consideration to be apportioned in the instance above would be £6,500, not £5,000. The apportionment must be a fair one the usual recital that for the purposes of stamp duty it has been agreed that the consideration for the property conveyed shall be a sum named, and for the property passing by delivery another sum, is not considered conclusive, and upon adjudication further evidence, such as the production of a valuation or a balance sheet, is required. If property capable of transfer by delivery is actually conveyed, the true consideration must be stated in the conveyance, and ad valorem conveyance duty paid thereon, for stamp duty is chargeable according to the tenor of the instrument (Introduction, p 2.) A recital that chattels have been delivered does not attract any duty

The cases upon conveyance of an interest in a partnership are Potter v Commissioners (10 Ex. R 147, 14 L J R. 345, 18 Jur 778), Christie v. Commissioners (2 Ex. 46), Phillips v Commissioners (2 Ex 399), and Troup v Commissioners (7 Times L R 610). In Philips v Commissioners, the price of the interest conveyed was declared to be "allowed in account appropriated and paid out of the assets of the partnership"; but ad valorem duty was held to be payable notwithstanding. In Troup v. Commissioners, the shares and interests of outgoing partners, in goodwill and book debts, were conveyed in consideration of a price in money to a continuing partner, and the point was taken that to be effective the conveyance as to book debts must be perfected by notice to the debtors under Section 25 of The Judicature Act, 1873, but the Court held that ad valorem conveyance duty was rightly charged.

The declaration in a deed of dissolution of partnership that the partnership is dissolved does not attract any further duty.

When upon a dissolution partnership assets are divided *in specie* the transaction is not a sale, even when one partner takes all the business assets, and the other a mortgage debt owing to the firm, together with a sum of money for equality (MacLeod v Commissioners, 12 Rettie, 4th Series, 1045, 22 Sco. L R 674)

It is not necessary, however, to incur the great expense of ad valorem stamp duty in effecting a dissolution of partnership "If the retiring partner, instead of assigning his interest, takes the amount due to him from the firm, gives a receipt for the money, and acknowledges that he has no more claims on his copartners, they will practically obtain all they want, and such a transaction, even if carried out by deed, could hardly be held to amount to a sale, and no ad valorem stamp, it is apprehended, would be payable " (Lindley on Partnership, p 867.) A deed of dissolution containing a recital that the stock-in-trade and chattels have been delivered, a declaration of the dissolution, a mutual release from the covenants in the partnership deed, and a covenant for further assurance if called upon, is, however, chargeable with ad valorem duty, unless it can be shown that the dissolution is carried out upon terms arranged by a previous instrument—*e g*, the deed creating the partnership

Direction as to duty in certain cases.

58. (1) Where property contracted to be sold for one consideration for the whole is conveyed to the purchaser in separate parts or parcels by different instruments, the consideration is to be apportioned in such manner as the parties think fit, so that a distinct consideration for each separate part or parcel is set forth in the conveyance relating thereto, and such conveyance is to be charged with ad valorem duty in respect of such distinct consideration.

The apportionment may be made without regard to the actual value of the separate parcels, provided that the whole of the consideration is accounted for and ad valorem conveyance duty paid upon it.

(2) Where property contracted to be purchased for one consideration for the whole by two or more persons jointly, or by any person for himself and others, or wholly for others, is conveyed in parts or parcels by separate instruments to the persons by or for whom the same was purchased for distinct parts of the consideration, the conveyance of each separate part or parcel is to be charged with ad valorem duty in respect of the distinct part of the consideration therein specified.

(3) Where there are several instruments of conveyance for completing the purchaser's title to property sold, the principal instrument of conveyance only is to be charged with ad valorem duty, and the other instruments are to be respectively

charged with such other duty as they may be liable to, but the last-mentioned duty shall not exceed the ad valorem duty payable in respect of the principal instrument.

A conveyance in confirmation of a duly stamped conveyance, which is defective or for any reason inoperative, is not the "principal instrument of conveyance," and is duly stamped with ten shillings, or the ad valorem conveyance duty if such duty is less than ten shillings (Doe dem Priest v. Western, 2 Q. B 249; 11 L J, Q B 17)

(4) Where a person having contracted for the purchase of any property, but not having obtained a conveyance thereof, contracts to sell the same to any other person, and the property is in consequence conveyed immediately to the sub-purchaser, the conveyance is to be charged with ad valorem duty in respect of the consideration moving from the sub-purchaser.

I.e, whether the consideration for the sub-sale be greater or less than the consideration in the original contract

(5) Where a person having contracted for the purchase of any property but not having obtained a conveyance contracts to sell the whole, or any part or parts thereof, to any other person or persons, and the property is in consequence conveyed by the original seller to different persons in parts or parcels, the conveyance of each part or parcel is to be charged with ad valorem duty in respect only of the consideration moving from the sub-purchaser thereof, without regard to the amount or value of the original consideration.

(6) Where a sub-purchaser takes an actual conveyance of the interest of the person immediately selling to him, which is chargeable with ad valorem duty in respect of the consideration moving from him, and is duly stamped accordingly, any conveyance to be afterwards made to him of the same property by the original seller shall be chargeable

only with such other duty as it may be liable to, but the last-mentioned duty shall not exceed the ad valorem duty

(33 & 34 Vict, Ch 97, Secs 74 and 76)

That is to say, the duty of ten shillings as a conveyance "not hereinbefore described" (*post*, p. 122), unless the ad valorem conveyance duty is less than ten shillings.

Certain contracts to be chargeable as conveyances on sale

59. (1) Any contract or agreement made in England or Ireland under seal, or under hand only, or made in Scotland, with or without any clause of registration, for the sale of any equitable estate or interest in any property whatsoever, or for the sale of any estate or interest in any property except lands, tenements, hereditaments, or heritages, or property locally situate out of the United Kingdom, or goods, wares, or merchandise, or stock, or marketable securities, or any ship or vessel, or part interest, share, or property of or in any ship or vessel, shall be charged with the same ad valorem duty, to be paid by the purchaser, as if it were an actual conveyance on sale of the estate, interest, or property contracted or agreed to be sold

(2) Where the purchaser has paid the said ad valorem duty, and before having obtained a conveyance or transfer of the property enters into a contract or agreement for the sale of the same, the contract or agreement shall be charged, if the consideration for that sale is in excess of the consideration for the original sale, with the ad valorem duty payable in respect of such excess consideration, and in any other case with the fixed duty of ten shillings or of sixpence, as the case may require

(3) Where duty has been duly paid in conformity with the foregoing provisions, the conveyance or transfer made to the purchaser or sub-purchaser, or any other person on his behalf or by his direction,

shall not be chargeable with any duty, and the Commissioners, upon application, either shall denote the payment of the ad valorem duty upon the conveyance or transfer, or shall transfer the ad valorem duty thereto upon production of the contract or agreement, or contracts or agreements duly stamped.

Or the adjudication stamp may be obtained upon the conveyance

(4) Provided that where any such contract or agreement is stamped with the fixed duty of ten shillings or of sixpence, as the case may require, the contract or agreement shall be regarded as duly stamped for the mere purpose of proceedings to enforce specific performance or recover damages for the breach thereof

This Sub-section does not include the filing of a contract with the Registrar of Joint Stock Companies Such contracts are required to be fully stamped, under Sub-section (1), and any doubt as to duty must be solved by adjudication (Reg v Registrar of Joint Stock Companies, 21 Q B. D 131)

When it is necessary to file a contract immediately, the contract should be stamped with ten shillings if under seal, or sixpence if under hand only, and an abstract lodged for adjudication under Section 12 The Registrar of Joint Stock Companies will then accept the contract for filing, and any further duty to which it may be liable can be impressed after the assessment has been completed

(5) Provided also that where any such contract or agreement is stamped with the said fixed duty, and a conveyance or transfer made in conformity with the contract or agreement is presented to the Commissioners for stamping with the ad valorem duty chargeable thereon within the period of six months after the first execution of the contract or agreement, or within such longer period as the Commissioners may think reasonable in the circumstances of the case, the conveyance or transfer shall be stamped accordingly, and the same, and the said contract or agreement, shall be deemed to be duly stamped.

Nothing in this proviso shall alter or affect the provisions as to the stamping of a conveyance or transfer after the execution thereof.

(6) Provided also that the ad valorem duty paid upon any such contract or agreement shall be returned by the Commissioners in case the contract or agreement be afterwards rescinded or annulled, or for any other reason be not substantially performed or carried into effect, so as to operate as or be followed by a conveyance or transfer.

(52 & 53 Vict., Ch. 42, Sec. 15).

_ommissioners v. Angus & Company, Limited (23 Q. B. D. 79), was decided upon the law in force before the passing of the Revenue Act, 1889 (Section 15), repealed by this Act, and re-enacted with verbal alterations by Section 59.

Section 59 governs—

(a) Contracts for the sale of any equitable estate or interest in any property whatsoever; and it is to be observed that the word "whatsoever" is new, and removes the doubt whether a contract for the sale of any equitable estate or interest in the description of property excepted from the next part of the sub-section should be charged with ad valorem conveyance duty. Contracts for the sale of any equitable estate or interest in such property are chargeable with ad valorem duty, except as to "any ship or vessel, or part interest, share, or property of or in any ship or vessel," instruments relating to which are expressly exempted from all stamp duties by the General Exemption No. 2 at the end of the Act, p. 203.

If a contract for the sale of an equitable estate or interest in any property (except a ship or vessel, &c.) within Sub-section 1 is followed immediately by a conveyance, the duty may be impressed on the conveyance (Sub-section 5).

(b) Contracts for the sale of *any* estate or interest in any property, except—

(1) Lands, tenements, hereditaments, or heritages
(2) Property locally situate out of the United Kingdom.
(3) Goods, wares, or merchandise
(4) Stock or marketable security
(5) Any ship or vessel, &c.

Property locally situate out of the United Kingdom includes patents actually taken out in foreign countries at the date of the contract, concessions made by foreign governments, as of mining and other rights, where possession has been taken of the property the subject of the concession; mortgages of foreign property executed abroad; but a contract for the sale of such property containing a covenant for payment of money is liable to ad valorem covenant duty if it is executed in the United Kingdom, or if the money is to be paid in the United Kingdom, or if the contract is to be filed with the Registrar of Joint Stock Companies, or if a cause of action would arise in the United Kingdom (Section 14 (4), *ante*, p 33)

A convenient example of the operation of Section 59 is afforded by a contract for the sale of a business as a going concern to a limited company It is assumed that, except as to (2) and (6), the property is not incumbered or held in trust The property sold may include—

(1) Freeholds, leaseholds, and copyholds, and machinery, plant, and fixtures affixed thereto, unincumbered
(2) Freeholds, &c., subject to a mortgage
(3) Loose plant and machinery, stock-in-trade, furniture, &c
(4) Patents, licences, trade marks, and copyrights
(5) Foreign property
(6) Ships
(7) Book debts.
(8) Goodwill
(9) Cash, bills of exchange, and promissory notes.
(10) Benefit of contracts
(11) Mortgage debts owing to the firm

The consideration for the sale is, say, £100,000, to be satisfied by the payment of £10,000 in cash, issue of debentures for £20,000, and the allotment of 7,000 shares of £10 each. Debentures and all shares in a new company are taken at par, unless the form of the contract admits of a distinction between preference shares and ordinary shares, in which case an affidavit as to the value of ordinary shares will be accepted

The £100,000 must be apportioned among the different heads of property, and ad valorem duty paid on the contract for the portion of the consideration apportioned to (2), (4), (7), (8), and (10), and to the consideration apportioned to (2) must be added the amount owing on the mortgage for principal and interest at the date of the contract

When the unincumbered freeholds, &c, are conveyed, ad valorem conveyance duty must be paid upon the consideration apportioned to them.

(3), (5), and (6) are excepted from the charge of duty, and no duty is payable in respect of (9) Mortgage debts (11) pass by transfer, and are not considered to be within the operation of the section

The following table may assist the explanation :—

	Apportionment of £100,000.	Amounts on which Duty is Payable on the Contract
	£	£
1 Freeholds, leaseholds, and copyholds, and machinery, &c, affixed thereto, unincumbered	8,300	—
2 Freeholds, &c, subject to a mortgage for £1,000	250	250
		Mortgage & interest 1,016
		1,266
3. Loose plant, &c.	42,000	—
4. Patents, &c	5,000	5,000
5 Foreign property	200	—
6 Ships	2,000	—
7 Book debts	23,700	23,700
8 Goodwill	10,000	10,000
9 Cash at bankers', bills, and notes	3,650	—
10 Benefit of contracts	500	500
11 Mortgage debts	4,400	—
	£100,000	£40,466

If as a further consideration the purchaser undertakes to pay the liabilities of the business owing on a certain date, the amount of such liabilities must be ascertained and included (Section 57) in the consideration to be apportioned for the purposes of stamp duty No "set-off," against liabilities, of book debts owing to the firm, stock-in-trade, or any other description of property sold is permissible, except cash, bills, and notes, which may be deducted from trade liabilities, though not from mortgages If the sale is to take effect from a day past, and the purchaser undertakes to pay liabilities incurred after that date only, such liabilities are not to be included in the consideration.

A contract made upon the reconstruction of a company for the transfer of the property of the old company to the new company, in consideration of the exchange of shares of equal or less nominal value in the new company for shares in the old company, share for share, is not considered to be a contract for sale within the section, and no ad valorem conveyance duty is payable, even though the contract should be expressed to be made upon sale. Regard must be had to the substance of the transaction, rather than the form of the instrument (Introduction, p. 2.)

60. Where upon the sale of any annuity or other right not before in existence such annuity or other right is not created by actual grant or conveyance, but is only secured by bond, warrant of attorney, covenant, contract, or otherwise, the bond or other instrument, or some one of such instruments, if there be more than one, is to be charged with the same duty as an actual grant or conveyance, and is for the purposes of this Act to be deemed an instrument of conveyance on sale *As to sale of an annuity or right not before in existence.*

(33 & 34 Vict, Ch 97, Sec. 75)

This Section does not reach a sale of property in consideration of an annuity where there is no conveyance or written contract chargeable under Section 59. The instrument creating the annuity in such a case is chargeable with the duty of two shillings and sixpence for every five pounds of the annuity under the head "Bond, Covenant, or Instrument of any kind whatsoever". A voluntary grant of an annuity, without a covenant to pay, is liable to duty of ten shillings only

The corresponding words in 48 Geo III., Ch 149, Sec 22, from which this section is derived, were "annuity, easement, servitude, or other right not before in existence"

61. (1) In the cases hereinafter specified the principal instrument is to be ascertained in the following manner:— *Principal instrument, how to be ascertained.*

> (a) Where any copyhold or customary estate is conveyed by a deed, no surrender being necessary, the deed is to be deemed the principal instrument

(b) In other cases of copyhold or customary estates, the surrender or grant, if made out of court, or the memorandum thereof, and the copy of court roll of the surrender or grant, if made in court, is to be deemed the principal instrument

(c) Where in Scotland there is a disposition or assignation executed by the seller, and any other instrument is executed for completing the title, the disposition or assignation is to be deemed the principal instrument.

(2) In any other case the parties may determine for themselves which of several instruments is to be deemed the principal instrument, and may pay the ad valorem duty thereon accordingly.

(33 & 34 Vict, Ch 97, Sec. 77.)

When freeholds and copyholds are sold together, it is usual to apportion the consideration; and if ad valorem duty on the sum apportioned as the price of the freeholds is paid on the conveyance, no further duty, ten shillings or otherwise, is chargeable upon the conveyance by reason of its containing a covenant to surrender the copyholds. If the interest in the copyholds is equitable only, the covenant to surrender transfers that interest, and is chargeable with ad valorem duty

CONVEYANCE or TRANSFER by way of security of any property (*except such stock as aforesaid*), or of any security.

See **Mortgage**, &c, and **Marketable Security**.   £ s d.

CONVEYANCE or TRANSFER of any kind not hereinbefore described   ..   0 10 0

And *see* Section 62

Conveyances on any Occasion except Sale or Mortgage.

<small>What is to be deemed</small>   62. Every instrument, and every decree or order of any court or of any commissioners, whereby any

property on any occasion, except a sale or mortgage, is transferred to or vested in any person, is to be charged with duty as a conveyance or transfer of property.

<small>a conveyance on any occasion, not being a sale or mortgage</small>

Provided that a conveyance or transfer made for effectuating the appointment of a new trustee is not to be charged with any higher duty than ten shillings.

(33 & 34 Vict, Ch 97, Sec 78.)

A conveyance for a nominal consideration, or in consideration of natural love and affection, is liable to the duty of ten shillings, whether under hand or seal.

If an instrument contains the declaration by deed under Section 65 of The Conveyancing Act, 1881, for enlarging the residue of a long term into a fee simple, it is liable to the duty of ten shillings in addition to whatever other duty it may bear.

The proviso to this section applies principally to transfers of inscribed Canadian and colonial stocks, which are otherwise liable to ad valorem conveyance duty, whether made on sale or otherwise, and transfers of mortgages, &c., otherwise liable to the duty of sixpence for every £100. In practice it is extended to transfers of such stocks and securities made upon the discharge of a trustee under Section 32 of The Conveyancing Act, 1881, to transfers by executors of a testator to the trustees of the will, and to transfers into court except in lunacy. The adjudication stamp should be obtained

COPY or EXTRACT (*attested or in any manner authenticated*) of or from—

(1) An instrument chargeable with any duty.

(2) An original will, testament, or codicil.

(3) The probate or probate copy of a will or codicil.

(4) Any letters of administration or any confirmation of a testament

(5) Any public register (*except any register of births, baptisms, marriages, deaths, or burials*).

(C) The books, rolls, or records of any court.

In the case of an instrument chargeable with duty not amounting to one shilling } The same duty as such instrument.

"Court" here is held, by reference to the repealed Stamp Acts, to mean Court of Judicature, and does not include manorial courts

	£	s	d.
In any other case	. 0	1	0

Exemptions.

(1) Copy or extract of or from any law proceeding.

(2) Copy or extract in Scotland of or from the commission of any person as a delegate or representative to the convention of royal burghs or the general assembly or any presbytery or church court

And *see* Section 63.

Attested Copies and Extracts.

Stamping of certain copies and extracts after attestation

63. An attested or otherwise authenticated copy or extract of or from—

(1) An instrument chargeable with any duty;

(2) An original will, testament, or codicil;

(3) The probate or probate copy of a will or codicil,

(4) Letters of administration or a confirmation of a testament;

may be stamped at any time within fourteen days after the date of the attestation or authentication on payment of the duty only

(33 & 34 Vict, Ch 97, Sec 79)

The duty applies only to such copies as are evidence *per se*, and the word "copy" means an authenticated copy receivable as evidence in the first instance *Per* Lord Abinger, C.B., in Braythwaite *v* Hitchcock (6 Jur. 976, 10 M. & W 494, 2 Dowl N R. 444), where an examined copy of a deed produced by a witness to prove the original, with which he had compared the copy, was allowed to be read, although unstamped, the original being in the possession of the opposite party, and not produced upon notice (*See also* Smith *v.* Maguire, 1 F. & F 199.)

COPY or EXTRACT (*certified*) of or from any register of births, baptisms, marriages, deaths, or burials . .   £   s   d.
         0   0   1

Exemptions.

(1) Copy or extract furnished by any clergyman, registrar, or other official person pursuant to and for the purposes of any Act, or furnished to any general or superintending registrar under any general regulation.

(2) Copy or extract for which the person giving the same is not entitled to any fee or reward

And *see* Section 64.

This charge applies to copies of or extracts from registers in the United Kingdom only

Certified Copies and Extracts from Registers of Births, &c

64. The duty upon a certified copy or extract of or from any register of births, baptisms, marriages, deaths, or burials is to be paid by the person requiring the copy or extract, and may be denoted by an adhesive stamp, which is to be cancelled by the person by whom the copy or extract is signed before he delivers the same out of his hands, custody, or power [Duty may be denoted by adhesive stamp.]

(33 & 34 *Vict.*, *Ch* 97, *Sec* 80)

COPYHOLD and CUSTOMARY ESTATES — Instruments relating thereto.

Upon a sale thereof *See* **Conveyance on Sale.**

Upon a Mortgage thereof. *See* **Mortgage, &c**

Upon a demise thereof. *See* **Lease or Tack.**

Upon any other occasion.

	£ s. d.
Surrender or grant made out of court, or the memorandum thereof, and copy of court roll of any surrender or grant made in court	0 10 0

And *see* Sections 65, 66, 67, and 68.

Copyhold and Customary Estates.

Provisions as to payment of duty

65. (1) No instrument is to be charged more than once with duty by reason of relating to several distinct tenements, in respect whereof several fines or fees are due to the lord or steward of the manor.

(2) The copy of court roll of a surrender or grant made out of court shall not be admissible or available as evidence of the surrender or grant, unless the surrender or grant, or the memorandum thereof, is duly stamped, of which fact the certificate of the steward of the manor on the face of the copy shall be sufficient evidence

(3) The entry upon the court rolls of a surrender or grant shall not be admissible or available as evidence of the surrender or grant unless the surrender or grant, if made out of court, or the memorandum thereof, or the copy of court roll of the surrender or grant, if made in court, is duly stamped, of which fact the certificate of the steward

of the manor in the margin of the entry shall be sufficient evidence.

(33 & 34 Vict., Ch. 97, Secs. 81 and 82.)

"Grant" means voluntary grant, as of waste, not an act of admittance (Scriven on Copyholds, 190). Admittances were specifically charged with duty under repealed Acts, but the charge was not re-enacted by The Stamp Act, 1870, and they are not liable to any duty under the present law.

66. (1) All the facts and circumstances affecting the liability to duty of the copy of court roll of any surrender or grant made in court, or the amount of duty with which any such copy of court roll is chargeable, are to be fully and truly stated in a note to be delivered to the steward of the manor before the surrender or grant is made.

<small>Facts affecting duty to be stated in note.</small>

(2) The steward of every manor shall refuse—
(a) To accept in court any surrender, or to make in court any grant, until such a note as is required by this section has been delivered to him; or
(b) To enter on the court rolls, or accept any presentment of, or admit any person to be tenant under or by virtue of, any surrender or grant made out of court, or any deed which is not duly stamped:

And in any case in which he does not so refuse shall incur a fine of fifty pounds.

(3) If any person, with intent to defraud Her Majesty,—
(a) Makes in court any surrender before such a note as aforesaid has been delivered to the steward of the manor, or
(b) Being employed or concerned in or about the preparation of any such note as aforesaid, neglects or omits fully and truly to state therein all the above-mentioned facts and circumstances;

he shall incur a fine of fifty pounds.

(33 & 34 Vict., Ch. 97, Secs. 83 and 84.)

Steward to make out only stamped copies

67. The steward of every manor shall, within four months from the day on which any surrender or grant is made in court, make out a duly stamped copy of court roll of such surrender or grant, and have the same ready for delivery to the person entitled thereto, and in default of so doing shall incur a fine of fifty pounds, and the duty payable in respect of the copy of court roll shall be a debt to Her Majesty from the steward, whether he has received it or not, and if he has not received the duty the same shall also be a debt to Her Majesty from the person entitled to the copy.

(33 & 34 *Vict*, *Ch* 97, *Sec* 85.)

This Section, being merely a fiscal regulation, would not increase the penalty payable upon the admission in evidence of an unstamped copy of court roll.

Steward may refuse to proceed except on payment of his fees and duty

68. The steward of any manor may, before he accepts in court any surrender or makes in court any grant, demand the payment of his lawful fees in relation to the surrender or grant, together with the duty payable on the copy of court roll thereof, and may refuse to proceed in the matter or to deliver the copy of court roll to any person until the fees and duty are paid.

(33 & 34 *Vict*, *Ch* 97, *Sec*. 86.)

COST BOOK MINES. *See* **Transfer.**

COUNTERPART. *See* **Duplicate.**

COVENANT for securing the payment
or repayment of money, or the transfer or retransfer of stock.

See **Mortgage**, &c.

COVENANT in relation to any annuity
upon the original creation and sale thereof

See **Conveyance on Sale,** and Section 60

COVENANT in relation to any annuity (*except upon the original creation and sale thereof*) or to other periodical payments

See **Bond, Covenant, &c.**

COVENANT. Any separate deed of covenant (*not being an instrument chargeable with ad valorem duty as a conveyance on sale or mortgage*) made on the sale or mortgage of any property, and relating solely to the conveyance or enjoyment of, or the title to, the property sold or mortgaged, or to the production of the muniments of title relating thereto, or to all or any of the matters aforesaid.

Where the ad valorem duty in respect of the consideration or mortgage money does not exceed 10s. ...	A duty equal to the amount of such ad valorem duty
In any other case	0 10 0

Under this head are charged covenants to surrender copyholds, whether on sale or mortgage, except a covenant to surrender made on the sale of an equitable interest only, and a covenant to surrender made on a mortgage which contains a covenant to pay principal and interest and the usual mortgage clauses. In such cases ad valorem conveyance or mortgage duty is chargeable, and the subsequent surrender is liable to the duty of ten shillings if made upon sale, or sixpence per £100 up to a maximum duty of ten shillings if made upon a mortgage. (*See* Section 87 [4] and [5])

CUSTOMARY ESTATES. *See* **Copyhold.**

DEBENTURE for securing the payment or repayment of money or the transfer or retransfer of stock.

See **Mortgage, &c**, and **Marketable Security.**

k

DEBENTURE or CERTIFICATE for entitling any person to receive any allowance by way of drawback or otherwise payable out of the revenue of customs or excise, for or in respect of any goods, wares, or merchandise exported or shipped to be exported from the United Kingdom to any part beyond the sea.

	£	s.	d.
Where the allowance to be received does not exceed £10	0	1	0
Exceeds £10, and does not exceed £50	0	2	6
Exceeds £50	0	5	0

Relief from stamp duty on debentures or certificates for allowance in respect of British spirits exported or for exportation was formerly conceded, but this concession was withdrawn by Official Circular of 15th March, 1894 Stamp duty is not charged, however, in respect of allowances payable for British spirits shipped as stores

DECLARATION of any use or trust of or concerning any property by any writing, not being a will, or an instrument chargeable with ad valorem duty as a settlement . . . 0 10 0

Such a declaration under seal is chargeable with the duty of 10s as a deed

DECLARATION (*Statutory*). *See* **Affidavit.**

DECREET ARBITRAL. *See* **Award.**

DEED whereby any real burden is declared or created on lands or heritable subjects in Scotland

See **Mortgage,** &c , and Section 86.

DEED containing an obligation to infeft any person in heritable subjects in Scotland, under a clause of reversion, as a security for money.

See **Mortgage**, &c , and Section 86.

DEED containing an obligation to infeft or seize in an annuity to be uplifted out of heritable subjects in Scotland

See **Bond, Covenant,** &c

DEED of any kind whatsoever, not described in this Schedule	£	s.	d
	0	10	0

An instrument under seal is not necessarily a deed. Sealing and delivery as a deed are essential.

In Brown v Vawser (4 East, 584), decided before a particular duty was charged upon awards, an award under seal not *delivered* as a deed was held not to be liable to deed duty In Reg. v Morton (42 L. J., M. C 58), "letters of orders" under the episcopal seal of the Bishop of Bath and Wells were held not to be a deed The Court observed, "An instrument must be treated as a deed if it confers any right or passes any interest or is a confirmation of an act which confers a right or passes an interest or gives a title or authority," and instanced documents which were not "deeds," though under seal a will under seal and delivered, warrants of magistrates, certificates of admission to learned societies; certificates of shares under the seal of a company

In the old case of Chanter v Johnson (11 M. & W. 408; 14 L. J., Ex. 289), a licence under seal to use a patented article was held by Parke, B , not to be a deed "It does not purport to be sealed and delivered as a deed, it rather resembles an award or a warrant of a magistrate, which, though under seal, are not deeds."

An appointment of a valuer under The Lands Clauses Consolidation Act, 8 & 9 Vict , Ch. 18, Sec 19, though under seal, is not a deed, nor is an instrument under the seal of the Charity Commissioners certifying their approval of the appointment of trustees at a meeting held under the Charitable Trusts Acts; nor the mandates of bishops and archdeacons for induction to a living, &c.

An instrument under the seal of a company sealed in

Scotland is not liable to duty as a deed unless it contains a clause of registration.

Instruments under seal of a company or corporation, sealed in England or Ireland, are liable to deed duty in the same manner as those executed by an individual, even though they are such as would ordinarily be under hand; as to which see 30 & 31 Vict., Ch. 131, Sec 37. The assessment of the duty of ten shillings as a deed upon a contract under the seal of a company was allowed by the Court of Appeal in Commissioners v. Angus & Company, Limited (23 Q. B. D. 579).

DEFEAZANCE. Instrument of defeazance of any conveyance, transfer, disposition, assignation, or tack, apparently absolute, but intended only as a security for money or stock.

See **Mortgage**, &c, and Section 86

In respect of marketable securities under hand only, see **Agreement**, and Section 23

	£	s.	d.
DELIVERY ORDER	0	0	1

And see Sections 69, 70, and 71.

Delivery Orders.

<small>Provisions as to duty on delivery order</small>

69. (1) For the purposes of this Act the expression "delivery order" means any document or writing entitling or intended to entitle any person therein named, or his assigns, or the holder thereof, to the delivery of any goods, wares, or merchandise of the value of forty shillings or upwards lying in any dock or port, or in any warehouse in which goods are stored or deposited on rent or hire, or upon any wharf, such document or writing being signed by or on behalf of the owner of such goods, wares, or merchandise, upon the sale or transfer of the property therein.

(2) A delivery order is to be deemed to have been given upon a sale of, or transfer of the property in, goods, wares, or merchandise of the value of forty shillings or upwards, unless the contrary is expressly stated therein.

(3) The duty upon a delivery order may be denoted by an adhesive stamp, which is to be cancelled by the person by whom the instrument is made, executed, or issued.

(33 & 34 Vict., Ch. 97, Secs 87, 89, and 91.)

70. (1) If any person—

Penalty for use of unstamped or untrue order

(a) Untruly states, or knowingly allows to be untruly stated, in a delivery order, either that the transaction to which it relates is not a sale or transfer of property, or that the goods, wares, or merchandise to which it relates are not of the value of forty shillings; or

(b) Makes, signs, or issues any delivery order chargeable with duty, but not being duly stamped; or

(c) Knowingly, either himself, or by his servant or any other person, delivers, or procures, or authorises the delivery of, any goods, wares, or merchandise mentioned in any delivery order which is not duly stamped, or which contains to his knowledge any false statement with reference either to the nature of the transaction, or the value of the goods, wares, or merchandise,

he shall incur a fine of twenty pounds.

(2) But a delivery order is not, by reason of the same being unstamped, to be deemed invalid in the hands of the person having the custody of, or delivering out, the goods, wares, or merchandise therein mentioned, unless such person is proved to have been party or privy to some fraud on the revenue in relation thereto.

(33 & 34 Vict., Ch. 97, Sec. 91.)

71. The duty upon a delivery order is, in the absence of any special stipulation, to be paid by the person to whom the order is given, and any person

By whom duty on delivery order to be paid

from whom a delivery order chargeable with duty is required may refuse to give it, unless or until the amount of the duty is paid to him.

(33 & 34 Vict., Ch 97, Sec 90.)

DEPOSIT of title deeds. *See* **Mortgage, &c**, and Section 86

DEPUTATION or APPOINTMENT of a gamekeeper . . . . £ s. d. 0 10 0

DISPENSATION. *See* **Faculty.**

DISPOSITION of heritable property in Scotland to singular successors or purchasers

    See **Conveyance on Sale.**

DISPOSITION of heritable property in Scotland to a purchaser, containing a clause declaring all or any part of the purchase money a real burden upon, or affecting, the heritable property thereby disponed, or any part thereof

    See **Conveyance on Sale, Mortgage, &c**, and Section 86

DISPOSITION in Scotland, containing constitution of feu or ground annual right

    See **Conveyance on Sale,** and Section 56.

DISPOSITION in security in Scotland.

    See **Mortgage, &c**

DISPOSITION of any wadset, heritable bond, &c

    See **Mortgage, &c**

DISPOSITION in Scotland of any property or of any right or interest therein not described in this Schedule   0 10 0

DOCK WARRANT. *See* **Warrant for Goods.**

DOCKET made on passing any instrument under the Great Seal of the United Kingdom ... 0 2 0   £ s. d.

DRAFT for money. *See* **Bill of Exchange.**

DUPLICATE or COUNTERPART of any instrument chargeable with any duty—

    Where such duty does not amount to 5s .. . { The same duty as the original instrument.

    In any other case ... 0 5 0

And *see* Section 72.

Duplicates and Counterparts.

72. The duplicate or counterpart of an instrument chargeable with duty (except the counterpart of an instrument chargeable as a lease, such counterpart not being executed by or on behalf of any lessor or grantor), is not to be deemed duly stamped unless it is stamped as an original instrument, or unless it appears by some stamp impressed thereon that the full and proper duty has been paid upon the original instrument of which it is the duplicate or counterpart. — *Provision as to duplicates and counterparts.*

(33 & 34 *Vict*, Ch. 97, Sec. 93.)

The counterpart of an instrument chargeable as a lease is admissible in evidence without a denoting stamp, as an independent instrument if stamped with five shillings, or the proper ad valorem lease duty if such duty is less than five shillings. The counterpart of any other instrument than a lease, and the duplicate of *every* instrument liable to greater duty than five shillings, is not duly stamped with the five shilling duty unless it bears the denoting stamp (Section 11) showing the amount of the duty which has been impressed on the original, but the denoting stamp does not indicate in terms that the "full and proper duty" has been paid upon the original. Instruments presented for denoting are carefully scrutinised, and the denoting stamp is refused, except in very doubtful cases, unless the requirements of the denoting officer are satisfied. In doubtful cases the denoting stamp is given, and the parties are allowed to run their own risk as to objection to the admissibility in evidence of the instrument, against which the denoting stamp affords no protection whatever. The only valid protection obtainable is by the adjudication of the original under Section 12, and the duplicate or counterpart should then be stamped with a stamp which denotes that the original has been "adjudged duly stamped"

EIK to a REVERSION. *See* **Mortgage,** &c., and Section 86.

EQUITABLE MORTGAGE. *See* **Mortgage,** &c., and Sections 23 and 86.

EXCHANGE or EXCAMBION—Instruments effecting—

	£	s.	d
In the case specified in Section 73 *see* that Section			
In any other case	0	10	0

Exchange and Partition or Division.

As to exchange, &c.

73. Where upon the exchange of any real or heritable property for any other real or heritable property, or upon the partition or division of any real or heritable property, any consideration exceeding in amount or value one hundred pounds is paid or given, or agreed to be paid or given, for equality, the principal or only instrument whereby the exchange or partition or division is effected is to be charged with the same ad valorem duty as a conveyance on sale for the consideration, and with that duty only; and where in any such case there are several instruments for completing the title of either party, the principal instrument is to be ascertained, and the other instruments are to be charged with duty in the manner hereinbefore provided in the case of several instruments of conveyance

(33 & 34 Vict., Ch. 97, Sec. 94.)

The consideration paid or given for equality must be paid or given by party to party. It does not include mortgage debts, or other incumbrances upon the properties exchanged or partitioned which either party undertakes to pay, the provisions of Section 57 not being applicable to instruments of this class.

This Section is applied in administration to leaseholds.

A partition is not a sale (Henniker v Henniker, 22 L. J., Q. B. 94, 1 E. & B 54); and the special regulations under "Conveyance on Sale" do not apply.

EXEMPLIFICATION or CONSTAT, under the Great Seal of the United Kingdom of Great Britain and Ireland, of any letters patent or grant made or to be made by Her Majesty, or by any of her royal precedessors, of any honour, dignity, promotion, franchise, liberty, or privilege, or of any lands, office, or other thing whatsoever 5 0 0

EXEMPLIFICATION under the seal of any court in England or Ireland of any record or proceeding therein . 3 0 0

EXTRACT. *See* **Copy or Extract.**

FACTORY, in the nature of a letter or power of attorney in Scotland.

    See **Letter or Power of Attorney.**

FACULTY, LICENCE, COMMISSION, or DISPENSATION for admitting or authorising any person to act as a notary public—

    In England . . 30 0 0
    In Scotland or Ireland . 20 0 0

FACULTY or DISPENSATION of any
other kind—   £   s. d.
  In England   .   .   .   30 0 0
  In Ireland   .   .   .   25 0 0

"Faculty or Dispensation of any other kind" covers personal faculties granted by prerogative e.g., the Archbishop of Canterbury has the privilege of granting faculties or degrees of M.A., M.D., and D.D.

Faculties and licences relating to consecrated buildings, &c., are now exempt from duty. (See under "Licence," post, p 155.)

FEU CONTRACT in Scotland. *See* **Conveyance on Sale,** and Section 56.

FOREIGN SECURITY. *See* **Marketable Security,** and Section 82.

FURTHER CHARGE or FURTHER SECURITY. *See* **Mortgage,** &c., and Section 86.

GRANT or LETTERS PATENT under the Great Seal or wafer Great Seal of the United Kingdom of Great Britain and Ireland, or of the Great Seal of Ireland, or the Seal of the Duchy or County Palatine of Lancaster, or under the Seal kept and used in Scotland in place of the Great Seal formerly used there—   £   s. d.

(1) Of the honour or dignity of a
      duke . .   350 0 0
    Of the honour or dignity of a
      marquis   ...   300 0 0
    Of the honour or dignity of an
      earl   250 0 0
    Of the honour or dignity of a
      viscount   200 0 0

		£	s	d.
	Of the honour or dignity of a baron	150	0	0
	Of the honour or dignity of a baronet	100	0	0
(2)	Of a congé d'élire to any dean and chapter for the election of an archbishop or bishop.			
(3)	Of the Royal Assent to, or signification of, the election made by any dean and chapter, or of the nomination and presentation by Her Majesty, in default of such election, of any person to be an archbishop or bishop	30	0	0
(4)	Of or for the restitution of the temporalities to any archbishop or bishop			
(5)	Of any other honour, dignity, or promotion whatsoever			
(6)	Of any franchise, liberty, or privilege to any person or body politic or corporate			

And *see* Section 74.

Grants of Honours and Dignities.

74. (1) Where two or more honours or dignities are granted by the same letters patent to the same person, such letters patent are to be charged with the proper duty in respect of the highest in point of rank only. Duty to be charged in respect of highest rank.

(2) Where any honour or dignity is granted to any person in remainder, the letters patent are to

be charged with such further duty in respect of every remainder as would be payable for an original grant of the same honour or dignity.

(33 & 34 Vict, Ch. 97, Sec 95.)

GRANT or WARRANT OF PRECE-   £   s   d.
DENCE to take rank among nobility,
under the sign manual of Her Majesty ...100   0   0

GRANT or LICENCE under the sign manual of Her Majesty to take and use a surname and arms, or a surname only.

    In compliance with the injunctions of any will or settlement   .. 50   0   0

    Upon any voluntary application .. 10   0   0

GRANT of arms or armorial ensigns only, under the sign manual of Her Majesty, or by any of the Kings of Arms of England, Scotland, or Ireland   10   0   0

GRANT of copyhold or customary estates. *See* **Conveyance—Copyhold.**

GRANT of the custody of the person or estate of a lunatic   ..   . 2   0   0

HERITABLE BOND. *See* **Mortgage,** &c., and Section 86

INSURANCE. *See* **Policy.**

LEASE or TACK.

  (1) For any definite term not exceeding a year—

    Of any dwelling-house or part of a dwelling-house at a rent not exceeding the rate of £10 per annum .   0   0   1

(2) For any definite term less than a year—

 (a) Of any furnished dwelling-house or apartments where the rent for such term exceeds £25 .   £ s d.
   0 2 6

 (b) Of any lands, tenements, or heritable subjects except or otherwise than as aforesaid { The same duty as a lease for a year at the rent reserved for the definite term.

A lease from week to week or month to month is not a lease for a "definite term" and is chargeable with duty under (3)

(3) For any other definite term or for any indefinite term—

  Of any lands, tenements, or heritable subjects—

  Where the consideration, or any part of the consideration, moving either to the lessor or to any other person, consists of any money, stock, or security ·

  In respect of such consideration { The same duty as a conveyance on a sale for the same consideration.

The amount of premium or consideration, whether moving to the lessor or to any other person, should be stated in the instrument, and ad valorem conveyance duty must be paid in respect thereof. This is especially important when a lease is granted by the ground landlord to the purchaser of a house from the builder. The purchase money should be set forth on the face of the lease, whether the builder is or is not a party to the instrument, and in default the penalties imposed by Section 5 are incurred: see Attorney-General v Brown (3 Ex. R. 662; 18 L J, Ex. 336) and the Act of Indemnity consequent upon that case (13 & 14 Vict., Ch. 97, Sec. 10), and Gingell v. Perkins (4 Ex R 720, 19 L. J, Ex. 129). In the latter case the Court held that the release of a debt in consideration of the grant of lease was a consideration in the nature of premium, and that the instrument should be stamped with ad valorem conveyance duty accordingly

Where the consideration or any part of the consideration is any rent.

In respect of such consideration:
If the rent, whether reserved, as a yearly rent or otherwise, is at a rate or average rate

	If the term does not exceed 35 years, or is indefinite	If the term exceeds 35 years, but does not exceed 100 years	If the term exceeds 100 years.
	£ s. d.	£ s. d.	£ s. d.
Not exceeding £5 per annum	0 0 6	0 3 0	0 6 0
Exceeding—			
£5 and not exceeding £10	0 1 0	0 6 0	0 12 0
£10 ,, ,, £15	0 1 6	0 9 0	0 18 0
£15 ,, ,, £20	0 2 0	0 12 0	1 4 0
£20 ,, ,, £25	0 2 6	0 15 0	1 10 0
£25 ,, ,, £50	0 5 0	1 10 0	3 0 0
£50 ,, ,, £75	0 7 6	2 5 0	4 10 0
£75 ,, ,, £100	0 10 0	3 0 0	6 0 0
£100— For every full sum of £50, and also for any fractional part of £50 thereof	0 5 0	1 10 0	3 0 0

(4) Of any other kind whatsoever not hereinbefore described ... ... £ s. d. 0 10 0

And *see* Sections 75, 76, 77, and 78.

Lease "of any other kind whatsoever," &c. (4), is held in administration to apply only to leases of lands, tenements, or heritable subjects, not to leases of chattels. It also includes a lease at will

The words "average rate" were inserted in The Stamp Act, 1870, to meet Pearson *v.* Commissioners (3 Ex. 242), in which it was held under the old law that a lease for forty-five years at a substantial rent for twenty-three years, and a peppercorn afterwards, was chargeable as a lease at a rent for twenty-three years. In administration, however, duty is still charged by relation to the period during which a beneficial rent is payable, and "average rate" has application where the fixed amount of beneficial rent varies from one year to another

A lease for a term of years, determinable upon the dropping of a life or lives, is a lease for an "indefinite term," chargeable with the lowest rate of duty

A lease at a rent reducible to a lower amount if the tenant performs some covenant, as to buy beer of the lessor only, is chargeable with ad valorem duty on the higher amount.

"Lands, tenements, or heritable subjects" includes all interests in land. A lease of sporting rights, or the surface of a wall for advertising purposes, is liable to ad valorem lease duty.

A lease at a rent not stated but ascertainable is liable to duty on the amount of the rent. (Parry v Deere, 5 A. & E. 551; 2 H. & W. 395.)

A lease containing an option of purchase of the property demised is sufficiently stamped with ad valorem lease duty. (Worthington v. Warrington, 17 L. J., C. P 117; 5 C. B 635.) If the option extends to property other than that demised, a deed stamp or agreement stamp is necessary in addition to the ad valorem duty (Lovelock v Frankland, 16 L J, Q. B 182; 8 A. & E. 371) A lease containing the covenant of a surety for payment of the rent is sufficiently stamped with lease duty (Price v. Thomas, 2 B & Ad. 218) A lease containing a contract for the sale of fixtures is liable to ad valorem lease duty and a deed or agreement stamp (Corder v. Drakeford, 3 Taunt 382; Clayton v. Burtenshaw, 5 B & C. 41.) A lease at a fixed rent and an indefinite royalty is liable to ad valorem duty and ten shillings. A lease of hereditaments and furniture at a gross rent is liable to ad valorem duty on the amount of the rent, but if there is a separate reservation of the rent for the furniture, ad valorem lease duty is not chargeable upon that rent, and ad valorem duty would be charged if there is a covenant to pay such rent under the head "Bond, Covenant, or Instrument of any kind," &c.

In a lease of offices ad valorem duty is not charged in respect of sums payable by the lessee for gas, housekeeper's services, &c, unless expressly reserved as rent and recoverable by distress as an additional rent payable to the lessor. In a lease of a house ad valorem duty is not charged upon a payment reserved as a garden rate for keeping up a common garden Rent reserved for insurance of the property demised is not chargeable with any duty

An instrument whereby several parcels are leased to the same person is liable to ad valorem duty on the aggregate amount of the rents (Boase v. Jackson, 3 B & B. 185; Blount v Pearman, 1 Bing. N. C. 408), unless the power of re-entry and distress in respect of rent owing for a particular parcel is restricted to that parcel only, in which case the instrument is regarded as several leases, and separate duties are payable A lease of several parcels to different persons is liable to ad valorem duty on the separate rents (Doe dem. Copley v Day, 13 East, 241; Cooper v Flynn, 3 Ir. L R. 473)

Leases

Agreements for not more than thirty-five years to be charged as leases.

76. (1) An agreement for a lease or tack, or with respect to the letting of any lands, tenements, or heritable subjects for any term not exceeding thirty-five years, or for any indefinite term, is to be charged with the same duty as if it were an actual lease or tack made for the term and consideration mentioned in the agreement

(2) A lease or tack made subsequently to, and in conformity with, such an agreement, duly stamped, is to be charged with the duty of sixpence only.

(33 & 34 *Vict.*, *Ch.* 97, *Sec* 96.)

An agreement to *take* lands, &c, is not chargeable with ad valorem duty In Glen v Dungay (4 Ex. B 61) an agreement to hire, signed by the lessee only, was considered sufficiently stamped with an agreement stamp *Per cur.*, "Even if signed by the lessor, there is nothing to stamp as a lease It is a mere agreement which, but for the Statute of Frauds, need not have been in writing."

If the agreement is in two parts, the one to *let* and the other to *take* land, &c., for a term within this section, ad valorem lease duty is chargeable upon the part executed by the lessor, and the other part must be stamped as a duplicate or counterpart

If an agreement operates as a present demise, and gives the tenant an option to take a lease for a further term, such lease when granted must be stamped with ad valorem duty The sixpenny duty upon the lease is only applicable where the lease covers the whole term for which the agreement was made, and is in strict conformity with the agreement If the rent fixed by the agreement is increased, ad valorem lease duty besides the sixpence is chargeable upon the lease in respect of such increase; and any other variation of the terms attracts the further duty of ten shillings as a deed.

When a lease is stamped with sixpence under (2) the duty paid stamp (Section 11) is required.

An agreement in articles of partnership that premises the property of one of the partners shall be held in tenancy by the firm is not considered to be within the charge.

An attornment is not liable to lease duty. *See*, under "Agreements," *ante*, p. 56.

An agreement for a lease at a fixed rent and a further uncertain valuable consideration is liable to the ad valorem lease duty and ten shillings (Section 8 [2]), not sixpence. If it were a separate instrument made "for such consideration only," it would be chargeable with ten shillings as a "lease of any other kind whatsoever not hereinbefore described."

An agreement for a lease at an uncertain rent for any term not exceeding thirty-five years or for any indefinite term is liable to the duty of ten shillings.

76. (1) Where the consideration, or any part of the consideration, for which a lease or tack is granted or agreed to be granted, consists of any produce or other goods, the value of the produce or goods is to be deemed a consideration in respect of which the lease or tack or agreement is chargeable with ad valorem duty.

<small>Leases, how to be charged in respect of produce, &c.</small>

(2) Where it is stipulated that the value of the produce or goods is to amount at least to, or is not to exceed, a given sum, or where the lessee is specially charged with, or has the option of paying after any permanent rate of conversion, the value of the produce or goods is, for the purpose of assessing the ad valorem duty, to be estimated at the given sum, or according to the permanent rate.

(3) A lease or tack or agreement for a lease or tack made either wholly or partially for any such consideration, if it contains a statement of the value thereof, and is stamped in accordance with the statement, is, so far as regards the subject matter of the statement, to be deemed duly stamped, unless or until it is otherwise shown that the statement is

incorrect, and that the lease or tack or agreement is in fact not duly stamped

(33 & 34 Vict., Ch 87, Sec. 97.)

Directions as to duty in certain cases.

77. (1) A lease or tack, or agreement for a lease or tack, or with respect to any letting, is not to be charged with any duty in respect of any penal rent, or increased rent in the nature of a penal rent, thereby reserved or agreed to be reserved or made payable, or by reason of being made in consideration of the surrender or abandonment of any existing lease, tack, or agreement, of or relating to the same subject matter.

(2) A lease made for any consideration in respect whereof it is chargeable with ad valorem duty, and in further consideration either of a covenant by the lessee to make, or of his having previously made, any substantial improvement of or addition to the property demised to him, or of any covenant relating to the matter of the lease, is not to be charged with any duty in respect of such further consideration

(3) No lease for a life or lives not exceeding three, or for a term of years determinable with a life or lives not exceeding three, and no lease for a term absolute not exceeding twenty-one years, granted by an ecclesiastical corporation aggregate or sole, is to be charged with any higher duty than thirty-five shillings.

14 & 15 Vic c. 123.

(4) A lease for a definite term exceeding thirty-five years granted under The Trinity College (Dublin) Leasing and Perpetuity Act, 1851, is not to be charged with any higher duty than would have been chargeable thereon if it had been a lease for a definite term not exceeding thirty-five years.

(33 & 34 Vict., Ch. 97, Sec. 98)

(5) An instrument whereby the rent reserved by any other instrument chargeable with duty and duly stamped as a lease or tack is increased is not to be charged with duty otherwise than as a lease or tack

in consideration of the additional rent thereby made payable

(39 & 40 Vict., Ch. 16, Sec. 11.)

(1) Whether a rent is penal or not depends very much upon the rate, and the power of the lessor to prevent the continuance of the breach in respect of which the penal rent is payable, or recover damages in addition thereto. A rent of £20 per acre payable upon breaking up pasture is clearly penal, and so in a brewer's lease would be a covenant to pay as an additional rent double the value of beer bought from any other brewer; but if an option is left to the lessee to do a particular thing upon payment of a reasonable further rent, such as to use a private house as a school, the rent is not considered penal.

If the surrender of the old lease is contained in the new lease, the instrument is not chargeable with separate duty in respect of the surrender.

(2) In Boulton v. Commissioners (5 Ex. 82) it was held that a lease in consideration of an annual rent and a covenant of the lessee to complete buildings then in process of erection was liable to ad valorem duty on the rent, and a deed stamp for the covenant as a further valuable consideration. The Act 33 & 34 Vict., Ch. 44 (passed by way of indemnity and relief and repealed by S. L. R. Act, 1883), of which this section is substantially a repetition, was as follows:—

"No lease already made or hereafter to be made for any consideration or considerations in respect whereof it is chargeable with ad valorem stamp duty, and in further consideration either of a covenant by the lessee to make or of his having previously made any substantial improvement of or addition to the property demised to him, or of any usual covenant, shall be deemed to be or have been chargeable with any stamp duty in respect of such further consideration."

"Any covenant relating to the matter of the lease" has evidently a wider meaning than "usual covenant" in the former Act; and as to what are "usual covenants" see Hampshire v. Wickens (7 Ch. D. 661). In a brewer's lease they include a covenant to buy beer of the lessor.

78. (1) The duty upon an instrument chargeable with duty as a lease or tack of— *Duty in certain cases may be denoted by adhesive stamp*

    (a) Any dwelling-house, or part of a dwelling-house, for a definite term not exceeding a year at a rent not exceeding the rate of ten pounds per annum, or (*b*) Any furnished dwelling-house or apartments for any definite term less than a year;

and upon the duplicate or counterpart of any such instrument, may be denoted by an adhesive stamp, which is to be cancelled by the person by whom the instrument is first executed.

(2) Every person who executes, or prepares or is employed in preparing, any such instrument (except letters or correspondence) which is not, at or before the execution thereof, duly stamped, shall incur a fine of five pounds

(33 & 34 *Vict*., Ch. 97, *Secs* 99 *and* 100, 52 & 53 *Vict*., *Ch* 42, *Sec*. 7.)

LETTER OF ALLOTMENT and LETTER OF RENUNCIATION, or

any other document having the effect of a letter of allotment—

	£ s. d.
(1) Of any share of any company or proposed company ...	
(2) In respect of any loan raised, or proposed to be raised, by any company or proposed company, or by any municipal body or corporation ..	
(3) Issued or delivered in the United Kingdom, of any share of any foreign or colonial company or proposed company, or in respect of any loan raised or proposed to be raised by or on behalf of any foreign or colonial state, government, municipal body, corporation, or company ...	0 0 1

And **SCRIP CERTIFICATE, SCRIP,** or other document—

		£	s	d.
(1) Entitling any person to become the proprietor of any share of any company or proposed company			...	...
(2) Issued or delivered in the United Kingdom, and entitling any person to become the proprietor of any share of any foreign or colonial company or proposed company ...		0	0	1
(3) Denoting, or intended to denote, the right of any person as a subscriber in respect of any loan raised or proposed to be raised by any company or proposed company, or by any municipal body or corporation				...
(4) Issued or delivered in the United Kingdom, and denoting, or intended to denote, the right of any person as a subscriber in respect of any loan raised or proposed to be raised by or on behalf of any foreign or colonial state, government, municipal body, corporation, or company				

And *see* Section 79

Letters of Allotment or Renunciation, Scrip Certificates, and Scrip.

79. (1) Every person who executes, grants, issues, or delivers out any document chargeable with duty as a letter of allotment, letter of renunciation, or

<small>Provisions as to letters of allotment, &c.</small>

scrip certificate, or as scrip, before the same is duly stamped, shall incur a fine of twenty pounds

(2) The stamp duty of one penny on a letter of renunciation may be denoted by an adhesive stamp, which is to be cancelled by the person by whom the letter of renunciation is executed

(33 & 34 Vict., Ch. 97, Sec. 101; 43 & 44 Vict., Ch 20, Sec 56.)

LETTER of CREDIT. *See* **Bill of Exchange.**

LETTER OR POWER OF ATTORNEY, and COMMISSION, FACTORY, MANDATE, or other instrument in the nature thereof·

	£ s d.
(1) For the sole purpose of appointing or authorising a proxy to vote at any one meeting at which votes may be given by proxy, whether the number of persons named in such instrument be one or more ..	0 0 1

(34 Vict, Ch 4, Sec. 4.)

A proxy given for a particular meeting, and any adjournment thereof, falls under this charge

If the proxy is to vote at more than one meeting, or to vote generally at all meetings, the instrument for appointing or authorising the proxy is liable to the duty of ten shillings under (6) *See* also *re* English, Scottish, and Australian Chartered Bank [1893] 1 Ch, C A. 385; 42 W. R 4.

	£ s d
(2) By any petty officer, seaman, marine, or soldier serving as a marine, or his representatives, for receiving prize money or wages	0 1 0
(3) For the receipt of the dividends or interest of any stock—	
Where made for the receipt of one payment only	0 1 0
In any other case	0 5 0

If the letter of attorney, &c, given for the receipt of any dividend or interest of any stock authorises the attorney therein named to appoint another attorney for the same purposes, or empowers him to sue for recovery of the dividend or interest, it is liable to the duty of ten shillings

		£	s.	d
(4)	For the receipt of any sum of money, or any bill of exchange or promissory note for any sum of money, not exceeding £20, or any periodical payments not exceeding the annual sum of £10 (*not being hereinbefore charged*) ..	0	5	0
(5)	For the sale, transfer, or acceptance of any of the Government or Parliamentary stocks or funds—			
	Where the value of the stocks or funds does not exceed £20	0	5	0
	In any other case	0	10	0
(6)	Of any kind whatsoever not hereinbefore described ..	0	10	0

Exemptions

(1) Letter or power of attorney for the receipt of dividends of any definite and certain share of the Government or Parliamentary stocks or funds producing a yearly dividend less than £3

(2) Letter or power of attorney or proxy filed in the Probate Division of the High Court of Justice in England or Ireland or in any ecclesiastical court

(3) Order, request, or direction under hand only from the proprietor of any stock to any company or to any officer of any company or to any banker to pay the dividends

or interest arising from the stock to any person therein named.

And *see* Sections 80 and 81.

A letter or power of attorney only authorises the attorney to do that which the appointor of the attorney could do himself. Therefore the appointment of a steward of a manor by the lord is not chargeable as a letter of attorney, but the appointment of a deputy steward by a steward, or a deputy coroner by a coroner, where there are no fees or emoluments, is chargeable. If there are fees or emoluments the appointment is exempt from duty by the repeal of the duty upon appointments, p 48

In Reg. v Kelk (12 A. & E 559) an authority to act in the appointment of a special commissioner under a local Act was held to be a power of attorney.

In Allen v Morrison (3 M & R. 71; 8 B & C. 565) a power of attorney given by several persons, possessing a common interest in the subject matter of the power, to one was held liable to one stamp only.

The appointment of a receiver by writing under the hand of a mortgagee in accordance with Section 24 of The Conveyancing Act, 1881, is liable to the duty of ten shillings as a letter of attorney

Letters or Powers of Attorney and Voting Papers

Provisions as to proxies and voting papers.

80. (1) Every letter or power of attorney for the purpose of appointing a proxy to vote at a meeting, and every voting paper, hereby respectively charged with the duty of one penny, is to specify the day upon which the meeting at which it is intended to be used is to be held, and is to be available only at the meeting so specified, and any adjournment thereof

In Reg. v McInerney and others (30 L R, Ir. 49) it was held that a proxy to vote "at the next election" does not sufficiently "specify" the day of the meeting for which such proxy is to be available to fall within the penny duty

(2) The duty of one penny may be denoted by an adhesive stamp, which is to be cancelled by the person by whom the instrument is executed, and a

letter or power of attorney or voting paper charged with the duty of one penny is not to be stamped after the execution thereof by any person.

(3) Every person who makes or executes, or votes, or attempts to vote, under or by means of any such letter or power of attorney or voting paper, not being duly stamped, shall incur a fine of fifty pounds, and every vote given or tendered under the authority or by means of the letter or power of attorney or voting paper shall be void

81. A letter or power of attorney for the sale, transfer, or acceptance of any of the Government or Parliamentary stocks or funds, duly stamped for that purpose, is not to be charged with any further duty by reason of containing an authority for the receipt of the dividends on the same stocks or funds. *[margin: Power relating to Government stocks, how to be charged.]*

(33 & 34 Vict, Ch. 97, Secs. 102 and 103)

In re English, Scottish, and Australian Bank ([1893] 1 Ch., C. A. 385) a proxy (executed in Australia) to vote at "a meeting of creditors to be held in London" was held to be liable to the duty of ten shillings under (6), p. 151.

A proxy executed out of the United Kingdom may either be executed upon an adhesive stamp, or stamped with ten shillings, within thirty days after it has been received in the United Kingdom under Section 15.

	£	s	d.
LETTERS of MARQUE and REPRISAL	5	0	0

LETTERS PATENT. *See* **Grant.**

LETTER of REVERSION in Scotland.
See **Mortgage,** &c , and Section 86.

LICENCE for Marriage.
   Special—
      In England or Ireland   5   0   0
   Not special—
      In England   0   10   0

LICENCE under the seal of any archbishop, bishop, chancellor, or other ordinary, or by any ecclesiastical court in England or Ireland, or by any presbytery or other ecclesiastical power in Scotland:

	£ s d.
(1) To hold the office of lecturer, reader, chaplain, church clerk, chapel clerk, parish clerk, or sexton	
(2) For licensing a building for the performance of divine service within an ecclesiastical district formed under the provisions of the New Parishes Acts	0 10 0
(3) For licensing any chapel for the solemnization of marriages therein, pursuant to the provisions of the Act 6 & 7 Will 4, Ch. 85	
(4) For any other purpose	2 0 0

Exemptions.

(1) Licence granted to any spiritual person to perform divine service in any building approved by the archbishop or bishop in lieu of a church or chapel whilst the same is under repair or is rebuilding, or in any building so approved for the convenience of the inhabitants of a parish resident at a distance from a church or consecrated chapel

(2) Licence to hold a perpetual curacy

(3) Licence to a stipendiary curate, wherein the annual amount of the stipend is specified

(4) Licence for the purpose of authorising or enabling any person to

preach or exercise any other spiritual function, not being a licence to hold the office of lecturer, reader, or chaplain, and there being no salary or emolument for or attached to the exercise of the function for which such licence is granted

(5) Licence by any ecclesiastical authority for licensing or authorising any matter relating to a consecrated building or ground, or anything to be constructed, set up, taken down, or altered therein, or to be removed therefrom.

([5] from 41 & 42 Vict., Ch 15, Sec 27.)

LICENCE to act as a notary public. *See* **Faculty.**

LICENCE to use surname or arms. *See* **Grant.**

MARKETABLE SECURITY (*and Foreign or Colonial Share Certificate* — Repealed by 56 Vict, Ch 7, Sec. 4)

(1) Marketable security, (*a*) being a colonial government security, or (*b*) being a security not transferable by delivery, or (*c*) being a security transferable by delivery and bearing date or signed or offered for subscription before or on the sixth day of August, one thousand eight hundred and eighty-five—

For or in respect of the money thereby secured	The same ad valorem duty according to the nature of the security as upon a mortgage

(2) **Transfer, Assignment, Disposition, or Assignation** of a marketable security of any description—
 Upon a sale thereof—*see* Conveyance or Transfer on Sale
 Upon a mortgage thereof—*see* Mortgage of Stock or Marketable Security   £ s d
 In any other case than a sale or mortgage 0 10 0
 (51 & 52 *Vict.*, *Ch.* 8, *Sec* 13.)

(3) Marketable security (except a colonial government security) being a security transferable by delivery and bearing date or signed or offered for subscription after the sixth day of August, one thousand eight hundred and eighty-five—
 For every £10, and also for any fractional part of £10, of the money thereby secured .. 0 1 0
 (48 & 49 *Vict*, *Ch* 51, *Sec* 21.)

(4) Marketable security (except a colonial government security) being such security as last aforesaid given in substitution for a like security duly stamped in conformity with the law in force at the time when it became subject to duty—
 For every £20, and also for any fractional part of £20, of the money thereby secured . 0 0 6

The substituted security to be properly stamped with sixpence for every £20 must be given in substitution for a like security duly stamped—i e a security transferable by delivery "When a security payable to bearer or transferable otherwise than by an instrument of transfer is issued in lieu of a registered security transferable only by an instrument of transfer, the substituted security is chargeable with the duty of one shilling for every £10, and also for any fractional part thereof" (*Official Circular*, March, 1890). A substituted security chargeable with the lower rate of duty must also bear the substituted security stamp.

(5) *Marketable security transferable by delivery, whatever may be the date thereof, and wherever it may have been made or issued, or the interest may be payable*

On the occasion of the first transfer thereof by delivery in the United Kingdom, and on the occasion of the first transfer thereof by delivery in the United Kingdom in any year after the year in which such first transfer by delivery shall happen—

	£	s.	d.
Where the amount secured does not exceed twenty-five pounds	0	0	3
Exceeds twenty-five pounds and does not exceed fifty pounds	0	0	6
Exceeds fifty pounds, for every fifty pounds and any fractional part of fifty pounds of such amount	0	0	6

(51 & 52 Vict., Ch. 8, Sec 12; 53 & 54 Vict., Ch. 8, Sec 18.)

Exemption.

Any security, duly stamped with the duty of one shilling for every ten pounds, and also for any fractional part of ten pounds, of the money thereby secured, or duly stamped as a substituted security for any security so stamped where such substituted security bears an impressed stamp denoting that the security for which it was substituted was so duly stamped.

(6) Foreign or colonial share certificate.

On the occasion of the first delivery thereof in the United Kingdom, and on the occasion of the first delivery thereof in the United Kingdom in any year after the year in which such first delivery shall happen—

	£	s	d.
Where the nominal amount in money of the stock or debenture stock or funded debt does not exceed twenty-five pounds ..	0	0	3
Exceeds twenty-five pounds and does not exceed fifty pounds ..	0	0	6
Exceeds fifty pounds, for every fifty pounds and any fractional part of fifty pounds of such amount	0	0	6

And see Sections 82, 83, 84, and 85.

The parts of the above charge printed in italics, with Section 82 (2) and Section 85, seq, were repealed by Section 4 of The Customs and Inland Revenue Act, 1893 (56 Vict., Ch 7, 12th May, 1893), which is as follows:—

Repeal of annual duties in respect of marketable securities, and foreign or colonial share certificates

4. (1) The annual duties imposed by The Stamp Act, 1891, under the head "Marketable Security and Foreign or Colonial Share Certificate" in the First Schedule to the said Act, upon a marketable security transferable by delivery and upon a foreign or colonial share certificate shall cease to be payable.

(2) Sub-section 2 of Section 82 and Section 85 of the said Act, and the paragraphs numbered 5 and 6 under the head "Marketable Security and Foreign or Colonial Share Certificate" in the First Schedule to the said Act, and also the words "and Foreign or Colonial Share Certificate" of that head, are hereby repealed.

"*Transferable by delivery*" is interpreted as meaning "transferable otherwise than by an instrument of transfer." Thus a security payable to "A. B. or order" is transferable by delivery as soon as it is endorsed by A B, and a security to registered holder convertible into a security to bearer is transferable by delivery and must bear the duty under (3), even though there may be no intention of effecting the conversion immediately

Stock and share certificates are issued by many foreign companies with a blank space, to be filled in by any holder, for the name of the transferee, and a blank power of attorney to execute the surrender and obtain the cancellation of the certificate Until the name of the transferee is inscribed such instruments are transferable by delivery, and were formerly liable to duty under (6) Since the repeal of that charge, by 56 Vict., Ch 7, these instruments have not been chargeable

Marketable Securities.

82. (1) Marketable securities for the purpose of the charge of duty thereon include— *(Meaning of marketable securities for charge of duty, and foreign and colonial share certificate.)*

    (*a*) A marketable security made or issued by or on behalf of any company or body of persons corporate or unincorporate formed or established in the United Kingdom; and

    (*b*) A marketable security by or on behalf of any foreign state or government, or foreign or colonial municipal body, corporation, or company (hereinafter called a foreign security), bearing date or signed after the third day of June, one thousand eight hundred and sixty-two,

        (i.) Which is made or issued in the United Kingdom, or

        (ii.) Which, though originally issued out of the United Kingdom, has been, after the sixth day of August, one thousand eight hundred and eighty-five, or is offered for subscription, and given or delivered to a subscriber in the United Kingdom, or (iii.) Which, the interest thereon being payable in the United Kingdom, is assigned, transferred, or in any manner negotiated in the United Kingdom; and

(c) A marketable security by or on behalf of any colonial government which if the borrower were a foreign government would be a foreign security (hereinafter called a colonial government security).

(2) *For the purposes of this Act the expression "foreign or colonial share certificate" includes any document whatever, being* primâ facie *evidence of the title of any person as proprietor of, or as having the beneficial interest in, any share or shares or stock or debenture stock or funded debt of any foreign or colonial company or corporation where such person is not registered in respect thereof in a register duly kept in the United Kingdom*—Repealed by 56 Vict, Ch. 7, Sec 4

(34 Vict , Ch. 4, Sec 2, 48 & 49 Vict., Ch. 51, Sec. 21, 51 & 52 Vict , Ch 8, Sec 12)

" Marketable security " means a security of such a description as to be capable of being sold in any stock market in the United Kingdom.

The description "Marketable Security" embraces several duties which were separately charged under the old law. Of these, the principal are—

Mortgage Bond, Covenant, &c (of the class of marketable securities),
Foreign Security;
Security Transferable by Delivery

A *foreign security* under the old law, bearing date or signed before the 4th June, 1862, was not charged with any duty

Until the 31st March, 1871, the definition of a foreign security for the charge of duty was (33 & 34 Vic., Ch. 97, Sec 113, and preceding Acts)—

(1) Which is made or issued in the United Kingdom
(2) Upon which any interest is payable in the United Kingdom

(3) Which is assigned, transferred, or in any manner negotiated in the United Kingdom

Such a security, whether to bearer or registered holder, was chargeable with the duty of 2s 6d per £100

After 30th March, 1871, the definition of a foreign security for the charge of duty was as follows (34 Vict, Ch. 4, Sec. 2) :—

(1) Which is made or issued in the United Kingdom;
(2) Which, the interest thereon being payable in the United Kingdom, is assigned, transferred, or in any manner negotiated in the United Kingdom.

When by 48 & 49 Vict, Ch 51, Sec. 21 (6th August, 1885) the duty upon all securities transferable by delivery, except securities "by or on behalf of any colonial government," was increased, the definition of a foreign security was extended "to include a security which, though originally issued to the holder out of the [United] Kingdom, is offered by him for subscription, and [sold] or delivered to a subscriber in the United Kingdom." These words meet the case of Grenfell v. Commissioners (1 Ex D 242, 45 L. J, Ex. 465), and the definition has been altered only by the omission of the words "to the holder" and "by him" (Sub section 1 (b) ii. of Section 82, *ante*, p. 159)

The issue of a security is its "first execution by the company, who give thereby a right of action in favour of some person to whom that bond is given" (*Per Pollock, B, Grenfell v Commissioners*, 1 Ex D 242, 45 L J, Ex. 465.) Bonds of an American company tendered for and purchased by a firm in New York, issued to them with the name of the payee in blank, and sent to England for sale, were held not to fall within the charge As regards securities transferable by delivery, this case was set aside by the words cited above in 48 & 49 Vict, Ch 51, Sec 21.

83. Every person who in the United Kingdom makes, issues, assigns, transfers, negotiates, or offers for subscription, any foreign security or colonial government security not being duly stamped, shall incur a fine of twenty pounds.

(*34 Vict., Ch 4, Sec 3*)

Penalty on issuing, &c., foreign, &c., security not duly stamped.

Foreign securities brought from abroad for conversion, and exchanged by the banker operating the conversion for the other securities, are not "assigned, transferred, or negotiated in the United Kingdom"

MARKETABLE SECURITY

Foreign or colonial securities may be stamped without penalty

84. The Commissioners may at any time, without reference to the date thereof, allow any foreign security or colonial government security to be stamped without the payment of any penalty, upon being satisfied, in any manner that they may think proper, that it was not made or issued, and has not been transferred, assigned, or negotiated within the United Kingdom.

Annual duties to be denoted by adhesive stamps

85. (1) The duties charged upon a marketable security on the occasion of the first transfer by delivery thereof in any year, and upon a foreign or colonial share certificate on the occasion of the first delivery thereof in any year, are to be denoted by adhesive stamps appropriated by words and figures on the face thereof to the duties and the year.

(2) Every person who delivers or transfers, or is concerned as broker or agent in delivering or transferring, any instrument chargeable with any duty so payable, and not being duly stamped, shall incur a fine of twenty pounds.

(3) Where the holder of any foreign or colonial share certificate bearing the stamp for any year shall in the course of the year, cause himself to be registered in the register of the foreign or colonial company or corporation to which it relates, and shall obtain a new certificate consequent upon the registration, the Commissioners may, subject to such regulations as they may prescribe, stamp the new certificate for the same year without payment of duty.—Repealed by 56 Vict, Ch. 7, Sec. 4

(51 & 52 Vict, Ch. 8, Sec 12.)

MARRIAGE LICENCE. *See* **Licence.**

MARRIAGE SETTLEMENT. *See* **Settlement.**

MEMORIAL to be registered pursuant to any Act for the time being in force relating to the public registering of deeds in England or Ireland—

Where the instrument registered is chargeable with any duty not amounting to 2s 6d. } The same duty as the registered instrument

	£	s	d.
In any other case ...	0	2	6

MORTGAGE, BOND, DEBENTURE, COVENANT (except a marketable security otherwise specially charged with duty), and **WARRANT of ATTORNEY to confess and enter up judgment.**

(1) Being the only or principal or primary security (other than an equitable mortgage) for the payment or repayment of money—

	£	s	d.
Not exceeding £10	0	0	3
Exceeding £10 and not exceeding £25	0	0	8
Exceeding £25 and not exceeding £50	0	1	3
Exceeding £50 and not exceeding £100	0	2	6
Exceeding £100 and not exceeding £150	0	3	9
Exceeding £150 and not exceeding £200	0	5	0
Exceeding £200 and not exceeding £250	0	6	3
Exceeding £250 and not exceeding £300	0	7	6

Exceeding £300—

    For every £100, and also for any fractional part of £100, of the amount secured £ s d.
    0 2 6

(2) Being a collateral, or auxiliary, or additional, or substituted security (other than an equitable mortgage), or by way of further assurance for the above-mentioned purpose where the principal or primary security is duly stamped—

    For every £100, and also for any fractional part of £100, of the amount secured   0 0 6

(3) Being an equitable mortgage—

    For every £100, and any fractional part of £100, of the amount secured   0 1 0

(4) **Transfer, Assignment, Disposition, or Assignation** of any mortgage, bond, debenture, or covenant (except a marketable security), or of any money or stock secured by any such instrument, or by any warrant of attorney to enter up judgment, or by any judgment—

    For every £100, and also for any fractional part of £100, of the amount transferred, assigned, or disponed, exclusive of interest which is not in arrear   0 0 6

    And also where any further money is added to the money already secured   { The same duty as a principal security for such further money.

(5) **Reconveyance, Release, Discharge, Surrender, Resurrender,**

Warrant to Vacate, or Renunciation of any such security as aforesaid, or of the benefit thereof, or of the money thereby secured—

	£	s	d.
For every £100, and also for any fractional part of £100, of the total amount or value of the money at any time secured .	0	0	6

And see Sections 86, 87, 88, and 89

(1) This charge formerly included "Foreign Security," as to which *see*, now, "Marketable Security," and Sections 82, 83, and 84, and notes

The minimum charge of duty was reduced from eightpence upon Mortgages, &c., not exceeding £25, to threepence, by 46 & 47 Vict, Ch 55, Sec 15 (25th August, 1883).

(2) *Collateral, &c, Security*

When mortgaged property is sold in consideration of a fee farm rent, and the instrument of conveyance contains a declaration that the fee farm rent is to be subject to the same equity of redemption as that to which the property out of which it issues was subject previously, the conveyance is chargeable with sixpence per £100 as a substituted security, in addition to the ad valorem conveyance duty, but in administration, the greatest amount of substituted security duty charged in such a case is ten shillings

A trust deed for securing payment of debentures is not considered a collateral security If the debentures are duly stamped, the trust deed is passed on adjudication with a stamp of ten shillings If the trust deed is made for securing the payment of debenture stock, it is liable to ad valorem mortgage duty.

If bonds or debentures terminating at a fixed date are renewed by endorsement, the endorsement is liable to the duty of ten shillings as a deed (or ad valorem duty if of less amount) if under seal, and sixpence if under hand. (For what is a deed in Scotland see pp 131—2)

A formal mortgage made in accordance with an agreement, &c, accompanied with a deposit of title deeds for making a mortgage (Section 86 (1) [*e*]), liable to the duty of two shillings and sixpence per £100, is regarded as sufficiently stamped with ten shillings, or ad valorem duty at sixpence per £100 if less than ten shillings If the agreement is chargeable as an equitable mortgage, however, the duty on the formal mortgage must be at the rate of two shillings and sixpence per £100

The "duty paid stamp" (Section 11) is required upon instruments stamped with the duty imposed by (2)

(3) *Equitable Mortgage*

An equitable mortgage is liable to the duty of one shilling per £100, whether given as a primary or collateral security, and if an equitable mortgage is followed by a mortgage under seal, the latter is liable to the duty of two shillings and sixpence per £100 The "equitable mortgage" duty was imposed by 51 & 52 Vict., Ch 8, Sec. 15 (16th May, 1888)

(4) *Transfer, &c*

Transfer duty is charged on the *amount transferred*, even when the sum paid by transferee to transferor is of less amount.

Interest in arrear must be included in the amount upon which transfer duty is paid, except where the transfer is made upon the appointment of a new trustee, and falls under the proviso to Section 62

Transfer duty is not charged upon interest which has not accrued due at the date of the transfer

(5) *Reconveyance, &c*

The ad valorem duty is payable once only If a part only of the property mortgaged is reconveyed, the duty required upon adjudication is ten shillings, or ad valorem duty if such duty is less than ten shillings, and the ad valorem duty upon "the total amount of the money at any time secured" is charged when the last parcel of the mortgaged property is reconveyed

The reconveyance of a collateral security is liable to a maximum duty of ten shillings if the reconveyance of the primary security is duly stamped If the ad valorem duty is less than ten shillings, the reconveyance of the collateral security should be stamped with ad valorem duty

A bare receipt acknowledging the payment of principal and interest endorsed upon an instrument chargeable with mortgage duty is not liable to reconveyance duty, and is exempt from receipt duty under Exemption 11 (see "Receipt," *post*, p 186), but if a receipt endorsed upon any mortgage or upon an equitable mortgage which contains such words, for example, as "in full discharge" of the moneys secured, it is liable to ad valorem duty as a "discharge"

Before the passing of The Stamp Act, 1870, warrants to vacate were not liable to duty. Now, when copyholds mortgaged alone are vacated, the warrant to vacate is chargeable with ad valorem reconveyance duty, but as to copyholds mortgaged with freeholds, the ad valorem reconveyance duty is paid upon the reconveyance of the freeholds, and the warrant to vacate is not chargeable with any duty

When in consequence of copyholds mortgaged alone being situate in different manors there are several warrants to vacate, one of such warrants only is liable to ad valorem duty The others are not liable to any duty, but they should bear the adjudication stamp or the duty paid stamp

Mortgages, &c

86. (1) For the purposes of this Act the expression "mortgage" means a security by way of mortgage for the payment of any definite and certain sum of money advanced or lent at the time, or previously due and owing, or forborne to be paid, being payable, or for the repayment of money to be thereafter lent, advanced, or paid, or which may become due upon an account current, together with any sum already advanced or due, or without, as the case may be;

And includes—

(a) Conditional surrender by way of mortgage, further charge, wadset, and heritable bond, disposition, assignation, or tack in security, and eik to a reversion of or affecting any lands, estate, or property, real or personal, heritable or moveable, whatsoever and

(b) Any deed containing an obligation to infeft any person in annual rent, or in lands or other heritable subjects in Scotland, under a clause of reversion, but without any personal bond or obligation therein contained for payment of the money or stock intended to be secured and

(c) Any conveyance of any lands, estate, or property whatsoever in trust to be sold or

Meaning of "mortgage"

otherwise converted into money, intended only as a security, and redeemable before the sale or other disposal thereof, either by express stipulation or otherwise, except where the conveyance is made for the benefit of creditors generally, or for the benefit of creditors specified, who accept the provision made for payment of their debts, in full satisfaction thereof, or who exceed five in number: and

(d) Any defeazance, letter of reversion, back bond, declaration, or other deed or writing for defeating or making redeemable, or explaining or qualifying any conveyance, transfer, disposition, assignation, or tack of any lands, estate, or property whatsoever, apparently absolute, but intended only as a security and

(e) Any agreement (other than an agreement chargeable with duty as an equitable mortgage), contract, or bond accompanied with a deposit of title deeds for making a mortgage, wadset, or any other security or conveyance as aforesaid of any lands, estate, or property comprised in the title deeds, or for pledging or charging the same as a security and

(f) Any deed whereby a real burden is declared or created on lands or heritable subjects in Scotland and

(g) Any deed operating as a mortgage of any stock or marketable security

(2) For the purpose of this Act the expression "equitable mortgage" means an agreement or memorandum under hand only, relating to the deposit of any title deeds or instruments constituting or being evidence of the title to any property what-

ever (other than stock or marketable security), or creating a charge on such property

(33 & 34 Vict., Ch 97, Sec 105, 51 & 52 Vict, Ch 8, Secs 14 and 15.)

(1) *"Security by way of Mortgage"*

The same words in Locke King's Act (17 & 18 Vict, Ch. 113) have been held to include all charges and incumbrances, except a vendor's lien for unpaid purchase money

It should be observed that in all these sections "security" refers to the instrument, not to the subject matter of the incumbrance.

Duty, *qua* mortgage, can only be charged in respect of a "definite and certain sum of money advanced or lent at the time," &c. Therefore a charge of portions on real estate for the benefit of future children is not within the charge of mortgage duty But the introduction of "covenant" into this charge extended the charge of duty to numerous instruments which would not have been chargeable as mortgages. Thus, in the case mentioned, a *covenant* to pay the portions would attract ad valorem duty under this head, and generally it may be said that ad valorem covenant duty is payable (not of course in addition to mortgage duty) upon every instrument containing a covenant to pay a definite and certain, i.e., an ascertainable sum, whether "advanced or lent at the time," &c, or otherwise. The words "definite and certain" relate to the amount secured, not to the certainty of payment In Maxwell *v* Commissioners (4 Rettie, 4th Series, 1121) a bond for the payment of sums named as a provision for unborn children, £20,000 if two children, and £30,000 if three, was held under 13 & 14 Vict., Ch 97, to be a bond for the payment of a "definite and certain" sum of £30,000, and chargeable accordingly. In Mortimore *v* Commissioners (2 H & C 820) the sum named secured by a mortgage of a reversionary interest payable only in the event of the mortgagor surviving the tenant for life, was held to be a definite and certain sum, notwithstanding the contingency, and in Canning *v* Raper (1 E & B 164, 22 L. J, Q B 87) a mortgage to indemnify a surety was held to be liable to ad valorem mortgage duty upon the sum for which the surety had made himself liable, the Court observing that "a security for future contingent payments is as much within the words and meaning of the statute as a security for certain future payments"

The "definite and certain sum" in a mortgage is the principal sum only Duty is not payable for interest, even of interest in arrear, unless capitalised and made part of the principal sum (Barker *v* Smark, 7 M & W. 50), nor expenses and disbursements incidental to the mortgage for recovery of which no express provision is required (Doe dem Scruton *v* Snaith, 8 Bing 146, 1 Moore & Scott, 230, Doe dem Merceron *v* Bragg, 8 A & E 620; 3 Nev & P 644), nor expenses of the renewal of a lease for lives charged on the mortgaged premises (Wroughton *v* Turtle, 11 M & W 561, 1 Dow & L 473), nor costs (Lysaght *v* Warren, 10 Ir L. R 269), nor bankers' commission (Frith *v* Rotherham, 15 L J, Ex 133, 10 Jur 208), nor premiums on policies of life insurance, though they are to be considered as principal moneys and bear interest (Lawrence *v* Boston, 21 L J, Ex 49, 7 Ex R 28), and *see* Section 88 (3) The mortgagee is entitled, without express provision in the instrument, to add these charges to his debt, and the expression of that which the law allows does not affect stamp duty (Wroughton *v* Turtle, *ubi supra*) So a debenture or other security for a principal sum, and a sum by way of bonus—say £100 and £5 respectively—or for £100, redeemable for £105, is sufficiently stamped with duty on £100

The ad valorem duty must be calculated upon the amount secured, even though the value of the property be of less amount Thus the mortgage of a life policy of £500 to secure an advance of £1,000 must be stamped with mortgage duty upon £1,000

Section 58 (3) of The Copyhold Act, 1894 (57 & 58 Vict. Ch 46), enacts that a certificate of charge under that Act and a transfer thereof shall be chargeable with the like stamp duty as is chargeable in respect of a mortgage and a transfer of mortgage respectively

Recognisances, attornments, and charging orders under 23 & 24 Vict, Ch 106, are not liable to mortgage duty

The memorandum of a pledge of goods with power of sale is not within the mortgage charge (Attenborough *v.* Commissioners, 11 Ex R. 461, 25 L J, Ex. 22)

As to conveyances for the benefit of creditors, *see* Coates *v* Perry (3 B & B 45). An assignment of debts, upon trust that the assignee shall collect and receive the same, and out of the proceeds retain a sum owing to him by the assignor, and pay over the surplus, is not an assignment by way of charge, and not liable to duty as a mortgage (Burlinson *v.* Hall, 12 Q B D 347.)

A policy of life insurance is property for the purposes of this section (Caldwell *v* Dawson, 5 Ex R 1, 14 Jur. 316.)

There is no definition of "debenture" in the Stamp Acts. In British India Steam Navigation Company *v* Commissioners

(7 Q B D 165, 50 L J, Q B 517) an instrument with coupons attached, under the hands of directors of a company, resembling in form a promissory note, but headed "Debenture," was held to be liable to duty as a debenture per Lindley, J, "You may have a debenture which is nothing more than an acknowledgment of indebtedness" The same view was expressed in Levy v Abercorris Slate and Slab Company (37 Ch D 260), and in Edmonds v Blaina Furnaces Company (36 Ch D 215) Chitty, J, held that a debenture need not necessarily be one of a series But a debenture which covers the whole indebtedness of a company is not considered to be a marketable security, and for transfer duty, &c, falls under this charge

As to instruments falling under (c) it should be observed that the old case of Meek v. Bayliss (31 L J, Ch 448) has long been superseded, but in Pyle v Partridge (15 L J, Ex 129) a document referring to a previous deposit of title deeds was held not to be an instrument "accompanied by a deposit," &c

(2) "*Equitable Mortgage*"

(2) The instrument to be an equitable mortgage for the purpose of stamp duty must be under hand only, if under seal it falls under (1) [e], and is liable to duty under (1) or (2) in the charge The equitable mortgage duty is a relief from the higher duty of two shillings and sixpence per £100, and the instruments to which it is intended to apply are the simplest forms of equitable mortgage, containing little, if anything, more than a memorandum of the deposit of the title deeds, an undertaking to pay principal and interest, and an undertaking to execute a legal mortgage if called upon An equitable mortgage, though under hand, framed with the object of placing the equitable mortgagee in as good or nearly as good a position as if he had taken a legal mortgage—*e g*, by giving him a power of sale, power to enter into receipt of rents and profits, or declaring that he is to have the powers conferred upon mortgagees by Sections 19 to 24 and Section 67 of the Conveyancing Act, 1881, or otherwise going beyond the character of the instrument defined as an equitable mortgage by Section 86 (2)—is chargeable with the duty of two shillings and sixpence per £100, as falling under Section 86 [1] (e)

In administration "property" is not considered to include goods, and a memorandum of the deposit of bills of lading or dock warrants is not within the charge Such instruments were not chargeable under Section 15 of the Act 51 & 52 Vict., Ch 8, from which (2) is taken See Harris v Birch (9 M & W 59, 11 L J, Ex 219)

MORTGAGE.

Direction as to duty in certain cases.

87. (1) A security for the transfer or re-transfer of any stock is to be charged with the same duty as a similar security for a sum of money equal in amount to the value of the stock; and a transfer, assignment, disposition, or assignation of any such security, and a reconveyance, release, discharge, surrender, re-surrender, warrant to vacate, or renunciation of any such security, is to be charged with the same duty as an instrument of the same description relating to a sum of money equal in amount to the value of the stock

(2) A security for the payment of any rent charge annuity, or periodical payments by way of repayment, or in satisfaction or discharge of any loan, advance, or payment intended to be so repaid, satisfied, or discharged, is to be charged with the same duty as a similar security for the payment of the sum of money so lent, advanced, or paid

(3) A transfer of a duly stamped security, and a security by way of further charge for money or stock, added to money or stock previously secured by a duly stamped instrument, is not to be charged with any duty by reason of its containing any further or additional security for the money or stock transferred or previously secured, or the interest or dividends thereof, or any new covenant, proviso, power, stipulation, or agreement in relation thereto, or any further assurance of the property comprised in the transferred or previous security.

The substance of the transaction is to be looked to Thus in Wale v. Commissioners (4 Ex D 270) an instrument which was in form a new mortgage—the transaction being, in fact, the transfer of an old debt, and a further advance—was held to fall under the corresponding Section (109) in The Stamp Act, 1870

(4) Where any copyhold or customary lands or hereditaments are mortgaged alone by means of a conditional surrender or grant, the ad valorem duty is to be charged on the surrender or grant, if made

out of court, or the memorandum thereof, and on the copy of court roll of the surrender or grant, if made in court

If the covenant to surrender, containing the covenant to pay principal and interest and the usual mortgage clauses, is not immediately followed by a surrender upon which ad valorem duty is paid, the ad valorem duty should be impressed upon the covenant to surrender, and the surrender when taken may be stamped with a maximum duty of ten shillings, or sixpence per £100, as an instrument of further assurance, if the duty at that rate is less than ten shillings.

(5) Where any copyhold or customary lands or hereditaments are mortgaged, together with other property, for securing the same money or the same stock, the ad valorem duty is to be charged on the instrument relating to the other property, and the surrender or grant, or the memorandum thereof, or the copy of court roll of the surrender or grant, as the case may be, is not to be charged with any higher duty than ten shillings

The duty on the surrender or grant, &c., is at the rate of 6d per £100 under Sub-section 2 in the charge, with a maximum of 10s

(6) An instrument chargeable with ad valorem duty as a mortgage is not to be charged with any further duty by reason of the equity of redemption in the mortgaged property being thereby conveyed or limited in any other manner than to a purchaser, or in trust for, or according to the direction of, a purchaser

(33 & 34 Vict, Ch. 97, Secs 106, 108, 109, 110, and 111)

If the instrument operates to vest the equity of redemption in a purchaser it is liable to conveyance duty as well as mortgage duty (Dart, V & P., 6th ed 795)

88. (1) A security for the payment or repayment of money to be lent, advanced, or paid, or which may become due upon an account current, either with or without money previously due, is to be charged, where the total amount secured or to be

Security for future advances, how to be charged.

ultimately recoverable is in any way limited, with the same duty as a security for the amount so limited

(2) Where such total amount is unlimited, the security is to be available for such an amount only as the ad valorem duty impressed thereon extends to cover, but where any advance or loan is made in excess of the amount covered by that duty the security shall for the purpose of stamp duty be deemed to be a new and separate instrument, bearing date on the day on which the advance or loan is made.

Sub section 2 applies to instruments dated before as well as after the Act

(3) Provided that no money to be advanced for the insurance of any property comprised in the security against damage by fire, or for keeping up any policy of life insurance comprised in the security, or for effecting in lieu thereof any new policy, or for the renewal of any grant or lease of any property comprised in the security upon the dropping of any life whereon the property is held, shall be reckoned as forming part of the amount in respect whereof the security is chargeable with ad valorem duty

(33 & 34 Vict, Ch 97, Sec 107, 51 & 52 Vict, Ch. 8, Sec 15.)

As to accounts current, the sufficiency of the stamp is to be judged by the amount owing for principal and interest at the time the balance is struck between the parties, without regard to figures that might be arrived at if dated balances were taken For instance, a security limited to £5,000 is sufficiently stamped if at the time the mortgagee determines to enforce his security only £5,000 is owing, although if an account had been struck at a previous time the debt would have amounted to £8,000

In Morgan v. Pike (14 C B 473) a security without limit, stamped with the adjudication stamp, was put in evidence, and the Court, treating the adjudication stamp as a nullity, held the security good for the amount it was stamped to cover

The provision for increasing the amount of duty upon a security without limit when the amount of advance, which the security has been stamped to cover, has been reached, is new in this Act A similar facility was provided for equitable mortgages by 51 & 52 Vict., Ch 8, Sec 15

89. The exemption from stamp duty conferred by the Act of the Session held in the sixth and seventh years of King William the Fourth, chapter thirty-two, for the regulation of benefit building societies, shall not extend to any mortgage made after the thirty-first day of July one thousand eight hundred and sixty-eight, except a mortgage by a member of a benefit building society for securing the repayment to the society of money not exceeding five hundred pounds

Exemption from stamp duty in favour of benefit building societies restricted.

(33 & 34 Vict, Ch 97, Sec 112, 31 & 32 Vict., Ch 24, Sec 11)

By The Building Societies Act, 1874 (37 & 38 Vict., Ch 42, Sec 7), the Act 6 & 7 Will IV, Ch 32, was repealed "except as to any subsisting society certified under that Act, until such society shall have obtained a certificate of incorporation under this Act." By Section 41 of The Building Societies Act, 1874, the exemption from stamp duty was re-enacted, with a proviso that such exemption should not extend to any mortgage The effect of this legislation is that unincorporated societies still enjoy the benefit of the exemption from stamp duty on mortgages not exceeding £500, and further charges where the amount of the further charge does not exceed £500, and that incorporated building societies are not entitled to any exemption from mortgage duty

MORTGAGE OF STOCK or Marketable
Security — Under hand only *See* **Agreement,** and Section 23

By deed *See* **Mortgage,** and Section 86

MUTUAL DISPOSITION or Conveyance in Scotland *See* **Exchange or Excambion.**

NOTARIAL ACT of any kind whatsoever (*except a protest of a bill of exchange or promissory note, or any notarial instrument to be expeded and recorded in any register of sasines*)

£	s.	d.
0	1	0

And *see* **Protest, Seisin,** and Section 90.

Notarial Acts

Duty may be denoted by adhesive stamp

90. The duty upon a notarial act, and upon the protest by a notary public of a bill of exchange or promissory note, may be denoted by an adhesive stamp, which is to be cancelled by the notary

(33 & 34 Vict, Ch. 97, Sec 118.)

The attestation by a formal notarial act of the execution of an instrument abroad must be stamped under Section 15 (3) if the instrument is to be used in the United Kingdom The most common example is the attestation by a formal notarial act of the execution of a power of attorney Only formal notarial attestations are regarded as being liable to duty as notarial acts.

ORDER for the payment of money.
See **Bill of Exchange.**

PARTITION or DIVISION—Instruments effecting

	£	s	d.
In the case specified in Section 73, see that Section			
In any other case	0	10	0

PASSPORT

0 0 6

POLICY OF SEA INSURANCE—

(1) Where the premium or consideration does not exceed the rate of 2s 6d per centum of the sum insured ... 0 0 1

(2) In any other case—

(a) For or upon any voyage—
In respect of every full sum of £100, and also any fractional part of £100 thereby insured 0 0 3

(b) For time—
In respect of every full sum of £100, and also any fractional part of £100 thereby insured—
Where the insurance shall be made for any time not exceeding six months .. 0 0 3

	£	s	d.
Where the insurance shall be made for any time exceeding six months and not exceeding twelve months	0	0	6

And see Sections 91, 92, 93, 94, 95, 96, and 97.

(30 Vict., Ch. 23 ; 50 & 51 Vict., Ch. 15, Sec. 5.)

Policies of Insurance.

91. For the purposes of this Act the expression "policy of insurance" includes every writing whereby any contract of insurance is made or agreed to be made, or is evidenced; and the expression "insurance" includes assurance.

Meaning of "policy of insurance."

(28 & 29 Vict., Ch. 30, Sec. 117 ; 30 & 31 Vict., Ch. 23, Sec. 4.)

Policies of Sea Insurance.

92. (1) For the purposes of this Act the expression "policy of sea insurance" means any insurance (including re-insurance) made upon any ship or vessel, or upon the machinery, tackle, or furniture of any ship or vessel, or upon any goods, merchandise, or property of any description whatever on board of any ship or vessel, or upon the freight of, or any other interest which may be lawfully insured in or relating to, any ship or vessel, and includes any insurance of goods, merchandise, or property for any transit which includes not only a sea risk, but also any other risk incidental to the transit insured from the commencement of the transit to the ultimate destination covered by the insurance.

Meaning of "policy of sea insurance."

(2) Where any person, in consideration of any sum of money paid or to be paid for additional freight or otherwise, agrees to take upon himself any risk attending goods, merchandise, or property of any description whatever while on board of any ship or vessel, or engages to indemnify the owner of any such goods, merchandise, or property from

any risk, loss, or damage, such agreement or engagement shall be deemed to be a contract for sea insurance

(30 & 31 Vict., Ch. 23, Secs 4 and 12, 47 & 48 Vict., Ch 62, Sec. 8)

<small>Contract to be in writing 25 & 28 Vic. c. 63.</small>

93. (1) A contract for sea insurance (other than such insurance as is referred to in the fifty-fifth section of The Merchant Shipping Act Amendment Act, 1862) shall not be valid unless the same is expressed in a policy of sea insurance

(2) No policy of sea insurance made for time shall be made for any time exceeding twelve months.

(3) A policy of sea insurance shall not be valid unless it specifies the particular risk or adventure, the names of the subscribers or underwriters, and the sum or sums insured, and is made for a period not exceeding twelve months

(30 & 31 Vict, Ch 23, Secs 7 and 8)

Where a number of vessels were insured under a time policy, a specific sum being appropriated to each vessel, it was held that the stamp duty exigible under 30 Vict, Ch. 23 (repealed and replaced by this Act), must be calculated upon the aggregate amount of the insurance, and not upon the separate sums insured in respect of each vessel (Great Britain Steamship Premium Association and Others v. White, 29 Sco L R 104)

The Merchant Shipping Amendment Act, 1862, referred to in this section, was repealed by The Merchant Shipping Act, 1894 (57 & 58 Vict, Ch 60), Sections 502, 503, and 506 of which take the place of Sections 54 and 55 of the repealed Act The new sections are as follows —

502. The owner of a British sea-going ship, or any share therein, shall not be liable to make good to any extent whatever any loss or damage happening without his actual fault or privity in the following cases, namely,—

(i) Where any goods, merchandise, or other things whatsoever taken in or put on board his ship are lost or damaged by reason of fire on board the ship ; or

(ii.) Where any gold, silver, diamonds, watches, jewels, or precious stones taken in or put on board his ship, the true nature and value of which have not at the time of shipment been declared by the owner or shipper thereof to the owner or master of the ship in the bills of lading or otherwise in writing, are lost or damaged by reason of any robbery, embezzlement, making away with, or secreting thereof

503. (1) The owners of a ship, British or foreign, shall not where all or any of the following occurrences take place without their actual fault or privity; (that is to say,)

(a) Where any loss of life or personal injury is caused to any person being carried in the ship,

(b) Where any damage or loss is caused to any goods, merchandise, or other things whatsoever on board the ship;

(c) Where any loss of life or personal injury is caused to any person carried in any other vessel by reason of the improper navigation of the ship;

(d) Where any loss or damage is caused to any other vessel, or to any goods, merchandise, or other things whatsoever on board any other vessel, by reason of the improper navigation of the ship,

be liable to damages beyond the following amounts, &c

506. An insurance effected against the happening, without the owner's actual fault or privity, of any or all of the events in respect of which the liability of owners is limited under this part of this Act shall not be invalid by reason of the nature of the risk.

94. Where any sea insurance is made for a voyage and also for time, or to extend to or cover any time beyond thirty days after the ship shall have arrived at her destination and been there moored at anchor, the policy is to be charged with duty as a policy for a voyage, and also with duty as a policy for time. *(Policy for voyage and time chargeable with two duties)*

(30 & 31 Vict, Ch 23, Sec. 11, 47 & 48 Vict., Ch. 62, Sec 8)

95. (1) A policy of sea insurance may not be stamped at any time after it is signed or underwritten by any person, except in the two cases following; that is to say, *(No policy valid unless duly stamped)*

(a) Any policy of mutual insurance having a stamp impressed thereon may, if required, be stamped with an additional stamp, provided that at the time when the additional stamp is required the policy has not been signed or underwritten to an amount exceeding the sum or sums which the duty impressed thereon extends to cover.

(b) Any policy made or executed out of, but being in any manner enforceable within, the United Kingdom, may be stamped at any time within ten days after it has been first received in the United Kingdom on payment of the duty only.

(2) Provided that a policy of sea insurance shall for the purpose of production in evidence be an instrument which may legally be stamped after the execution thereof, and the penalty payable by law on stamping the same shall be the sum of one hundred pounds

(33 & 34 Vict., Ch 97, Sec 17, 30 & 31 Vict., Ch 23, Sec 9, 39 & 40 Vict Ch 6, Sec 2, 50 & 51 Vict., Ch. 15, Sec 6.)

Legal alterations in policies may be made under certain restrictions.

96. Nothing in this Act shall prohibit the making of any alteration which may lawfully be made in the terms and conditions of any policy of sea insurance after the policy has been underwritten, provided that the alteration be made before notice of the determination of the risk originally insured, and that it do not prolong the time covered by the insurance thereby made beyond the period of six months in the case of a policy made for a less period than six months, or beyond the period of twelve months in the case of a policy made for a greater period than six months, and that the articles insured remain the property of the same person or persons, and that no additional or further sum be insured by reason or means of the alteration

(30 & 31 Vict., Ch 23, Sec 10)

Penalty on assuring unless policy duly stamped

97. (1) If any person—

(a) Becomes an assurer upon any sea insurance, or enters into any contract for sea insurance, or directly or indirectly receives or contracts, or takes credit in account for any premium or consideration for any sea insurance, or knowingly takes upon himself any risk, or renders himself liable to pay, or pays, any sum of money upon any loss, peril, or contingency relative to any sea insurance, unless the insurance is expressed in a policy of sea insurance duly stamped, or

(b) Makes or effects, or knowingly procures to be made or effected, any sea insurance, or directly or indirectly gives or pays, or renders himself liable to pay, any premium or consideration for any sea insurance, or enters into any contract for sea insurance, unless the insurance is expressed in a policy of sea insurance duly stamped, or

(c) Is concerned in any fraudulent contrivance or device, or is guilty of any wilful act, neglect, or omission, with intent to evade the duties payable on policies of sea insurance, or whereby the duties may be evaded,

he shall for every such offence incur a fine of one hundred pounds

(2) Every broker, agent, or other person negotiating or transacting any sea insurance contrary to the true intent and meaning of this Act, or writing any policy of sea insurance upon material not duly stamped, shall for every such offence incur a fine of one hundred pounds, and shall not have any legal claim to any charge for brokerage, commission, or agency, or for any money expended or paid by him with reference to the insurance, and any money paid to him in respect of any such charge shall be deemed to be paid without consideration, and shall remain the property of his employer

(3) If any person makes or issues, or causes to be made or issued, any document purporting to be a copy of a policy of sea insurance, and there is not

at the time of the making or issue in existence a policy duly stamped whereof the said document is a copy, he shall for such offence, in addition to any other fine or penalty to which he may be liable, incur a fine of one hundred pounds

(30 & 31 *Vict*, *Ch* 23, *Secs* 13, 14, 15, *and* 16.)

POLICY OF LIFE INSURANCE—

	£	s	d.
Where the sum insured does not exceed £10	0	0	1
Exceeds £10 but does not exceed £25	0	0	3
Exceeds £25 but does not exceed £500· For every full sum of £50, and also for any fractional part of £50, of the amount insured	0	0	6
Exceeds £500 but does not exceed £1,000 For every full sum of £100, and also for any fractional part of £100, of the amount insured	0	1	0
Exceeds £1,000 For every full sum of £1,000, and also for any fractional part of £1,000, of the amount insured	0	10	0

And *see* Sections 91, 98, and 100

The re insurance between insurance companies of a risk upon a duly stamped policy of life insurance is liable to the duty of sixpence as an agreement if under hand, ten shillings if under seal It is usual to endorse on the re-insurance a statement that the original policy is duly stamped

The sum insured upon which ad valorem duty is chargeable is the greatest amount payable according to the terms of the policy in any event, not including, of course, bonuses

POLICY of INSURANCE against
accident and policy of insurance for any payment agreed to be made during the sickness of any person, or his

	£	s.	d
incapacity from personal injury, or by way of indemnity against loss or damage of or to any property .	0	0	1

And *see* Sections 91, 98, 99, and 100.

A policy of re-insurance or guarantee between insurance companies of a risk upon a policy duly stamped under this charge is chargeable with the same duty as the original policy. *i.e* one penny.

In Mortgage Insurance Corporation, Limited, *v* Commissioners (57 L. J , Q B 179), a guarantee under hand for payment of a mortgage debt in default of payment by the mortgagor was held to be liable to the duty of sixpence as an agreement, and not to the duty of one penny as an indemnity against loss or damage of or to any property.

Policies of Insurance except Policies of Sea Insurance.

98. (1) For the purposes of this Act the expression "policy of life insurance" means a policy of insurance upon any life or lives or upon any event or contingency relating to or depending upon any life or lives except a policy of insurance against accident; and the expression "policy of insurance against accident" means a policy of insurance for any payment agreed to be made upon the death of any person only from accident or violence, or otherwise than from a natural cause, or as compensation for personal injury, and includes any notice or advertisement in a newspaper or other publication which purports to insure the payment of money upon the death of or injury to the holder or bearer of the newspaper or publication containing the notice only from accident or violence, or otherwise than from a natural cause

(2) A policy of insurance against accident is not to be charged with any further duty than one penny by reason of the same extending to any payment to be made during sickness or incapacity from personal injury

(52 & 53 *Vict*, *Ch* 42, Sec 20, 53 & 54 *Vict*, *Ch* 8, Sec 20.)

Marginal note: Meaning of policy of life insurance, and policy of insurance against accident.

POLICY OF INSURANCE

Duty on certain policies may be denoted by adhesive stamp

99. The duty of one penny upon a policy of insurance, other than a policy of sea insurance or life insurance, may be denoted by an adhesive stamp, which is to be cancelled by the person by whom the policy is first executed

(33 & 34 Vict, Ch 97, Sec 119, 44 & 45 Vict, Ch 12, Sec 44)

Penalty for not making out policy, or making, &c, any policy not duly stamped

100. Every person who—

(1) Receives, or takes credit for, any premium or consideration for any insurance other than a sea insurance, and does not within one month after receiving, or taking credit for, the premium or consideration, make out and execute a duly stamped policy of insurance, or

(2) Makes, executes, or delivers out, or pays or allows in account, or agrees to pay or allow in account, any money upon or in respect of any policy other than a policy of sea insurance which is not duly stamped,

shall incur a fine of twenty pounds

(33 & 34 Vict., Ch 97, Sec 118)

POWER OF ATTORNEY. *See* **Letter of Attorney.**

	£	s	d
PRECEPT OF CLARE CONSTAT to give seisin of lands or other heritable subjects in Scotland	0	5	0
PROCURATION, deed, or other instrument of	0	10	0

PROMISSORY NOTE. *See* **Bank Note, Bill of Exchange.**

PROTEST of any bill of exchange or promissory note   £ s. d

    Where the duty on the bill or note does not exceed 1s.   { The same duty as the bill or note.

    In any other case   0 1 0

And *see* Section 90.

PROXY. *See* **Letter or Power of Attorney.**

RECEIPT given for, or upon the payment of, money amounting to £2 or upwards   0 0 1

Exemptions.

(1) Receipt given for money deposited in any bank, or with any banker, to be accounted for and expressed to be received of the person to whom the same is to be accounted for.

(2) Acknowledgment by any banker of the receipt of any bill of exchange or promissory note for the purpose of being presented for acceptance or payment.

(3) Receipt given for or upon the payment of any Parliamentary taxes or duties, or of money to or for the use of Her Majesty.

(4) Receipt given by an officer of a public department of the State for money paid by way of imprest or advance, or in adjustment of an account, where he derives no personal benefit therefrom.

(5) Receipt given by any agent for money imprested to him on account of the pay of the army

(6) Receipt given by any officer, seaman, marine or soldier, or his representatives, for or on account of any wages, pay or pension, due from the Admiralty or Army Pay Office

(7) Receipt given for any principal money or interest due on an exchequer bill.

(8) Receipt written upon a bill of exchange or promissory note duly stamped, or upon a bill drawn by any person under the authority of the Admiralty, upon and payable by the Accountant-General of the Navy

(9) Receipt given upon any bill or note of the Bank of England or the Bank of Ireland

(10) Receipt given for the consideration money for the purchase of any share in any of the Government or Parliamentary stocks or funds, or in the stocks and funds of the Secretary of State in Council of India, or of the Bank of England, or of the Bank of Ireland, or for any dividend paid on any share of the said stocks or funds respectively

(11) Receipt indorsed or otherwise written upon or contained in any instrument liable to stamp duty, and duly stamped, acknowledging the receipt of the consideration money therein expressed, or the receipt of any principal money, interest, or annuity thereby secured or therein mentioned

This exemption includes receipts, endorsed, for the payment of instalments (Orme *v* Young, 4 Camp 386) The instrument on which the receipt is written or endorsed must be one that is liable to stamp duty see Skrine v. Elmore (2 Camp. 457), where a warranty of a horse, containing a receipt, exempt from agreement duty as an agreement relating to the sale of goods, was regarded as being liable to duty as a receipt The exemption does not extend to a receipt endorsed upon a policy of insurance for moneys payable thereunder

(12) Receipt given for any allowance by way of drawback or otherwise upon the exportation of any goods or merchandise from the United Kingdom.

(13) Receipt given for the return of any duty of customs upon a certificate of over entry

And see Sections 101, 102, and 103

Receipts.

101. (1) For the purposes of this Act the expression "receipt" includes any note, memorandum, or writing whereby any money amounting to two pounds or upwards, or any bill of exchange or promissory note for money amounting to two pounds or upwards, is acknowledged or expressed to have been received or deposited or paid, or whereby any debt or demand, or any part of a debt or demand, of the amount of two pounds or upwards, is acknowledged to have been settled, satisfied, or discharged, or which signifies or imports any such acknowledgment, and whether the same is or is not signed with the name of any person.

Provisions as to duty upon receipts

(2) The duty upon a receipt may be denoted by an adhesive stamp, which is to be cancelled by the person by whom the receipt is given before he delivers it out of his hands

(33 & 34 Vict, Ch. 97, Secs 120 and 121)

The definition in the old law (16 and 17 Vict, Ch 59) was "any note, memorandum, or writing whatsoever given to any person for or upon the payment of money whereby any sum of money debt or demand, or any part of any debt or demand *therein specified* shall be expressed or acknowledged to have been *paid, settled, balanced, or otherwise discharged or satisfied*, or which shall import or signify such acknowledgment, and whether the same shall or shall not be signed with the name of any person." Many of the old cases in which instruments in the form of receipts were held not to be chargeable were decided upon the ground that the instrument was not given upon the payment of any "debt or demand." A comparison of the definition shows that this is no longer material. An acknowledgment that money has been received or merely deposited, unless as to a deposit it falls within the bankers' exemptions (1) and (2), is chargeable with duty. (*See* Welsh's Trustees *v* Forbes, 12 Rettie, 4th Series, 851.)

A cheque is a bill of exchange for the purposes of the Stamp Act (Section 32), and a receipt for a cheque for £2 or upwards is liable to duty.

' For or upon the payment of money" does not mean contemporaneous payment only. A receipt given subsequently is liable, and if no receipt be given at the time a subsequent statement of account in which credit is expressed for a payment, as "By Cash £5," is chargeable. A receipt may be liable to duty though no cash or bill passes, as in Lucas *v* Jones (13 L J, Q B 208, 5 A & E, N S 949), where a discharge from rent due in consideration of an equal amount being written off a mortgage debt owing from the lessor to the lessee was held to be chargeable. If there are cross accounts between parties a stamped receipt must be given upon the document upon which the payment of a balance amounting to £2 is acknowledged (Brooks *v* Davis, 3 C & P 186.)

Any form of words will constitute a receipt. "Settled," with or without initials, at the foot of an account is a receipt (Spawforth *v* Alexander, 2 Esp 621.) In Reg *v* Overton (18 Jur 134, 1 C. C R 308, 23 L J., Mag 29) the judges held a signature in a book of account signifying the payment of money, though not accompanied by any written words importing payment, to be a valid receipt. A letter acknowledging the receipt of money, &c, is as much a receipt as a more formal document. In Rex *v* Boardman (2 Moo. & R 147) a mere signature without any words "settled" or "paid" was held a receipt.

A receipt for £70 "in settlement of all claims" was held by Huddleston, B, in White *v* South London Tramways Company (*Times* 13th December, 1889), to be liable to duty as an agreement. It was stamped as a receipt, and was, it is submitted, liable to both duties. See also Weish's Trustees *v* Forbes (12 Rettie, 4th Series, 851) on page 56, and Skrine *v.* Elmore (2 Camp. 457) on page 187

Receipts liable to duty, respecting which many mistakes are made, are—

Entries in the books of tradesmen, lodging-house keepers, &c., for payments on current accounts, &c., amounting to £2

Receipts given by employers to servants who collect or receive moneys for moneys so collected and paid over

Receipts for sums amounting to £2 paid on account

Receipts for club subscriptions amounting to £2

A receipt for a donation or subscription to an institution totally devoted to charitable purposes enjoys a practical exemption from duty, as the Commissioners do not enforce a penalty if it is given unstamped

A receipt for a fee marked on a barrister's brief has been passed on taxation unstamped. (*Re* Beaven, 23 L J, Ch 536.)

A receipt for money paid to an officer of the county court, *e.g.* a bailiff, is not chargeable with duty, the stamped receipt being given by the suitor in the county court books upon taking the money out of court. (Treasury Instructions.)

A receipt is not required to be given in a ready money transaction (Bussey *v.* Barrett, 9 M. & W. 312), or upon the order to "deliver" given by an auctioneer to a purchaser at an auction where no credit is given, but if a written receipt is given it must be stamped

102. A receipt given without being stamped may be stamped with an impressed stamp upon the terms following; that is to say,

Terms upon which receipts may be stamped after execution

(1) Within fourteen days after it has been given, on payment of the duty and a penalty of five pounds;

(2) After fourteen days, but within one month, after it has been given, on payment of the duty and a penalty of ten pounds;

and shall not in any other case be stamped with an impressed stamp

A receipt executed out of the United Kingdom may be executed upon an adhesive stamp, or, if executed unstamped, it falls under the provisions of Section 15.

Penalty for offences in reference to receipts.

103. If any person—

(1) Gives a receipt liable to duty and not duly stamped; or

(2) In any case where a receipt would be liable to duty refuses to give a receipt duly stamped; or

(3) Upon a payment to the amount of two pounds or upwards gives a receipt for a sum not amounting to two pounds, or separates or divides the amount paid with intent to evade the duty;

he shall incur a fine of ten pounds

(33 & 34 Vict., Ch. 97, Secs. 122 and 123.)

The only means known to the law of compelling a person to give a receipt is provided by this section, which applies to receipts liable to duty only. Information must be given to the Commissioners, who usually insist upon the giving of a stamped receipt as a condition of compromise of proceedings.

The obligation to provide the receipt stamp is virtually thrown upon the person to whom the payment is made. The provisions of Section 5 of 43 Geo. III., Ch. 126, whereby the debtor was required to present a stamped receipt to the payee before the offence of refusing to give a stamped receipt was complete, were repealed by 33 & 34 Vict., Ch. 99, and not re-enacted, and the law on the subject is now contained in Section 103 (2). The refusal must be a refusal to give a stamped receipt to the person entitled to take it, and a mere neglect or omission to comply with a request to send a stamped receipt by post is not considered a refusal for the purposes of the section.

An account of money expended in the purchase of provisions, &c., by a lodging-house keeper for his lodgers, for which he is to be repaid, may be separated from the amount payable for rent and extras without incurring the penalty imposed by Section 103 (3). If money amounting in the whole to £2 is paid upon separate accounts, or for weekly subscriptions or rents, separate receipts may be given.

RECONVEYANCE, RELEASE, or RENUNCIATION of any Security. *See* Mortgage, &c.

RELEASE or RENUNCIATION of any property, or of any right or interest in any property—
   Upon a sale. *See* **Conveyance on Sale.**
   By way of security *See* **Mortgage, &c.**   £ s. d.
   In any other case 0 10 0

  A renunciation of probate is not chargeable under this head, not being a release or renunciation of any property, &c

RENUNCIATION. *See* **Reconveyance and Release.**

RENUNCIATION, LETTER OF. *See* **Letter of Allotment.**

RESIGNATION. Principal or original instrument of resignation, or service of cognition of heirs, or charter or seisin of any houses, lands, or other heritable subjects in Scotland holding burgage, or of burgage tenure 0 5 0
And instrument of resignation of any lands or other heritable subjects in Scotland not of burgage tenure .. 0 5 0

REVOCATION of any use or trust of any property by any writing, not being a will 0 10 0

SCRIP CERTIFICATE or SCRIP. *See* **Letter of Allotment.**

SEISIN. Instrument of seisin given upon any charter, precept of clare constat, or precept from chancery, or upon any wadset, heritable bond, disposition, apprising, adjudication, or otherwise of any lands or heritable subjects in Scotland .. 0 5 0

And any **NOTARIAL INSTRUMENT** to be expeded and recorded in any register of sasines £ s. d.
0 5 0

SETTLEMENT. Any instrument, whether voluntary or upon any good or valuable consideration, other than a *bonâ fide* pecuniary consideration, whereby any definite and certain principal sum of money (whether charged or chargeable on lands or other hereditaments or heritable subjects, or not, or to be laid out in the purchase of lands or other hereditaments or heritable subjects or not), or any definite and certain amount of stock, or any security, is settled or agreed to be settled in any manner whatsoever.

For every £100, and also for any fractional part of £100, of the amount or value of the property settled or agreed to be settled
0 5 0

Exemption

Instrument of appointment relating to any property in favour of persons specially named or described as the objects of a power of appointment, where duty has been duly paid in respect of the same property upon the settlement creating the power or the grant of representation of any will or testamentary instrument creating the power

And *see* Sections 104, 105, and 106.

For an example of an Assessment of Settlement Duty see pp 270 to 272.

A settlement made for a *bonâ fide* pecuniary consideration is chargeable with ad valorem duty under the head "Conveyance on Sale"

SETTLEMENT.

The Act contains no definition of "Settlement" An assignment to trustees to hold to separate use is not considered to be a settlement unless it contains a restraint against anticipation, and an assignment of a fund upon trust to pay an annuity out of the income, and subject thereto in trust for the assignor, is not liable to settlement duty

"The words 'definite and certain' apply, not to the interest of the settlor or the nature of the interest, but to the amount of the stock". *per* Bowen, L J, in Onslow *v.* Commissioners ([1891] 1 Q B., C A 239) "The charge applies to every interest, whether vested, whether liable to be divested, whether contingent or not, in any sum of which it may be said that it is a definite and certain amount of stock" *per* Fry, L J, in the same case

Ad valorem duty is assessed in respect of amounts agreed to be paid or bequeathed to trustees to be held upon the trusts of the settlement, also upon a settlement of a vested reversion or any interest therein, whether absolute or defeasible. In Stucley *v* Commissioners (5 Ex. 85) the Court upheld the assessment of ad valorem duty upon the settlement of an absolute reversionary interest in stock and securities vested in the trustees of an earlier settlement, and the same was held in Onslow *v* Commissioners (*ubi supra*), though the trustees of the earlier settlement had power to vary the investments In Onslow's case ad valorem duty upon the settlement of money defeasible upon the birth of a brother or sister of the settlor was assessed by the Commissioners and allowed by the Court

The duty is calculated, under Section 6 (*ante*, p 21), upon the value of the trust funds, the subject of the reversionary interest, as if in possession.

The settlement of a vested reversion liable to be divested by the adverse exercise of a power of appointment limited to a class, of whom the reversioner is one, is chargeable with ad valorem duty, but where the power of appointment is general the ad valorem duty is not charged

Ad valorem duty was not formerly assessed in respect of contingent interests in reversion as opposed to vested interests, or vested interests liable to be divested, except in the case where the contingency which would defeat the settlor's interest was the birth of issue to a lady past the age of child-bearing Since the decision in Onslow *v* Commissioners, however, ad valorem duty is assessed in all cases where the interest settled is the best existing or visible interest, contingencies by which it may be defeated notwithstanding See Example of Assessment of Settlement Duty, *post*, pp 270 to 272

The ordinary covenant to settle any other property than that specifically described in the settlement, to which the covenantor is entitled at the date of the settlement, binds all such other property of the covenantor, and if any of this is money, stock, or securities for money in possession, or a vested interest in any trust fund, the settlement is charged with ad valorem duty on the amount ascertainable. When after-acquired property subsequently comes into the trust fund by force of such a covenant, no further duty is then payable. The covenant to settle after-acquired property renders the settlement liable to the further duty of ten shillings under Section 4 (1) as a deed.

A covenant to make up funds settled, or that may come into settlement, to a definite and certain sum—say £20,000—renders the settlement liable to ad valorem settlement duty on £20,000.

Settlements of the proceeds of sale of real estate and leaseholds unsold, or furniture, and settlements containing covenants to expend definite sums in the purchase of house or furniture, are not chargeable with ad valorem duty therefor.

A settlement of one half of the property of which the settlor shall die possessed, or a share in a business, or an interest in a law suit, or a debt owing from a bankrupt's estate, does not attract ad valorem duty, there being no "definite and certain" sum.

A settlement of land, which by conversion is money in equity, is not liable to ad valorem duty. (Stucley v Commissioners, *ubi supra*.)

An order of the Court effecting a settlement, in accordance with the terms of a will, of a fund bequeathed in trust for A. till his marriage, the fund to be then settled on his wife and children, was held to be chargeable with ad valorem duty in Gowan v Gowan (17 Ch D 778).

Settlements

As to settlement of policy or security

104. (1) Where any money which may become due or payable upon any policy of life insurance, or upon any security not being a marketable security, is settled or agreed to be settled, the instrument whereby the settlement is made or agreed to be made is to be charged with ad valorem duty in respect of that money.

(2) Provided as follows:

(a) Where, in the case of a policy, no provision is made for keeping up the policy, the ad valorem duty is to be charged only on the value of the policy at the date of the instrument.

(b) If in any such case the instrument contains a statement of the said value, and is stamped in accordance with the statement, it is, so far as regards the policy, to be deemed duly stamped, unless or until it is shown that the statement is untrue, and that the instrument is in fact insufficiently stamped

(33 & 34 Vict., Ch. 97, Sec 124.)

A settlement of a "single premium" policy is chargeable with duty upon the amount assured. A "single premium" policy is one on which all the premiums are paid up in one sum

A settlement of a policy containing the ordinary covenant for payment of premiums and keeping up the policy is not an instrument wherein "no provision is made for keeping up the policy," and ad valorem duty is chargeable for the amount assured. In the old case, Sanville v. Commissioners (10 Ex R. 159, 23 L. J., Ex. 270), such a covenant was held not to attract ad valorem duty, because (per Pollock, C B, re Alsager's Settlement, 10 L T R. 238) there was no special fund out of which the premiums on the policy were to be paid. The law was amended in 1864, by 27 Vict., Ch 18, Sec 12, which in effect made chargeable settlements containing any "covenant, contract, or provision for keeping up the policy or for payment of premiums," and upon that enactment the present law and practice are based

The provision for keeping up the policy need not necessarily be in the settlement. Duty is chargeable if such a provision binding on the settlor of the policy exists in any other instrument. If a reversionary interest in a fund of which a policy forms part is settled, the value of the policy for purposes of assessment must be computed in accordance with Section 104.

Duty is charged in respect of any bonus that may have been added to a policy falling under Section 104, up to the date of settlement, and the amount of the bonus should be stated when the settlement is brought for adjudication.

A covenant to effect a policy for a definite sum, either forthwith or within a stated period, or without any stipulation as to time, attracts ad valorem duty on such sum if the settlement contains also a provision for keeping up the policy See re Arthur's Estate (14 Ch D 603, 49 L. J, Ch 556) for the general principle

Moneys which may become payable under accident policies are not within the charge. They are covered by the deed stamp.

The statement of value referred to in Section 104 (2) (b) is not regarded as conclusive when a settlement is submitted for adjudication. A certificate of the surrender value from the insurance company is required.

Settlements, when not to be charged as securities. **105.** An instrument chargeable with ad valorem duty as a settlement in respect of any money, stock, or security is not to be charged with any further duty by reason of containing provision for the payment or transfer of the money, stock, or security, or by reason of containing, where the money, stock, or security is in reversion or is not paid or transferred upon the execution of the instrument, provision for the payment by the person entitled in possession to the interest or dividends of the money, stock, or security, during the continuance of such possession, of any annuity or yearly sum not exceeding interest at the rate of four pounds per centum per annum upon the amount or value of the money, stock, or security.

(53 & 54 Vict., Ch. 97, Sec. 125.)

The duty payable upon such a covenant would, but for this provision, be at the rate of two shillings and sixpence for every five pounds or fractional part of five pounds of the annuity or yearly sum under the head "Bond, Covenant, or Instrument of any kind whatsoever," in the Schedule, *ante*, p. 85.

Ad valorem settlement duty being chargeable in respect of a definite sum covenanted to be paid by a settlor after death, or at any future period, or upon any contingency, the principle of Section 105 was applied under The Stamp Act, 1870, to a covenant by such settlor for the payment, meanwhile, of an annuity not exceeding interest at the rate of four per cent. upon such definite sum; also to the similar covenant by a tenant for life of real estate or person in enjoyment of the income of any property charged with the payment of a portion, or other definite sum, upon the settlement of such portion or sum, whether the charge is created for the purposes of the settlement or is of prior date. This practice is now confirmed by Section 105.

Four per cent. is regarded in practice as an abatement of duty. If the amount of the annuity exceeds interest at the rate of four per cent. upon the definite sum, duty at the rate of two shillings and sixpence for every five pounds, or fractional part of five pounds, is charged in respect of such excess.

The abatement of duty is allowed, whether the covenant for payment of the annuity is contained in the settlement or a separate instrument.

A covenant in a settlement to make up the annual income of a settled fund, in respect of which ad valorem settlement duty has been paid, to a specified sum, is charged with ad valorem duty at the rate of two shillings and sixpence for every five pounds or fractional part of five pounds of the difference between the present income of the fund and the specified sum. The adjudication stamp should be obtained.

106. (1) Where several instruments are executed for effecting the settlement of the same property, and the ad valorem duty chargeable in respect of the settlement of the property exceeds ten shillings, one only of the instruments is to be charged with the ad valorem duty

Where several instruments, one only to be charged with ad valorem duty

(2) Where a settlement is made in pursuance of a previous agreement upon which ad valorem settlement duty exceeding ten shillings has been paid in respect of any property, the settlement is not to be charged with ad valorem duty in respect of the same property

The adjudication stamp should be obtained upon the settlement.

(3) In each of the aforesaid cases the instruments not chargeable with ad valorem duty are to be charged with the duty of ten shillings

Where an ad valorem duty of lower amount than ten shillings is applicable, the ten shilling stamp is not necessary (Lant v Peace, 3 Nev. & Per. 329.) Thus, the transfer of a mortgage for £1,200 to the trustee of a settlement in which such mortgage is included would be properly stamped with the duty of sixpence per one hundred pounds = six shillings

(33 & 34 Vict, Ch 97, Sec 105.)

SHARE WARRANT issued under the provisions of The Companies Act, 1867, and **Stock Certificate to Bearer.**
And *see* Sections 107, 108, and 109.

{ A duty of an amount equal to three times the amount of the *ad valorem* stamp duty which would be chargeable on a deed transferring the share or shares or stock specified in the warrant or certificate if the consideration for the transfer were the nominal value of such share or shares or stock.

(44 *Vict.*, Ch 12, Sec 46, 50 & 51 *Vict.*, Ch. 15, Sec 7.)
The charge of duty, "A duty of an amount equal," &c., is taken verbatim from Section 33 of The Companies Act, 1867 (30 & 31 Vict, Ch 131)

Share Warrants.

Penalty for issuing share warrant not duly stamped

107. If a share warrant is issued without being duly stamped, the company issuing the same, and also every person who, at the time when it is issued, is the managing director or secretary, or other principal officer of the company, shall incur a fine of fifty pounds

(33 & 34 *Vict* Ch 97, Sec. 127)

Stock Certificates to Bearer

Meaning of "stock certificate to bearer" 38 & 39 Vic c. 83

108. For the purposes of this Act the expression "stock certificate to bearer" includes every stock certificate to bearer issued after the third day of June, one thousand eight hundred and eighty-one, under the provisions of The Local Authorities Loans Act, 1875, or of any other Act authorising the creation of debenture stock, county stock, corporation stock, municipal stock, or funded debt, by whatever name known

(38 & 39 *Vict*., *Ch.* 83.)

109. (1) Where the holder of a stock certificate to bearer has been entered on the register of the local authority as the owner of the share of stock described in the certificate, the certificate shall be forthwith cancelled so as to be incapable of being re-issued to any person. [Penalty for issuing stock certificate unstamped.]

(2) Every person by whom a stock certificate to bearer is issued without being duly stamped shall incur a fine of fifty pounds.

(44 & 45 *Vict.*, *Ch.* 12, *Sec.* 46.)

SUPERANNUATION ANNUITY. *See* Bond, Covenant, &c.

SURRENDER—

Of Copyholds. *See* **Copyhold.**

	£	s	d
Of any other kind whatsoever not chargeable with duty as a conveyance on sale or a mortgage	0	10	0

TACK of Lands, &c., in Scotland. *See* Lease or Tack.

TACK in SECURITY. *See* Mortgage, &c.

TRANSFER. *See* Conveyance or Transfer.

TRANSFER.

	£	s	d
Any request or authority to the purser or other officer of any mining company, conducted on the cost book system, to enter or register any transfer of any share, or part of a share, in any mine, or any notice to such purser or officer of any such transfer	0	0	6

And *see* Section 110.

Transfer of Shares in Cost Book Mines

<small>Duty may be denoted by adhesive stamp</small>

110. (1) The duty upon a request or authority to the purser or other officer of a mining company conducted on the cost book system to enter or register the transfer of any share or part of a share of the mine, and the duty upon a notice to such purser or officer of any such transfer, may be denoted by an adhesive stamp, which is to be cancelled by the person by whom the request, authority, or notice is written or executed

(2) Every person who writes or executes any such request, authority, or notice, not being duly stamped, and every purser or other officer of any such company who in any manner obeys, complies with, or gives effect to any such request, authority, or notice, not being duly stamped, shall incur a fine of twenty pounds

(33 & 34 Vict., Ch 97, Sec 128)

VALUATION. *See* Appraisement.

VOTING PAPER. Any instrument for

	£	s	d
the purpose of voting by any person entitled to vote at any meeting of any body exercising a public trust, or of the shareholders, or members, or contributors to the funds of any company, society, or institution	0	0	1

And *see* Section 80

The charge in The Stamp Act, 1870, was taken from 27 & 28 Vict., Ch 18, Sec. 1, and Schedule C, which described "meeting," and charged duty upon voting papers to be used "at any such meeting." In Reg *v* Strachan (7 Q B 463), decided on that Act, the charge was held not to apply to voting papers used at a meeting of the town council of a municipal borough, convened under 7 Will IV and 1 Vict, Ch 78, Secs 13 & 14, for the election of aldermen, and *per* Quain, J, "the charge applies to meetings of charities, dock companies, and other companies at which voting by proxy is allowed" In the present Act, the charge has been framed so that it corresponds with the decision in Reg *v* Strachan

A voting paper to be within this charge must be one that can only be used for voting at a meeting. Voting papers which may be sent by letter where there is no meeting, such as those for the election of candidates to charitable institutions, are not liable to duty.

The exemption of Parliamentary voting papers for the elections at the Universities by 24 & 25 Vict., Ch 58, Sec 6, and other Acts, was quite unnecessary. Such voting papers are not chargeable

WADSET. *See* **Mortgage,** &c

WARRANT OF ATTORNEY to confess and enter up a judgment given as a security for the payment or repayment of money, or for the transfer or re-transfer of stock

See **Mortgage,** &c

	£ s. d.
WARRANT OF ATTORNEY of any other kind	0 10 0
WARRANT FOR GOODS	0 0 3

Exemptions.

(1) Any document or writing given by an inland carrier acknowledging the receipt of goods conveyed by such carrier.

(2) A weight note issued together with a duly stamped warrant, and relating solely to the same goods, wares, or merchandise

And *see* Section 111

Warrants for Goods.

111. (1) For the purposes of this Act the expression "warrant for goods" means any document or writing, being evidence of the title of any person therein named, or his assigns, or the holder

Provisions as to warrants for goods

thereof, to the property in any goods, wares, or merchandise lying in any warehouse or dock, or upon any wharf, and signed or certified by or on behalf of the person having the custody of the goods, wares, or merchandise

(2) The duty upon a warrant for goods may be denoted by an adhesive stamp, which is to be cancelled by the person by whom the instrument is made, executed, or issued

(3) Every person who makes, executes, or issues, or receives, or takes by way of security or indemnity, any warrant for goods not being duly stamped, shall incur a fine of twenty pounds

(33 & 34 *Vict.*, Ch 97, Secs 88, 89, & 92)

WARRANT under the sign manual of Her Majesty

£ s d
0 10 0

WRIT—

(1) Of **Acknowledgment** under The Registration of Leases (Scotland) Act, 1857 . ..
(2) Of **Acknowledgment** by any persons infeft in lands in Scotland in favour of the heir or disponee of a creditor fully vested in right of an heritable security constituted by infeftment . .
(3) Of **Resignation** and **Clare Constat**

0 5 0

GENERAL EXEMPTIONS FROM ALL STAMP DUTIES.

(1) Transfers of shares in the Government or Parliamentary stocks or funds

(2) Instruments for the sale, transfer, or other disposition, either absolutely or by way of mortgage, or otherwise, of any ship or vessel, or any part, interest, share, or property of or in any ship or vessel

This exemption includes bottomry bonds. Freight is considered a part of the ship inseparably appurtenant thereto (*per* Erle, C J., in Willis *v.* Palmer, 7 C B, N S. 358), and instruments for the sale, &c., thereof are exempt. The exemption does not extend to instruments relating to shares in a single ship company.

(3) Instruments of apprenticeship, bonds, contracts, and agreements entered into in the United Kingdom for or relating to the service in any of Her Majesty's colonies or possessions abroad of any person as an artificer, clerk, domestic servant, handicraftsman, mechanic, gardener, servant in husbandry, or labourer

(4) Testaments, testamentary instruments, and dispositions *mortis causâ* in Scotland.

(5) Bonds given to sheriffs or other persons in Ireland upon the replevy of any goods or chattels, and assignments of such bonds

(6) Instruments made by, to, or with the Commissioners of Works for any of the purposes of the Act 15 & 16 Vict, Ch 28

PART III.

SUPPLEMENTAL

Duty on Capital of Companies

Charge of duty on capital of limited liability companies

112. A statement of the amount which is to form the nominal share capital of any company to be registered with limited liability shall be delivered to the Registrar of Joint Stock Companies in England, Scotland, or Ireland, and a statement of the amount of any increase of registered capital of any company now registered or to be registered with limited liability shall be delivered to the said Registrar, and every such statement shall be charged with an ad valorem stamp duty of two shillings for every one hundred pounds and any fraction of one hundred pounds over any multiple of one hundred pounds of the amount of such capital or increase of capital as the case may be

(51 Vict, Ch 8, Sec 11, 52 Vict, Ch 7, Sec 16)

Charge of duty on capital of companies with limited liability otherwise than under the Companies Acts.

113. (1) Where by virtue of any letters patent granted by Her Majesty, or any Act, the liability of the holders of shares in the capital of any corporation or company is limited otherwise than by registration with limited liability under the law in that behalf, a statement of the amount of nominal share capital of the corporation or company shall be delivered by the corporation or company to the Commissioners within one month after the date of the letters patent or the passing of the Act, and in case of any increase of the amount of nominal share capital of any corporation or company, whether now existing or to be hereafter formed, being authorised by any letters patent or Act, a statement of the amount of such increase shall be delivered by the corporation or company to the Commissioners within the like period

(2) The statement shall be charged with an ad valorem stamp duty of two shillings for every one hundred pounds and any fraction of one hundred pounds over any multiple of one hundred pounds of the amount of such capital or increase of capital as the case may be, and shall be duly stamped accordingly when the same is delivered to the Commissioners

(3) In the case of neglect to deliver such a statement as is hereby required to be delivered, the corporation or company shall be liable to pay to Her Majesty a sum equal to ten pounds per centum upon the amount of duty payable, and a like penalty for every month after the first month during which the neglect shall continue

(52 Vict, Ch. 7, Sec 17)

Upon the conversion by an Act of Parliament of Debenture Stock of the Milford Docks Company into First Preference Debenture Stock, the Debenture Stock was cancelled, and an amount of First Preference Stock issued *Held* that the issue of this First Preference Stock was an increase of "nominal share capital" within the meaning of Section 17 of The Customs and Inland Revenue Act, 1889 (52 Vict, Ch 7), and consequently Sections 112 and 113 of The Stamp Act, 1891. *Per* Cave, J "'Amount of nominal share capital' means the amount of nominal capital belonging to the shareholders, outside of the capital which they have borrowed." (Attorney-General v. The Milford Docks Company, 69 L T R 453)

Composition for certain Stamp Duties

114. (1) By way of composition for stamp duty chargeable on transfers of any stock of the Government of Canada which may be inscribed in books kept in the United Kingdom, or of any Colonial stock to which The Colonial Stock Act, 1877, applies, the Government of Canada or other colony, as the case may be, shall pay to the Commissioners a sum as stamp duty calculated at the rate of one shilling and threepence for every ten pounds and any fraction of ten pounds of the nominal amount of

Composition for stamp duty on transfers of Canadian and colonial stock 40 & 41 Vic. c. 59.

such stock inscribed in the name of each and every stockholder at the date of the composition—

With the addition—

(a) When the period within which the stock is to be redeemed or paid off, or during which annual or other payments in respect of the redemption or payment off of the same are required to be made, exceeds sixty years, but does not exceed one hundred years from that date, of threepence for every such ten pounds or fraction of ten pounds; or

(b) When the said period exceeds one hundred years, or no period is fixed for such redemption or payment off, or no such annual or other payments are required to be made, of sixpence for every such ten pounds or fraction of ten pounds,

and in consideration of the payment transfers of the stock in respect of which the composition has been paid shall be exempt from stamp duty

(2) All sums certified by the Commissioners to have been received by way of composition for stamp duty on transfers of stock under this section shall be paid over to the National Debt Commissioners, and shall be applied by them towards the reduction of the National Debt in such manner as the Treasury from time to time direct

(37 & 38 Vict, Ch 26, Sec 4, 40 & 41 Vict, Ch. 59, Sec 3, 43 & 44 Vict, Ch. 20, Secs 53, 54, and 55)

The scope of this Section has been extended by Section 39 of The Finance Act, 1894 (57 & 58 Vict, Ch 30), which is as follows —

39. The provisions contained in Section 114 of The Stamp Act, 1891, in reference to the composition for stamp duty chargeable on transfers of certain stocks, shall extend to the stock of any foreign State or Government which is inscribed in the books of the Bank of England.

115. (1) Any county council or corporation or company may enter into an agreement with the Commissioners, if the Commissioners in their discretion think proper, for the delivery of an account showing the nominal amount of all the stock and funded debt of such county council, corporation, or company, or the amount thereof in respect of which payment has been made, if the whole sums payable in respect thereof have not been paid, and after such agreement has been entered into the account shall be immediately delivered to the Commissioners, and a like account shall be delivered half-yearly in each year

(2) The agreement shall specify the officer of the county council, corporation, or company, whether secretary, treasurer, accountant, or other officer, by whom the accounts are to be delivered, and such officer shall observe the rules in the first part of the Second Schedule to this Act, and is in those rules referred to by the expression "accountable officer"

(3) There shall be charged by way of composition upon the aggregate amount appearing on every half-yearly account delivered to the Commissioners for every one hundred pounds and any fraction of one hundred pounds of such amount the duty of sixpence as a stamp duty, and so soon as any account has been delivered, and payment of the duty hereby imposed has been made, transfers of any stock or funded debt included in such account, and also any share warrants or stock certificates relating to such stock or funded debt, shall be exempt from duty.

(4) If the duty charged is not paid upon the delivery of the account, it shall be a debt due to Her Majesty from the county council, corporation, or company on whose behalf the account is delivered

Composition for stamp duty by county councils, &c

(5) In the case of wilful neglect to deliver such an account as is hereby required to be delivered, or to pay the duty in conformity with this section, the county council or corporation or company shall be liable to pay to Her Majesty a sum equal to ten pounds per centum upon the amount of duty payable, and a like penalty for every month after the first month during which the neglect continues.

(6) Where an agreement for composition under this section has been entered into by any county council or corporation or company, such county council or corporation or company shall have power, in addition to any fee exigible upon registration of any transfer of stock, or funded debt, as the case may be, or upon issue of any share warrant, or stock certificate relating thereto, to require payment of an amount not exceeding the amount of duty which would have been chargeable upon the transfer or share warrant, or stock certificate, if no such agreement had been entered into

(50 & 51 Vict, Ch. 15, Secs 8, 9, 12, 15, and 16.)

The Inland Revenue Act, 1880 (43 & 44 Vict., Ch 20, Secs 53 & 54), authorised the payment of composition for stamp duty on transfers of debenture stock, &c., issued under the authority of The Local Authorities Loans Act, 1875, by the council of any city or municipal borough. It was replaced by the provisions of 50 & 51 Vict., Ch. 15 (with which Section 118 corresponds), which altered the rate and incidence of the compositions, and extended the privilege of compounding to all companies and corporations, as well as to county justices issuing "county stock." The compositions effected under the older Act hold good, but any increase of stock or debt must be compounded for under the provisions of this Act.

The descriptions of duties now compounded for are enumerated in Sub-section 3. If paid before the issue of share warrants and stock certificates, the composition covers the original duty thereon.

The Commissioners usually require security to be given for payment of composition by limited companies, either by a deposit of stock in joint names, or by the bond of Directors and approved sureties.

116. (1) Where any person issuing policies of insurance against accident shall, in the opinion of the Commissioners, so carry on the business of such insurance as to render it impracticable or inexpedient to require that the duty of one penny be charged and paid upon the policies, the Commissioners may enter into an agreement with that person for the delivery to them of quarterly accounts of all sums received in respect of premiums on policies of insurance against accident.

Composition for stamp duty on policies of insurance against accident

(2) The agreement shall be in such form and shall contain such terms and conditions as the Commissioners may think proper, and the person with whom the agreement is entered into shall observe the rules in the second part of the Second Schedule to this Act

(3) After an agreement has been entered into between the Commissioners and any person and during the period for which the agreement is in force, no policy of insurance against accident issued by that person shall be chargeable with any duty, but in lieu of and by way of composition for that duty there shall be charged on the aggregate amount of all sums received in respect of premiums on policies of insurance against accident a duty at the rate of five pounds per centum as a stamp duty

(4) If the duty charged is not paid upon the delivery of the account it shall be a debt due to Her Majesty from the person by or on whose behalf the account is delivered

(5) In the case of wilful neglect to deliver such an account as is hereby required or to pay the duty in conformity with this section the person shall be liable to pay to Her Majesty a sum equal to ten pounds per centum upon the amount of duty payable, and a like penalty for every month after the first month during which the neglect continues

(52 & 53 Vict, Ch 42, Sec. 20)

The Railway Passengers' Assurance Company and the Ocean, Railway, and General Accident Company have long enjoyed the privilege of compounding for insurance duty upon railway tickets, at the rate of five per cent., under private Acts, and this privilege was extended by 52 & 53 Vict., Ch 42, Sec 20, to "newspapers and other publications" containing notices and advertisements which purported to insure the payment of money upon the death of the holder or bearer of the newspaper or publication containing the notice or advertisement only from accident or violence, or otherwise than from a natural cause The provisions of the present law give the Commissioners a wide discretion as to an extension of the system

Miscellaneous.

Conditions and agreements as to stamp duty void

117. Every condition of sale framed with the view of precluding objection or requisition upon the ground of absence or insufficiency of stamp upon any instrument executed after the sixteenth day of May one thousand eight hundred and eighty-eight, and every contract, arrangement, or undertaking for assuming the liability on account of absence or insufficiency of stamp upon any such instrument or indemnifying against such liability, absence, or insufficiency, shall be void
(51 *Vict*, *Ch* 8, *Sec* 20)

A purchaser is entitled to insist that all deeds forming part of the chain of title, including a discharged mortgage, shall be stamped with ad valorem duty at the vendor's expense, even though the mortgagee join in the conveyance (Whiting v Loames, 17 Ch D 10, affirmed 14 Ch D. 823 *See* also *ex parte* Birkbeck Freehold Land Society, 24 Ch D. 119)

In the old case of Abbot v Stratton (3 J & L 616), Sir Edward Sugden declined to give effect to an agreement in a loan transaction that the security should remain unstamped, the borrower to pay the penalty if at any time it should become necessary to stamp the security, upon the ground that the agreement was an attempt to evade the stamp law

Assignment of policy of life assurance to be stamped before payment of money assured

118. (1) No assignment of a policy of life insurance shall confer on the assignee therein named, his executors, administrators, or assigns, any right to sue for the moneys assured or secured thereby, or to give a valid discharge for the same, or any part thereof, unless the assignment is duly stamped, and no payment shall be made to any person claiming under any such assignment unless the same is duly stamped.

(2) If any payment is made in contravention of this section, the stamp duty not paid upon the assignment, together with the penalty payable on stamping the same, shall be a debt due to Her Majesty from the person by whom the payment is made   (51 *Vict.*, Ch. 8, Sec 19)

Section 19 of The Customs and Inland Revenue Act, 1888 (51 & 52 Vict., Ch 8), with which the Section above corresponds, was enacted to check the laxity of practice of insurance companies in paying out moneys assured to persons who claimed under unstamped assignments   This Section reaches all assignments, whether made on sale, mortgage, settlement, or by way of gift, which would fall under Section 14 (4), *ante*, p. 33, and it is necessary to bear in mind that an instrument containing an assignment of a policy of life insurance—as, for example, a settlement—must be fully stamped with regard to any operation that it may have other than as an assignment of the policy

The Section has retrospective action, but in practice the Commissioners do not require payment of duty upon instruments executed before the coming into operation of 51 Vict, Ch 8, Sec 18 (May 16th, 1888, when the non-payment of ad valorem duty was made penal), relating to previous dealings with a policy which subsequently to such dealings has again become vested in the insurer   Thus if the insurer has mortgaged his policy and redeemed it, and has afterwards mortgaged it again, the instruments by which the former mortgage and the reconveyance, if executed before May 16th, 1888, and any intermediate dealings, were effected are not regarded as falling within this Section   This rule does not, of course, affect the right of an insurance company to call for any documents which are necessary to establish the title of an assignee   it only fixes a limit beyond which payment of stamp duty is not enforced

A policy issued in India, and payable either in India or the United Kingdom, is not liable to stamp duty until the premiums or the moneys assured are paid in the United Kingdom   It then falls under the provisions of Section 15 (3) of this Act, but previous assignments executed abroad are not chargeable   If the policy was originally issued in the United Kingdom, each assignment, whether executed in the

United Kingdom or elsewhere, must be duly stamped as an instrument relating to property situate in the United Kingdom under Section 14 (4). (See Whiting v Loames, 17 Ch D 10, affirmed 14 Ch D 243, and p 210.)

When a policy is mortgaged to secure advances "without limit" (Section 88 [2]), it is obligatory upon the insurance company to ascertain whether the amount owing upon the security exceeded the amount that the security was stamped to cover.

Instruments relating to Crown property

119. Except where express provision to the contrary is made by this or any other Act, an instrument relating to property belonging to the Crown, or being the private property of the Sovereign, is to be charged with the same duty as an instrument of the same kind relating to property belonging to a subject. (33 & 34 Vict, Ch 97, Sec. 5.)

As to instruments charged with duty of 35s

120. Any instrument which by any Act passed before the first day of January one thousand eight hundred and seventy-one and not relating to stamp duties is specifically charged with the duty of thirty-five shillings, shall be chargeable only with the duty of ten shillings in lieu of the said duty of thirty-five shillings.
(33 & 34 Vict, Ch 97, Sec 4.)

Recovery of penalties

121. All fines imposed by this Act are to be sued for and recovered by information in the High Court in England in the name of the Attorney General for England, in Scotland in the name of the Lord Advocate, and in Ireland in the name of the Attorney General for Ireland.*
(33 & 34 Vict, Ch 97, Sec 26.)

---

* POWER TO REWARD INFORMERS.—The Commissioners may at their discretion reward any person who informs them of any offence against any Act relating to inland revenue, or assists in the recovery of any fine or penalty, provided that a reward exceeding fifty pounds shall not be paid in any case without the consent of the Treasury

POWER TO MITIGATE FINES AND STAY PROCEEDINGS.—The Commissioners may in their discretion mitigate any fine or penalty incurred under this Act or any other Act relating to inland revenue, or stay or compound any proceedings for recovery thereof or for the condemnation of any seizure, and may restore anything seized, and may also after judgment further mitigate or entirely remit any such fine or penalty, and order any person imprisoned for any offence against inland revenue to be discharged before the term of his imprisonment has expired
(53 & 54 Vict., Ch 21, Secs. 32 and 35.)

122. (1) In this Act, unless the context otherwise Definitions.
requires,—

The expression "Commissioners" means Commissioners of Inland Revenue

The expression "material" includes every sort of material upon which words or figures can be expressed:

The expression "instrument" includes every written document·

The expression "stamp" means as well a stamp impressed by means of a die as an adhesive stamp:

The expression "stamped," with reference to instruments and material, applies as well to instruments and material impressed with stamps by means of a die as to instruments and material having adhesive stamps affixed thereto.

The expressions "executed" and "execution," with reference to instruments not under seal, mean signed and signature·

The expression "money" includes all sums expressed in British or in any foreign or colonial currency·

The expression "stock" includes any share in any stocks or funds transferable at the Bank of England or at the Bank of Ireland, and India promissory notes, and any share in the stocks or funds of any foreign or colonial state or government, or in the capital stock or funded debt of any county council, corporation, company, or society in the United Kingdom, or of any foreign or colonial corporation, company, or society

This definition does not include shares which partake of the character of real estate, as Founders' Shares and King's Shares in the New River Company, Shares in the River Don, River Avon, Droitwich, Kennet and Avon Navigations, Aire and Calder Canal, Leeds Cloth Market, nor shares in a quasi partnership formed for the purpose of being registered as a limited liability company under Part VII of The Companies Act, 1862

The expression "marketable security" means a security of such a description as to be capable of being sold in any stock market in the United Kingdom

The true test of the applicability of this definition to a security is not whether the security is current (that is to say, quoted on any Stock Exchange), but whether it is a security of such a description "as to be capable according to the use and practice of stock markets of being there sold and bought" per Lord Shand in the Texas Land and Cattle Company, Limited, v Commissioners of Inland Revenue (26 Sco L R p 51) In that case the Court of Session held a debenture, one of a series issued from time to time as investors lent money to the company, not quoted on any Stock Exchange, to be a marketable security within the meaning of this definition Mortgages of rates, tolls, &c, which are transferred and registered much in the same manner as mortgages and other securities created under The Companies Clauses Act, 1845, and The Companies Acts, 1861 and 1867, &c, are within the definition

The expression "steward" of a manor includes deputy steward

(2) In the application of this Act to Scotland expressions referring to the High Court shall be construed as referring to the Court of Session sitting as the Court of Exchequer

(33 & 34 Vict, Ch 97, Sec 2)

Repeal, Commencement; Short Title

Repeal
123. The enactments specified in the Third Schedule to this Act are hereby repealed from and after the commencement of this Act to the extent specified in the third column of that Schedule

Commencement
124. This Act shall come into operation on the first day of January one thousand eight hundred and ninety-two

Short title
125. This Act may be cited as The Stamp Act, 1891

SECOND SCHEDULE.

RULES AS TO COMPOSITION FOR STAMP DUTIES

First Part

1. Every account shall be made in such form and shall contain all such particulars as the Commissioners shall require

2. Every account shall be a full and true account of all stock and funded debt existing at the time of the delivery of the account, and of the amount thereof in respect of which payment has been made, if the whole sums payable in respect thereof have not been paid

3. In the case of any company or corporation formed within the United Kingdom, and having registers abroad in which stock or funded debt may be registered, the stock or funded debt of such company or corporation shall not for the purposes of the account include the stock or funded debt for the time being registered abroad

4. In the case of any colonial or foreign company or corporation having registers in the United Kingdom in which stock or funded debt are registered, the stock or funded debt for the time being registered in the United Kingdom shall for the purposes of the account be regarded as constituting all the stock or funded debt of the company or corporation

5. Where the first account shall be delivered at any time between two half-yearly days, such account shall be charged with an amount of duty proportionate to the period between the date of the delivery of the account and the first succeeding half-yearly day

Section 118.

Section 115.   6 Accounts shall be delivered to the Commissioners on or within seven days before the first day of February and the first day of August in each year

7 The duty shall be paid upon the delivery of the account

(50 & 51 Vict., Ch 15, Secs 10, 11, and 13.)

Second Part.

Section 116.   1. Every account shall be made in such form and shall contain all such particulars as the Commissioners shall require

2 Every account shall be a full and true account of all unstamped policies of insurance against accident issued during the quarter of a year ending on the quarterly day next preceding the delivery thereof, and of all sums of money received for or in respect of such policies so issued during that quarter, and of all sums of money received and not already accounted for in respect of any other unstamped policies of insurance against accident issued at any time before the commencement of that quarter

3 Accounts shall be delivered to the Commissioners within twenty days after the fifth day of April, the fifth day of July, the tenth day of October, and the fifth day of January in each year.

4. The duty shall be paid upon the delivery of the account

(52 & 53 Vict, Ch 42, Sec 20)

THIRD SCHEDULE

Enactments Repealed

Session and Chapter.	Title or Short Title.	Extent of Repeal
57 Geo. III, Ch 41	An Act to repeal two Acts passed in the fifty-fourth and fifty-fifth years of His present Majesty relating to the office of the Agent-General, and for transferring the duties of the said office to the office of the Paymaster-General and Secretary at War	Section eight
9 & 10 Vict., Ch. 17	An Act for the abolition of the exclusive privilege of trading in burghs in Scotland	Section one, from "Provided always" to the end of the section.
28 & 29 Vict, Ch 30	An Act to grant certain duties of customs and inland revenue.	Sections one and two, and Schedule B.
30 & 31 Vict., Ch 23.	An Act to grant and alter certain duties of customs and inland revenue, and for other purposes relating thereto	Except sections seventeen and eighteen.
33 & 34 Vict., Ch 24.	An Act for making further provision respecting the borrowing of money by the Metropolitan Board of Works	Sections three and four.
33 & 34 Vict, Ch. 97.	The Stamp Act, 1870	Except section twenty-five so far as it relates to provision (3) and sections twenty-seven and twenty-eight

ENACTMENTS REPEALED

Session and Chapter.	Title or Short Title.	Extent of Repeal.
34 & 35 Vict., Ch 4	An Act to amend The Stamp Act, 1870, in relation to foreign securities, mortgages of stock, and proxy papers	The whole Act.
34 & 35 Vict, Ch 103	An Act to amend the law relating to the customs and inland revenue	Section twenty-six.
36 & 37 Vict, Ch 18	The Customs and Inland Revenue Act, 1873.	Section five
37 & 38 Vict, Ch 19	An Act to amend The Stamp Act, 1870, in regard to the stamp duty payable by advocates in Scotland on admission as barristers in England or Ireland, and by barristers in England or Ireland on admission as advocates in Scotland.	The whole Act
37 & 38 Vict, Ch 26	The Canadian Stock Stamp Act, 1874.	The whole Act
39 & 40 Vict, Ch 6	The Sea Insurance (Stamping of Policies) Amendment Act, 1876.	The whole Act
39 & 40 Vict, Ch 16	The Customs and Inland Revenue Act, 1876	Section eleven
40 & 41 Vict, Ch 59	The Colonial Stock Act, 1877	Section two, and the first paragraph of section three
41 & 42 Vict, Ch 15	The Customs and Inland Revenue Act, 1878	Section twenty-seven
43 & 44 Vict, Ch 20	The Inland Revenue Act, 1880	Sections fifty-three to fifty six.
44 & 45 Vict, Ch 12	The Customs and Inland Revenue Act, 1881	Sections forty-four to forty-seven
45 & 46 Vict, Ch 72	The Revenue, Friendly Societies, and National Debt Act, 1882.	Sections eight to ten, thirteen, fourteen, and seventeen.
46 & 47 Vict, Ch 55	The Revenue Act, 1883	Section fifteen

Session and Chapter.	Title or Short Title.	Extent of Repeal.
47 & 48 Vict., Ch. 62	The Revenue Act, 1884	Sections eight to ten
48 & 49 Vict., Ch 51.	The Customs and Inland Revenue Act, 1885	Section twenty-one
5 & 51 Vict , Ch 15	The Customs and Inland Revenue Act, 1887	Sections five to sixteen.
51 & 52 Vict., Ch. 8.	The Customs and Inland Revenue Act, 1888	Sections ten to twenty, and the First Schedule.
52 & 53 Vict., Ch 7.	The Customs and Inland Revenue Act, 1889.	Sections sixteen and seventeen.
52 & 53 Vict , Ch 42.	The Revenue Act, 1889	Sections fifteen to seventeen, and twenty
53 & 54 Vict , Ch. 8	The Customs and Inland Revenue Act, 1890.	Sections eighteen to twenty-one.

THE STAMP DUTIES MANAGEMENT ACT, 1891.

ARRANGEMENT OF SECTIONS

Application of Act

Section		Page
1	Act to apply to all stamp duties	222

Mode of Recovering Money received for Duty.

2	Moneys received for duty and not appropriated to be recoverable in High Court	222

Sale of Stamps.

3	Power to grant licences to deal in stamps	223
4	Penalty for unauthorised dealing in stamps, &c	224
5	Provisions as to determination of a licence	224
6	Penalty for hawking stamps	225
7	Postage stamps	225
8	Discount	225

Allowance for Spoiled Stamps

9	Procedure for obtaining allowance	226
10	Allowance for misused stamps	228
11	Allowance how to be made	229
12	Stamps not wanted may be repurchased by the Commissioners	229

Offences relating to Stamps.

13	Certain offences in relation to dies and stamps provided by Commissioners to be felonies	230
14	Making paper in imitation of paper used for stamp duties	232
15	Possession of paper, plates, or dies used for stamp duties	232
16	Proceedings for detection of forged dies, &c	233
17	Proceedings for detection of stamps stolen or obtained fraudulently	233

Section		Page
18	Licensed person in possession of forged stamps to be presumed guilty until contrary is shown	234
19	Mode of proceeding when stamps are seized	235
20	As to defacement of adhesive stamps	235
21	Penalty for frauds in relation to duties	236

Miscellaneous

22	As to discontinuance of dies	236
23	Application of Act to excise labels	237
24	Declarations, how to be made	237
25	Mode of granting licences	237
26	Recovery of fines	238
27	Definitions	238

Repeal, Commencement, Short Title

28.	Repeal	239
29.	Commencement	239
30.	Short title	239
SCHEDULE		240

THE STAMP DUTIES MANAGEMENT ACT, 1891.

(54 & 55 VICT, CHAPTER 38.)

An Act to Consolidate the Law relating to the Management of Stamp Duties. [21st July, 1891.

BE IT ENACTED by the QUEEN'S MOST EXCELLENT MAJESTY, by and with the advice and consent of the Lords Spiritual and Temporal, and Commons, in this present Parliament assembled, and by the authority of the same, as follows:—

Application of Act.

Act to apply to all stamp duties.

1. All duties for the time being chargeable by law as stamp duties shall be under the care and management of the Commissioners, and this Act shall apply to all such duties and to all fees which are for the time being directed to be collected or received by means of stamps.

(33 & 34 *Vict.*, *Ch* 98, *Sec* 4, 38 & 39 *Vict*, *Ch.* 23, *Sec.* 13; 42 & 43 *Vict*, *Ch* 58, *Sec* 5)

Mode of recovering Money received for Duty

Moneys received for duty and not appropriated to be recoverable in High Court.

2. (1) Every person who, having received any sum of money as or for any duty, or any fee collected by means of a stamp, does not apply the money to the due payment of the duty or fee, and improperly withholds or detains the same, shall be accountable for the amount of the duty or fee, and the same shall be a debt from him to Her Majesty, and recoverable as such accordingly

(2) The Commissioners may sue out of the High Court in England or Ireland, or of the Court of Session sitting as the Court of Exchequer in Scot-

land, as the case may require, a writ of summons commanding any such person to deliver an account of every sum of money so received by him, and withheld or detained, and to pay the money to them, together with the costs of the proceedings, or to show cause to the contrary

(3) If cause is shown, the court shall make such order as to the court seems just

(13 & 14 Vict., Ch 97, Sec. 8; 28 & 29 Vict, Ch 104, Sec 55, 33 & 34 Vict, Ch 97, Sec 28.)

Sale of Stamps.

3. (1) The Commissioners may, in their discretion, grant a licence to any person to deal in stamps at any place to be named in the licence

(2) The licence shall specify the full name and place of abode of the person to whom the same is granted, and a description of every house, shop, or place in or at which he is authorised to deal in stamps.

(3) Every person to whom a licence is granted shall give security in the sum of one hundred pounds in such manner and form as the Commissioners shall prescribe, and, if by bond, the bond shall be exempt from stamp duty.

(4) One licence and one bond only shall be required for any number of persons in partnership, and the licence may at any time be revoked by the Commissioners

(5) Every person licensed to deal in stamps shall cause to be visibly and legibly painted, and shall keep so painted in letters of not less than one inch in length on some conspicuous place on the outside of the front of every house, shop, or place in or at which he is licensed to deal in stamps, his full name, together with the words " Licensed to sell

Power to grant licences to deal in stamps.

stamps," and for every neglect or omission so to do shall incur a fine of ten pounds

(3 & 4 Vict., Ch. 96, Secs. 24 and 25; 33 & 34 Vict., Ch. 98, Secs. 5, 6, and 8.)

Penalty for unauthorised dealing in stamps, &c.

4. (1) If any person who is not duly appointed to sell and distribute stamps deals in any manner in stamps, without being licensed so to do, or at any house, shop, or place not specified in his licence, he shall, for every such offence, incur a fine of twenty pounds.

(2) If any person who is not duly appointed to sell and distribute stamps, or duly licensed to deal in stamps, has, or puts upon his premises, either in the inside or on the outside thereof, or upon any board or any material whatever exposed to public view, and whether the same be affixed to his premises or not, any letters importing or intending to import that he deals in stamps, or is licensed so to do, he shall incur a fine of ten pounds.

(33 & 34 Vict., Ch. 98, Secs. 7 and 9.)

Provisions as to determination of a licence

5. (1) If the licence of any person to deal in stamps expires or is revoked, or if any person licensed to deal in stamps dies or becomes bankrupt, and any such person at the expiration or revocation of his licence, or at the time of his death or bankruptcy, has in his possession any stamps, such person, or his executor or administrator, or the receiver or trustee or official assignee under his bankruptcy, may, within six months after the expiration or revocation of the licence, or after the death or bankruptcy, as the case may be, bring or send the stamps to the chief office or to one of the head offices.

(2) The Commissioners may in any such case pay to the person bringing or sending stamps the amount of the duty thereon, deducting therefrom the proper discount, if proof to their satisfaction is furnished that the same were actually in the possession of the person whose licence has expired

or been revoked, or so dying or becoming bankrupt, for the purpose of sale, at the time of the expiration or revocation of the licence, or of his death, or bankruptcy, and that the stamps were purchased or procured by that person at the chief office or at one of the head offices, or from some persons duly appointed to sell and distribute stamps, or duly licensed to deal in stamps

(33 & 34 Vict., Ch. 98, Sec 10.)

6. (1) If any person, whether licensed to deal in stamps or not, hawks or carries about for sale or exchange, any stamps, he shall in addition to any other fine or penalty to which he may be liable incur a fine of twenty pounds *Penalty for hawking stamps*

(2) In default of payment of the fine, on summary conviction the offender shall be imprisoned for any term not exceeding two months

(3) All stamps which are found in the possession of the offender shall be forfeited, and shall be delivered to the Commissioners, to be disposed of as they think fit

(4) Any person may arrest a person found committing an offence against this section, and take him before a justice having jurisdiction where the offence is committed, who shall hear and determine the matter.

(33 & 34 Vict., Ch. 98, Sec 11.)

7. Notwithstanding anything in this Act contained, it shall be lawful for any person in the service or employment of the Post Office, without any other licence or authority than this Act, to sell postage stamps at any place, and in any manner. *Postage stamps*

(23 & 24 Vict., Ch. 111, Sec 22; 33 & 34 Vict., Ch. 98, Sec 12.)

8. Upon the sale of stamps such discount shall be allowed to the purchasers thereof as the Treasury direct *Discount*

(33 & 34 Vict., Ch. 98, Sec 13.)

Q

Allowance for Spoiled Stamps

Procedure for obtaining allowance

9. Subject to such regulations as the Commissioners may think proper to make, and to the production of such evidence by statutory declaration or otherwise as the Commissioners may require, allowance is to be made by the Commissioners for stamps spoiled in the cases hereinafter mentioned; that is to say,

(1) The stamp on any material inadvertently and undesignedly spoiled, obliterated, or by any means rendered unfit for the purpose intended, before the material bears the signature of any person or any instrument written thereon is executed by any party·

(2) Any adhesive stamp which has been inadvertently and undesignedly affixed or rendered unfit for use and has not in the opinion of the Commissioners been affixed to any material:

(3) Any adhesive stamp representing a fee capable of being collected by means of such stamp which has been affixed to material, provided that a certificate from the proper officer is produced to the effect that the stamp should be allowed·

(4) The stamp on any bill of exchange signed by or on behalf of the drawer which has not been accepted or made use of in any manner whatever or delivered out of his hands for any purpose other than by way of tender for acceptance:

(5) The stamp on any promissory note signed by or on behalf of the maker which has not been made use of in any manner whatever or delivered out of his hands:

(6) The stamp on any bill of exchange or

promissory note which from any omission or error has been spoiled or rendered useless, although the same, being a bill of exchange, may have been accepted or indorsed, or, being a promissory note, may have been delivered to the payee, provided that another completed and duly stamped bill of exchange or promissory note is produced identical in every particular, except in the correction of the error or omission, with the spoiled bill or note

(7) The stamp used for any of the following instruments; that is to say,

    (a) An instrument executed by any party thereto, but afterwards found to be absolutely void from the beginning·

    (b) An instrument executed by any party thereto, but afterwards found unfit, by reason of any error or mistake therein, for the purpose originally intended:

    (c) An instrument executed by any party thereto which has not been made use of for any purpose whatever, and which, by reason of the inability or refusal of some necessary party to sign the same or to complete the transaction according to the instrument, is incomplete and insufficient for the purpose for which it was intended

    (d) An instrument executed by any party thereto, which by reason of the refusal of any person to act under the same, or for want of enrolment or registration within the time required by law, fails of the intended purpose or becomes void:

    (e) An instrument executed by any party thereto which is inadvertently and undesignedly spoiled, and in lieu whereof another instrument made between the same parties and for the same purpose is executed and duly stamped, or which becomes useless in consequence of the transaction intended to be thereby effected being effected by some other instrument duly stamped

Provided as follows:—

(a) That the application for relief is made within six months after the stamp has been spoiled or become useless, or in the case of an executed instrument after the date of the instrument, or, if it is not dated, within six months after the execution thereof by the person by whom it was first or alone executed, or within such further time as the Commissioners may prescribe in the case of any instrument sent abroad for execution, or when from unavoidable circumstances any instrument for which another has been substituted cannot be produced within the said period.

(b) That in the case of an executed instrument no legal proceeding has been commenced in which the instrument could or would have been given or offered in evidence, and that the instrument is given up to be cancelled;

(c) That in the case of stamps used for medicines or playing cards, the medicines or cards bearing the stamps are produced to an officer and the stamps are removed therefrom in his presence

(30 & 31 *Vict*, *Ch* 23, *Sec* 17, 33 & 34 *Vict*, *Ch* 98, *Sec* 14.)

Allowance for misused stamps

10. When any person has inadvertently used for an instrument liable to duty a stamp of greater value than was necessary, or has inadvertently used a stamp for an instrument not liable to any duty, the Commissioners may, on application made within six months after the date of the instrument, or, if it is not dated, within six months after the execution thereof by the person by whom it was first or alone executed, and upon the instrument, if liable to duty, being stamped with the proper duty, cancel and allow as spoiled the stamp so misused.

(33 & 34 Vict., Ch 98, Sec 15.)

11. In any case in which allowance is made for spoiled or misused stamps the Commissioners may give in lieu thereof other stamps of the same denomination and value, or, if required, and they think proper, stamps of any other denomination to the same amount in value, or, in their discretion, the same value in money, deducting therefrom the discount allowed on the purchase of stamps of the like description

Allowance, how to be made.

(33 & 34 Vict., Ch. 98, Sec 16.)

12. When any person is possessed of a stamp which has not been spoiled or rendered unfit or useless for the purpose intended, but for which he has no immediate use, the Commissioners may, if they think fit, repay to him the value of the stamp in money, deducting the proper discount, upon his delivering up the stamp to be cancelled, and proving to their satisfaction that it was purchased by him at the chief office or at one of the head offices, or from some person duly appointed to sell and distribute stamps or duly licensed to deal in stamps, within the period of six months next preceding the application and with a bonâ fide intention to use it

Stamps not wanted may be re-purchased by the Commissioners.

(33 & 34 Vict, Ch 98, Sec 17)

The claim for signed bills and promissory notes must be made by the drawer or maker thereof within six months of the dates of such bills or notes

The substituted bill or note should in strictness be produced by the drawer at the time of making the declaration; but if this should be inconvenient, it may be produced by the claimant's clerk with the spoiled bill, and the drawer may make the declaration at his convenience within six months of the date of the spoiled bill

In all cases the stamps for allowance must be delivered to the revenue officials to be cancelled

Claims for allowance of spoiled and useless stamps are to be made in accordance with the following regulations —

The owner of the stamps (i e, the person for whose use and business the stamps are purchased), or his clerk, authorised by him in writing, must, attend in person to make a statutory declaration on an official form before a distributor of stamps, or at Somerset House, respecting the property in the stamps, the reason for making the claim, and the grounds on which the claim is based The declaration is not liable to stamp duty

The name, address, and occupation of the claimant must be written in full at the head of the declaration, and the declaration must be signed by him at the foot

In the case of a claim in respect of an executed instrument, the reason of the instrument becoming useless must be fully set forth in the declaration

The instrument used in lieu (if any) must be produced to the officer duly stamped and executed

A spoiled instrument must be presented in a complete state without mutilation, and the stamps thereon examined and counted by the officer, no instrument being received which does not fall within the conditions above set forth

Offences relating to Stamps.

Certain offences in relation to dies and stamps provided by Commissioners to be felonies

13. Every person who does, or causes or procures to be done, or knowingly aids, abets, or assists in doing, any of the acts following; that is to say,

(1) Forges a die or stamp;

(2) Prints or makes an impression upon any material with a forged die;

(3) Fraudulently prints or makes an impression upon any material from a genuine die;

(4) Fraudulently cuts, tears, or in any way removes from any material any stamp, with

intent that any use should be made of such stamp or of any part thereof;

(5) Fraudulently mutilates any stamp, with intent that any use should be made of any part of such stamp,

(6) Fraudulently fixes or places upon any material, or upon any stamp, any stamp or part of a stamp which, whether fraudulently or not, has been cut, torn, or in any way removed from any other material, or out of or from any other stamp,

(7) Fraudulently erases or otherwise either really or apparently removes from any stamped material any name, sum, date, or other matter or thing whatsoever thereon written, with the intent that any use should be made of the stamp upon such material;

(8) Knowingly sells or exposes for sale or utters or uses any forged stamp, or any stamp which has been fraudulently printed or impressed from a genuine die,

(9) Knowingly and without lawful excuse (the proof whereof shall lie on the person accused) has in his possession any forged die or stamp or any stamp which has been fraudulently printed or impressed from a genuine die, or any stamp or part of a stamp which has been fraudulently cut, torn, or otherwise removed from any material, or any stamp which has been fraudulently mutilated, or any stamped material out of which any name, sum, date, or other matter or thing has been fraudulently erased or otherwise either really or apparently removed,

shall be guilty of felony, and shall on conviction be liable to be kept in penal servitude for any term not exceeding fourteen years, or to be imprisoned with or without hard labour for any term not exceeding two years

(3 & 4 Vict, Ch. 18, Sec 22, 33 & 34 Vict., Ch. 98, Sec. 18, 42 & 43 Vict., Ch 58, Sec 5.)

Making paper in imitation of paper used for stamp duties

14. Every person who without lawful authority or excuse (the proof whereof shall lie on the person accused)—

(a) Makes or causes or procures to be made, or aids or assists in making, or knowingly has in his custody or possession, any paper in the substance of which shall appear any words, letters, figures, marks, lines, threads, or other devices peculiar to and appearing in the substance of any paper provided or used by or under the direction of the Commissioners for receiving the impression of any die, or any part of such words, letters, figures, marks, lines, threads, or other devices, and intended to imitate or pass for the same; or

(b) Causes or assists in causing any such words, letters, figures, marks, lines, threads, or devices as aforesaid, or any part of such words, letters, figures, marks, lines, threads, or other devices, and intended to imitate or pass for the same, to appear in the substance of any paper whatever,

shall be guilty of felony, and shall on conviction be liable to be kept in penal servitude for any term not exceeding seven years, or to be imprisoned with or without hard labour for any term not exceeding two years

(3 & 4 Vict , Ch 96, Sec 29, 42 & 43 Vict , Ch 58, Sec 5; 45 & 46 Vict , Ch 72, Sec 13)

Possession of paper, plates, or dies used for stamp duties

15. Every person who without lawful authority or excuse (the proof whereof shall lie on the person accused) purchases or receives or knowingly has in his custody or possession—

(a) Any paper manufactured and provided by or under the direction of the Commissioners, for the purpose of being used for receiving the impression of any die before such paper shall have been duly stamped and issued for public use; or

(b) Any plate, die, dandy-roller, mould, or other implement peculiarly used in the manufacture of any such paper,

shall be guilty of a misdemeanour, and shall on conviction be liable to be imprisoned with or without hard labour for any term not exceeding two years.

(3 & 4 Vict., Ch. 96, Sec. 30; 42 & 43 Vict., Ch. 58, Sec 5; 45 & 46 Vict., Ch 72, Sec. 13.)

16. On information given before a justice upon oath that there is just cause to suspect any person of being guilty of any of the offences aforesaid, such justice may, by a warrant under his hand, cause every house, room, shop, building, or place belonging to or occupied by the suspected person, or where he is suspected of being or having been in any way engaged or concerned in the commission of any such offence, or of secreting any machinery, implements, or utensils applicable to the commission of any such offence, to be searched, and if upon such search any of the said several matters and things are found, the same may be seized and carried away, and shall afterwards be delivered over to the Commissioners

Proceedings for detection of forged dies, &c.

(33 & 34 Vict., Ch. 98, Sec 19; 42 & 43 Vict., Ch 58, Sec. 5.)

17. (1) Any justice having jurisdiction in the place where any stamps are known or supposed to be concealed or deposited, may, upon reasonable suspicion that the same have been stolen or fraudulently obtained, issue his warrant for the seizure thereof, and for apprehending and bringing before himself or any other justice within the same juris-

Proceedings for detection of stamps stolen or obtained fraudulently

diction the person in whose possession or custody the stamps may be found, to be dealt with according to law.

(2) If the person does not satisfactorily account for the possession of the stamps, or it does not appear that the same were purchased by him at the chief office or at one of the head offices, or from some person duly appointed to sell and distribute stamps or duly licensed to deal in stamps, the stamps shall be forfeited, and shall be delivered over to the Commissioners.

(3) Provided that if at any time within six months after the delivery any person makes out to the satisfaction of the Commissioners that any stamps so forfeited were stolen or otherwise fraudulently obtained from him, and that the same were purchased by him at the chief office or one of the head offices, or from some person duly appointed to sell and distribute stamps, or duly licensed to deal in stamps, such stamps may be delivered up to him

(33 & 34 Vict., Ch 98, Sec 23.)

Licensed person in possession of forged stamps to be presumed guilty until contrary is shown.

18. (1) If any forged stamps are found in the possession of any person appointed to sell and distribute stamps, or being or having been licensed to deal in stamps, that person shall be deemed and taken, unless the contrary is satisfactorily proved, to have had the same in his possession knowing them to be forged, and with intent to sell, use, or utter them, and shall be liable to the punishment imposed by law upon a person selling, using, uttering, or having in possession forged stamps knowing the same to be forged

(2) If the Commissioners have cause to suspect any such person of having in his possession any forged stamps, they may by warrant under their hands authorise any person to enter between the hours of nine in the morning and seven in the

evening into any house, room, shop, or building of or belonging to the suspected person, and if on demand of admittance, and notice of the warrant, the door of the house, room, shop, or building, or any inner door thereof, is not opened, the authorised person may break open the same and search for and seize any stamps that may be found therein or in the custody or possession of the suspected person

(3) All officers of the peace are hereby required, upon request by any person so authorised, to aid and assist in the execution of the warrant

(4) Any person who—

(a) Refuses to permit any such search or seizure to be made as aforesaid; or

(b) Assaults, opposes, molests, or obstructs any person so authorised in the due execution of the powers conferred by this section or any person acting in his aid or assistance,

and any officer of the peace who, upon any such request as aforesaid, refuses or neglects to aid and assist any person so authorised in the due execution of his powers shall incur a fine of fifty pounds

(33 & 34 Vict, Ch 98, Secs 20 and 22)

19. Where stamps are seized under a warrant, the person authorised by the warrant shall, if required, give to the person in whose custody or possession the stamps are found an acknowledgment of the number, particulars, and amount of the stamps, and permit the stamps to be marked before the removal thereof

Mode of proceeding when stamps are seized.

(33 & 34 Vict, Ch 98, Sec 21)

20. Every person who by any writing in any manner defaces any adhesive stamp before it is used shall incur a fine of five pounds · Provided that any person may with the express sanction of the Commissioners, and in conformity with the conditions which they may prescribe, write upon or otherwise

As to defacement of adhesive stamps

appropriate an adhesive stamp before it is used for the purpose of identification thereof.

(33 & 34 Vict., Ch 98, Sec 25)

Penalty for frauds in relation to duties

21. Any person who practises or is concerned in any fraudulent act, contrivance, or device, not specially provided for by law, with intent to defraud Her Majesty of any duty shall incur a fine of fifty pounds

(33 & 34 Vict, Ch 97, Sec 25; 45 & 46 Vict, Ch. 72, Sec 15)

Miscellaneous

As to discontinuance of dies

22. Whenever the Commissioners determine to discontinue the use of any die, and provide a new die to be used in lieu thereof, and give public notice thereof in the London, Edinburgh, and Dublin Gazettes, then from and after any day to be stated in the notice (such day not being within one month after the same is so published) the new die shall be the only lawful die for denoting the duty chargeable in any case in which the discontinued die would have been used, and every instrument first executed by any person, or bearing date after the day so stated, and stamped with the discontinued die, shall be deemed to be not duly stamped·

Provided as follows.

(a) If any instrument stamped as last aforesaid, and first executed after the day so stated at any place out of the United Kingdom, is brought to the Commissioners within fourteen days after it has been received in the United Kingdom, then upon proof of the facts to the satisfaction of the Commissioners the stamp thereon shall be cancelled, and the instrument shall be stamped with the same amount of duty by means of the lawful die, without the payment of any penalty

(b) All persons having in their possession any material stamped with the discontinued die, and which by reason of the providing of such new die has been rendered useless. may at any time within six months after the day stated in the notice send the same to the chief office or one of the head offices, and the Commissioners may thereupon cause the stamp on such material to be cancelled, and the same material, or, if the Commissioners think fit, any other material, to be stamped with the new die, in lieu of and to an equal amount with the stamp so cancelled.

(33 & 34 Vict., Ch. 98, Sec 24.)

23. The provisions of this Act in reference to offences relating to stamps shall apply to any label now or hereafter provided by the Commissioners for denoting any duty of excise, and any label so provided shall be deemed to be included in the term "stamp" as defined by this Act.

Application of Act to excise labels.

(45 & 46 Vict, Ch 41, Sec 5.)

24. Any statutory declaration to be made in pursuance of or for the purposes of this or any other Act for the time being in force relating to duties may be made before any of the Commissioners, or any officer or person authorised by them in that behalf, or before any commissioner for oaths or any justice or notary public in any part of the United Kingdom, or at any place out of the United Kingdom, before any person duly authorised to administer oaths there

Declarations, how to be made

(55 Geo. III, Ch 184, Secs 52 and 53, 33 & 34 Vict., Ch 97, Sec 27, Ch 98, Sec. 27.)

25. Any licence or certificate to be granted by the Commissioners under this or any other Act for the time being in force relating to duties may be granted by such officer or person as the Commissioners may authorise in that behalf

Mode of granting licences.

(12 & 13 Vict., Ch. 1, Sec 16.)

Recovery of fines.

26. All fines imposed by this Act or by any Act for the time being in force relating to stamp duties charged in respect of medicines or playing cards may be proceeded for and recovered in the same manner and in the case of summary proceedings with the like power of appeal as any fine or penalty under any Act relating to the excise

(42 *Geo III*, *Ch.* 56, *Secs* 25 *and* 28, 52 *Geo III*, *Ch* 105, *Sec.* 2, 25 *& 26 Vict.*, *Ch.* 22, *Sec* 41.)

Definitions

27. In this Act, unless the context otherwise requires,—

The expression "Commissioners" means Commissioners of Inland Revenue

The expression "officer" means officer of Inland Revenue

The expression "chief office" means chief office of Inland Revenue :

The expression "head offices" means the head offices of Inland Revenue in Edinburgh and Dublin :

The expression "duty" means any stamp duty for the time being chargeable by law :

The expression "material" includes every sort of material upon which words or figures can be expressed.

The expression "instrument" includes every written document.

The expression "die" includes any plate, type, tool, or implement whatever used under the direction of the Commissioners for expressing or denoting any duty, or rate of duty, or the fact that any duty or rate of duty or penalty has been paid, or that an instrument is duly stamped, or is not chargeable with any duty or for denoting any fee, and also any part of any su_ plat , type, tool, or implement ·

The expressions "forge" and "forged" include counterfeit and counterfeited:

The expression "stamp" means as well a stamp impressed by means of a die as an adhesive stamp for denoting any duty or fee:

The expression "stamped" is applicable as well to instruments and material impressed with stamps by means of a die as to instruments and material having adhesive stamps affixed thereto:

The expressions "executed" and "execution," with reference to instruments not under seal, mean signed and signature.

The expression "justice" means justice of the peace.

(33 & 34 Vict., Ch. 98, Sec 2.)

Repeal, Commencement, Short Title.

28. The enactments specified in the Schedule to this Act are hereby repealed from and after the commencement of this Act to the extent specified in the third column of that Schedule. Repeal.

Provided that all bonds and securities given under or in pursuance of any enactment hereby repealed shall have the same effect as if they had been given in pursuance of this Act.

29. This Act shall come into operation on the first day of January, one thousand eight hundred and ninety-two. Commencement.

30. This Act may be cited as The Stamp Duties Management Act, 1891. Short title.

SCHEDULE

Session and Chapter	Title or Short Title	Extent of Repeal
39 & 40 Geo III, Ch 72	An Act to amend several laws relating to the duties on stamped vellum, parchment, and paper	The whole Act
42 Geo III, Ch 56	An Act to repeal an Act passed in the twenty-fifth year of the reign of His present Majesty for granting stamp duties on certain medicines and for charging other duties in lieu thereof, and for making effectual provision for the better collection of the said duties	Sections eighteen, twenty-five, and twenty-eight
52 Geo III, Ch 150	An Act to amend an Act passed in the forty-fourth year of His Majesty's reign for granting stamp duties in Great Britain, so far as regards the duties granted on medicines and on licences for vending the same	Section two, from "to be recovered" to the end of the section, and three
55 Geo III, Ch 184	An Act for repealing the stamp duties on deeds, law proceedings, and other written or printed instruments, and the duties on fire insurances, and on legacies and successions to personal estate upon intestacies now payable in Great Britain, and for granting other duties in lieu thereof	Sections fifty-two and fifty-three
3 & 4 Vict, Ch 96	An Act for the regulation of the duties of postage	Sections nineteen, twenty-one from "and all" to the end of the section, and twenty-two to thirty

ENACTMENTS REPEALED.

Session and Chapter.	Title or Short Title	Extent of Repeal.
13 & 14 Vict., Ch 97.	An Act to repeal certain stamp duties, to grant others in lieu thereof, and to amend the laws relating to the stamp duties	The whole Act
23 & 24 Vict., Ch. 111	An Act for granting to Her Majesty certain duties of stamps, and to amend the law relating to the stamp duties	Section twenty-two.
25 & 26 Vict., Ch 22	An Act to continue certain duties of Customs and Inland Revenue for the service of Her Majesty, and to grant, alter, and repeal certain other duties	Section forty-one.
30 & 31 Vict., Ch. 28	An Act to grant and alter certain Duties of Customs and Inland Revenue, and for other purposes relating thereto	Sections seventeen and eighteen
33 & 34 Vict., Ch 97	The Stamp Act, 1870	Section twenty-five so far as it relates to provision (3), and sections twenty-seven and twenty-eight
33 & 34 Vict., Ch. 98.	The Stamp Duties Management Act, 1870.	The whole Act
38 & 39 Vict, Ch. 22	The Post Office Act, 1875	The second, fourth, and fifth paragraphs of section six.
38 & 39 Vict., Ch 23	The Customs and Inland Revenue Act, 1875.	Section thirteen.
45 & 46 Vict., Ch 41.	The Customs and Inland Revenue Act, 1882.	Sub section three of section five
45 & 46 Vict., Ch. 72.	The Revenue, Friendly Societies, and National Debt Act, 1882	Section fifteen.

APPENDIX.

SPECIAL EXEMPTIONS IN STATUTES NOT OTHERWISE RELATING TO STAMP DUTIES.

The Bankruptcy Act, 1883 (46 & 47 Vict., Ch. 52).

S. 144. Every deed, conveyance, assignment, surrender, admission, or other assurance relating solely to freehold, leasehold, copyhold, or customary property, or to any mortgage, charge, or other incumbrance on, or any other estate, right, or interest in any real or personal property which is part of the estate of any bankrupt, and which after the execution of such deed, conveyance, assignment, surrender, admission, or other assurance, either at law or in equity, is or remains the estate of the bankrupt or of the trustee under the bankruptcy, and every power of attorney, proxy paper, writ, order, certificate, affidavit, bond, or other instrument or writing relating solely to the property of any bankrupt, or to any proceeding under any bankruptcy, shall be exempt from stamp duty (except in respect of fees under this Act)

It is evidently the intention of the High Court to give a very wide interpretation to this Section

"For the purposes of Section 144, 'bankruptcy' shall include any proceeding under the Act, whether before or after the adjudication, and whether an adjudication is made or not, and 'bankrupt' shall include any debtor proceeded against under the Act"—Rule 52 of the Rules made pursuant to Section 127 of The Bankruptcy Act, 1883.

In the old case of Flather v Stubbs (2 A. & E 614) a contract with the assignees of a bankrupt for the purchase of houses was held to be within the exemption from duty in 6 Geo IV, Ch 16, Sec 98, the terms of which were not quite so wide as those of the present exemption

"Proceeding" means any legal proceedings

An order of the Court under Section 55 (6) of The Bankruptcy Act, 1883, for the vesting of disclaimed property in the person entitled thereto, is exempt as an order not chargeable as a conveyance

The conveyance, upon sale by the trustee of all or any part of the bankrupt's estate, is liable to ad valorem conveyance duty. If the sale is made in consideration of the payment of a composition, ad valorem duty must be paid on the amount of the composition, plus (Section 57) any secured debt that the purchaser undertakes to pay.

When an adjudication of bankruptcy is annulled by the Court, as upon the payment in full of the debts of the bankrupt, the conveyance to him of property which upon adjudication vested in the trustee is liable to the duty of ten shillings as a conveyance not otherwise charged. "Bankrupt" is descriptive of the status of the debtor, and the exemption applies only to transactions which take place whilst, in the view of the law, he is in the state of bankruptcy.

The exemption is considered in administration to extend to receipts given by the trustee, receipts given by creditors for dividends, receipts for costs payable for work done for a trustee, and cheques drawn on a banking account kept solely for the purposes of the bankrupt's estate.

The Bankruptcy (Scotland) Act, 1856
(19 & 20 Vict., Ch. 79).

S. 184. All conveyances or assignations, instruments, discharges, writings, or deeds relating solely to the estate belonging to any bankrupt against whom sequestration has been or may be awarded, either under this or any former Act, and which estate, after the execution of such conveyances, assignations, instruments, discharges, writings, or deeds, shall be and remain the property of such bankrupt, for the benefit of his creditors, or the trustees appointed or chosen under or by virtue of such sequestration, and all discharges to such bankrupt, and all deeds, assignations, instruments, or writings for re investing such bankrupt in the estate, and all powers of attorney, commissions, factories, oaths, affidavits, articles of roup or sale, submissions, decrees arbitral, and all other instruments and writings whatsoever, relating solely to the estate of such bankrupt, and all other deeds or writings forming a part of the proceedings ordered under such sequestration, shall be exempt from all stamp duties or other government duty.

The Irish Bankrupt and Insolvent Act, 1857
(20 & 21 Vict., Ch. 60).

S. 400. No fees or stamp duties other than those authorised by the Act shall be payable in respect of any affidavit, certificate, bond, motion, or proceeding in bankruptcy or insolvency, or under this Act provided that nothing in this section contained shall exempt from stamp duty any deed, conveyance, assignment, or other assurance which now is by law liable to such duty

The Barracks Act, 1890
(53 & 54 Vict., Ch. 25).

S. 11. All contracts, conveyances, and other documents made in pursuance of or with a view to carrying into effect the purposes of this Act shall be exempted from stamp duty

The Building Societies Act, 1874 (37 & 38 Vict., Ch. 42).

S. 41. No rules of any society under this Act, nor any copy thereof, nor any power, warrant, or letter of attorney granted or to be granted by any person as trustee for the society for the transfer of any share in the public funds standing in his name, nor any receipts given for any dividend in any public stock or fund, or interest of exchequer bills, nor any receipt, nor any entry in any book of receipt for money deposited in the funds of the society, nor for any money received by any member, his executors or administrators, assigns, or attorneys, from the funds of the society, nor any transfer of any share, nor any bond or other security to be given to or on account of the society, or by any officer thereof, nor any order on any officer for payment of money to any member, nor any appointment of any agent, nor any certificate or other instrument for the revocation of any such appointment, nor any other instrument or document whatever required or authorised to be given, issued, signed, made, or produced in pursuance of this Act, or of the rules of the society, shall be subject or liable to or charged with any stamp duty or duties whatsoever, provided that the exemption shall not extend to any mortgage

The general rule as regards an exemption of this class is that it extends only to documents required or authorised for the purpose of carrying on the internal affairs of the society, or required or authorised for the purpose of bringing the society into a position to carry on business with the outside world, and this rule also extends to the transactions of friendly societies (*post*, p 239) It does not extend to all documents which may be necessary in the course of carrying on the business of the society, as in Royal Liver Society *v* Commissioners (5 Ex 78), where a mortgage to a friendly society was held not to be within the exemption from stamp duty in 18 and 19 Vict., Ch 63, Sec 37, the terms of which were almost identical with those of the above exemption In

Attorney-General v Gilpin (6 Ex 193), decided on 10 Geo IV, Ch 56, Sec 37 (applied, by 6 & 7 Will IV, Ch. 32, Sec. 4, to building societies, and almost identical in terms with the above), "order . required or authorised to be given . in pursuance of this Act or the rules of the society," was held to apply only to instruments falling within the ordinary transactions of a building society, and not to include an order for payment of money to a member upon withdrawal of his shares or for interest on a share In Attorney-General v Phillips (19 W R. 1146) a receipt given by a building society mortgagee in possession to a tenant, not a member of the society, was considered not to fall within the exemption (*Per* Martin, B) "The exemption means that those receipts are exempt from duty which were given for moneys deposited belonging to the funds of the society This is not such money. The fact that the money, after it was paid by the tenant, was deposited in those funds does not affect the question"

Instruments in the forms given in the schedule to the Act are exempt from duty The most important is the form of receipt to be endorsed on a mortgage or further charge, to which operation as a reconveyance is given by Section 42. Unless the statutory form is closely followed, the instrument will become liable to reconveyance duty Inasmuch as the statutory receipt vacates the mortgage, a warrant to vacate copyholds included in such mortgage is not liable to duty

Carriers Act (11 Geo. IV., & 1 Will. IV., Ch. 68).

S. 3. Such receipt (for any package or parcel, ackowledging the same to have been insured at an increased charge) shall not be liable to any stamp duty.

Cessio Bonorum (Scotland) (6 & 7 Will. IV., Ch. 56).

S. 20. And be it enacted that no fee fund dues shall be exigible in respect of any of the proceedings mentioned in this Act, nor shall any stamp duty or other government duty be exigible in respect of . any disposition which the debtor shall be ordained to execute in terms of this Act

Church Building Act (3 Geo. IV., Ch. 72).

S. 28. No deed of gift, or grant, security, contract, agreement, deed or conveyance, or other instrument, made for any of the purposes in the said recited Acts mentioned (58 Geo III, Ch 45, and 59 Geo III, Ch 134), or for any other purpose or under any of the provisions in the said recited

Acts mentioned, or for any other of the purposes or under any of the provisions in the said recited Acts, or either of them, or of this Act, or for the carrying into execution any of the powers, authorities, regulations, purposes, or provisions thereof or therein mentioned respectively, shall be subject to any of the duties upon stamped vellum, parchment, or paper, anything in any Act or Acts of Parliament to the contrary notwithstanding

This exemption is read as if embodied in subsequent Church Building Acts, of which the principal are 5 Geo. IV., Ch 103, 1 & 2 Will IV, Ch 38, 1 & 2 Vict., Ch 107, 3 & 4 Vict., Ch 60, 14 & 15 Vict, Ch 97, 36 & 37 Vict, Ch 50 (Places of Worship Sites Act, 1873, by which it is extended to sale)

Church Building Act (Scotland) (5 Geo. IV., Ch. 90).

S. 10. No stamp duty shall be paid for or in respect of any such conveyances or assurances, or of any lease to be granted under the powers contained in this Act

The Common Law Procedure Act, 1854 (17 & 18 Vict., Ch. 125).

S. 30. No document made or required under the provisions of this Act shall be liable to any stamp duty.

The Common Law Procedure Amendment Act (Ireland), 1856 (19 & 20 Vict., Ch. 102).

S. 36. No document made or required under the provisions of this Act shall be liable to any stamp duty

Companies (Colonial Registers) Act, 1883 (46 & 47 Vict., Ch. 30).

S. 7. An instrument of transfer of a share registered in a colonial register under this Act shall be deemed to be a transfer of property situated out of the United Kingdom, and, unless executed in any part of the United Kingdom, shall be exempt from British stamp duty

The Consecration of Churchyards Act, 1867 (30 & 31 Vict., Ch. 133).

S. 6. No deed of gift, or grant, security, contract, agreement, deed, or conveyance, or other instrument made for the purposes of this Act, or for carrying into execution any of the powers, authorities, or provisions of this Act, shall be subject to any of the duties upon stamped vellum, parchment, or paper, anything in any Act or Acts of Parliament to the contrary notwithstanding

The Contagious Diseases (Animals) Act, 1878 (41 & 42 Vict., Ch. 56).

S. 83. No stamp duty shall be payable on any appointment, certificate, declaration, or licence under this Act.

Copyhold Act, 1894 (57 & 58 Vict., Ch. 46).

S. 58. (1.) An agreement, valuation, or power of attorney under this Act shall not be chargeable with stamp duty

An Act to Amend the Law of Copyright (5 & 6 Vict., Ch. 45).

Assignment by entry in the Registry Book of the Stationers' Company, in the form given in the Schedule to the Act, of the interest or portion of the interest of the registered proprietor of the copyright in a book

S. 3. Such assignment shall be effectual in law, to all intents and purposes whatsoever, without being subject to any stamp or duty

County Treasurers Act (Ireland) (1 & 2 Vict., Ch. 53).

S. 1. All drafts to be drawn by any treasurer under the authority of the hereinbefore recited Act of the last Session of Parliament, or of this present Act, shall be exempt from any stamp duty whatever

Customs and Inland Revenue Act, 1889 (52 Vict., Ch. 7).

S. 13. Any person may cause an attested copy (which shall be exempt from stamp duty) of any document which creates a liability for payment of any succession duty, or duty hereinbefore imposed, &c , to be deposited with the Commissioners of Inland Revenue at their office, &c

Dispensary Houses (Ireland) Act, 1879 (42 & 43 Vict., Ch. 25).

S. 14. No order, mortgage, bond, obligation, security, contract, agreement, or other instrument whatsoever, executed under the provisions of this Act, nor any memorial thereof for registration, shall be liable to any stamp duty whatever.

Drainage Act (9 & 10 Vict., Ch. 101).

An Act to authorise the advance of public money to promote the improvement of land in Great Britain and Ireland by drainage

S. 47. No bond or other security given to the Commissioners under this Act, and no certificate or other instrument made under this Act, shall be chargeable with stamp duty

East India Loan Act, 1893 (56 & 57 Vict., Ch. 70).

S. 16. The provisions contained in Section 4 of the Act 5 & 6 Will IV, Ch 64, with respect to the composition and agreement for the payment by the East India Company of an annual sum in lieu of stamp duties on their bonds, and the exemption of their bonds from stamps duties, shall be applicable with respect to the bonds, debentures, and bills to be issued by the Secretary of State under the authority of this or any previous Act, as if such provisions were here and there repeated and re enacted with reference thereto

Education (Scotland) Act, 1872 (35 & 36 Vict., Ch. 62).

S. 39. The transference (of any school, with the site and house and land, if any, held and used in connection therewith, to a school board under this Act) may be effected by an ordinary disposition or other deed of conveyance by the persons vested with the title recorded in the register of sasines, and no stamp or other duty shall be exigible on such disposition or other deed

Friendly Societies Act, 1875 (38 & 39 Vict., Ch. 60).

S. 15. (2) Stamp duty shall not be chargeable upon any of the following documents —

(a) Power, warrant, or letter of attorney granted by any person as trustee for the transfer of any money of the society invested in his name in the public funds

(b) Order or receipt for money contributed to or received from the funds of the society by virtue of its rules or of this Act

(c) Bond given to or on account of the society, or by the treasurer or other officer thereof

(d) Draft or order, or form of policy, or appointment or revocation of appointment of agent, or other document required or authorised by this Act or by the rules of the society

Cheques drawn by the society on its banker are not within this exemption, nor are receipts given upon repayment of a loan by instalments or otherwise The exemption is interpreted with the same strictness as that relating to building societies Instruments in the forms given in the schedule are exempt from duty The most important is the form of receipt which vacates a mortgage by statutory authority, as in the case of a receipt endorsed upon a building society's mortgage, and the same rules are applicable. See also note to Building Societies Act, 1874, on pp 235, 236

The Glebe Loans (Ireland) Act, 1870 (33 & 34 Vict., Ch. 112).

S. 8. No mortgage, bond, obligation, security, contract, agreement, or other instrument whatsoever, executed under the provisions of this Act, nor any memorial thereof for registration, shall be liable to any stamp duty whatever

With the addition of "order," the exemption in The National School Teachers' Residences (Ireland) Act, 1875 (38 & 39 Vict Ch 82, Sec. 6), is the same

An Act for Regulating Hackney and Stage Carriages in and near London (6 & 7 Vict., Ch. 86).

S. 23. An agreement for the payment of any sum of money by a driver or conductor to a proprietor on account of the earnings of any hackney carriage or metropolitan stage carriage (which by Section 23 of the Act is required to be in writing) is not liable to any stamp duty

Inclosure Act (8 & 9 Vict., Ch. 118).

S. 163. No agreement, award, bond, or power of attorney made or confirmed or used under this Act shall be chargeable with any stamp duty

Income Tax Act (5 & 6 Vict., Ch. 35).

S 179. No receipt, certificate of payment, contract of composition, affidavit, appraisement, or valuation, made or given in pursuance and for the purposes of this Act, shall be liable to any stamp duty

Indian Prize Money Act (29 & 30 Vict., Ch. 47).

S. 8. Where, under the statutes at present in force, an order for the payment of prize money is liable to stamp duty, the amount of such duty may be paid by receipt or draft stamps affixed to the said order, equal in the total amount thereof to the stamp duty payable on an inland bill for a sum equal to that for which the order is given, and no order for any sum less than forty shillings shall be liable to stamp duty

Landed Property (Ireland) Act, 1847
(10 & 11 Vict., Ch. 32).

S. 59. No bond, obligation, or other security, contract, agreement, or other instrument whatever, taken or made to or by the said Commissioners, nor any affidavit, deposition, release, receipt, or discharge to be respectively taken or made under and by virtue of this Act to or by them, nor any power of attorney to receive from the said paymaster of civil services any money advanced on account of loans under this Act, nor any other instrument whatsoever executed under the provisions of this Act, nor any memorial thereof for registration, shall be liable to any stamp duty whatever

Land Tax Consolidation and Amendment Act
(42 Geo. III., Ch. 116).

S. 68. Where the moneys to be paid as the consideration for any sale, mortgage, or grant to be made by virtue of this Act by any person or persons (other than bodies politic or corporate, or companies, for feoffees or trustees for charitable or other public purposes) shall not exceed the sum of £1,000, the deed of sale, mortgage, or grant, or the enrolment thereof, and in cases of copyhold or customary estates the deed of sale or of grant or any copy of the entry upon the court rolls of such deed of sale or grant shall not be liable to any stamp duty whatever

S. 81. No deed or instrument whatever whereby any sale enfranchisement, mortgage, or grant shall be made of or out of any manors, messuages, lands, tenements, or hereditaments under the authority of the said last mentioned Commissioners (for regulating sales, &c), by virtue of this Act, shall be liable to any stamp duty whatever

45 Geo. III., Ch. 7 (amending above Act).

S. 1. No such assignment of land tax (i e, on purchase for the benefit of a living, &c) or any such deed of sale, mortgage, or grant, in pursuance of this Act, shall be liable to any stamp duty whatever

S. 107. No obligation to His Majesty, in pursuance of this Act, shall be liable to any stamp duty whatever

S. 173. And be it further enacted that no contract entered into for the redemption or purchase of any land tax, nor any assignment of any such contract or land tax, by virtue of the said recited Acts or this Act, nor any copy of the register thereof, nor any certificate or receipt which shall be given by virtue of the said recited Acts or of this Act, nor any transfer of any stock in the funds which shall be made by virtue of the said recited Acts or of this Act to the Commissioners for the Reduction of the National Debt, or any letter of attorney authorising any person or persons to transfer any such stock to the said Commissioners, or to accept any such stock previously to and for the purpose of transferring the same to them, nor any affidavits whatever to be made in pursuance of the said recited Acts or of this Act, shall be liable to any stamp duty whatever

Loan Societies Act (England) (3 & 4 Vict., Ch. 110).

S. 9. Debenture (for money deposited with the society) to be registered in the books

S. 12. Bond in the form in the Schedule to the Act by a treasurer or other person entrusted with receipt or custody of money or securities for money for the faithful execution of such office or trust

S. 14. No note which shall be signed for the repayment of any loan made under this Act, nor any receipt or entry in any book of receipt for money lent or paid, nor any draft or order, nor any appointment of any agent, nor any other instrument whatever required to be made in pursuance of this Act or of the rules of the society, shall be chargeable with any stamp duty whatever

Loan Societies Act (Ireland) (6 & 7 Vict., Ch. 91).

S. 26. And be it enacted that no note or security for the repayment of any loan made by any society established or acting under the provisions of this Act, nor any receipt or entry in any bank or receipt of money lent or paid, nor any debenture, or transfer, or draft, or order, nor any appointment of any agent, nor any bond nor security, nor other instrument or document whatever required or authorised to be given, issued, made, or provided in pursuance of the rules of any such society or of this Act, shall be subject to or chargeable with any stamp duty whatsoever

With regard to the Irish Reproductive Loan Fund Institution, *see* Section 47 of the same Act.

Local Loans Act, 1875 (38 & 39 Vict., Ch. 83).

S. 19. Any coupons issued in respect of any debenture or stock certificate to bearer under this Act shall, for the purposes of the Acts relating to stamp duties, be deemed to have been attached to and issued with such security

Lord Tenterden's Act (9 Geo. IV., Ch. 14)

S. 5. No memorandum or other writing made necessary by this Act shall be deemed to be an agreement within the meaning of any statute relating to the duties of stamps.

The exemption in Lord Tenterden's Act rarely comes into operation. In Morris v Dixon (4 Ad & E 845, 6 N & M 438) it was held to apply to an acknowledgment of a debt containing an undertaking by the debtor to pay as soon as his circumstances would permit. The money had been advanced in 1826, the acknowledgment was given in 1832; the debt was proved *aliunde*, and the acknowledgment produced merely to avoid the Statute of Limitations otherwise it would have been liable to duty as an agreement. In Jones v Rider (4 M & W 32) the exemption was declared to be applicable only to an instrument which could legally be stamped as an agreement, not to a promissory note. *See* also Parmiter v Parmiter (1 J & H 135, 30 L J, Ch 508)

Merchant Shipping Act, 1894 (57 & 58 Vict. Ch. 60.)

S. 108. (1) Every indenture of apprenticeship to the sea service shall be executed in duplicate, and shall be exempt from stamp duty

S. 196. (1) The wages of a seaman volunteering into the Navy may be paid by bill drawn upon the owner, and payable at sight to the order of the Accountant General of the Navy, and such bill shall be exempt from stamp duty

S. 309. (2) The bond (given by the master of an emigrant ship) shall be executed in duplicate, and shall be exempt from stamp duty

S. 320. (4) Contract tickets (for passengers) under this section shall be exempt from stamp duty

S. 342. (2) The bond (given by a passage broker) shall be renewed on each occasion of obtaining a licence, and shall not be liable to stamp duty

S. 395. (7) All such indentures and agreements (for the sea fishing service) made in conformity with this part (Part IV Fishing Boats) of this Act, shall be exempt from stamp duty

S. 563. Any bond, statement, agreement, or other document made or executed in pursuance of the provisions of this part (IX) of this Act relating to salvage by Her Majesty's ships, shall, if made or executed out of the United Kingdom, be exempt from stamp duty

S. 721. The following instruments shall be exempt from stamp duty —

(a) Any instruments used for carrying into effect the First Part of this Act

(b) Any instruments used by or under the direction of the Board of Trade in carrying into effect the Second, Fifth, Eleventh and Twelfth Parts of this Act, and

(c) Any instruments which are by those parts of this Act required to be in a form approved by the Board of Trade, if made in that form

Metropolitan Board of Works Loan Act
(33 & 34 Vict., Ch. 24).

S. 5. In consideration of the provisions for composition in this Act contained, transfers of metropolitan consolidated stock issued or to be issued, and stock certificates in respect thereof, and transfers of metropolitan annuities, are hereby, notwithstanding anything in the Principal Act, exempted from stamp duty

The Military Forces Localisation Act, 1872
(35 & 36 Vict., Ch. 68).

S. 12. All contracts, conveyances, and other documents made in pursuance of or with a view to carrying into effect the purposes of this Act shall be exempted from stamp duty

The Militia Law Amendment Act, 1854 (England and Wales)
(17 & 18 Vict., Ch. 105).

S. 20. All conveyances, leases, mortgages, awards, contracts, receipts, and other instruments made for the purpose of carrying into effect the provisions of this Act shall be exempt from stamp duty

The exemption in the Act for Scotland, 17 & 18 Vict, Ch 106, Sec. 41, is in similar terms, except that "bonds" is substituted for "mortgages"

An Act to provide for the Regulation of Municipal Corporations in England and Wales.
(5 & 6 Will. IV., Ch. 76.)

S. 22. No stamp duty shall be payable in respect of the admission, registry, or enrolment of any burgess according to the provisions of this Act

The same exemption, with the addition of the words "or freeman" after burgess, occurs in the Irish Act (3 & 4 Vict, Ch 108, Sec 48).

National Debt Redemption Act, 1893
(56 & 57 Vict., Ch. 64.)

S 4. (1) A power of attorney authorising the sale of any stock liable to redemption under this Act shall authorise the receipt of any money payable on redemption of that stock.

(2) A power of attorney given exclusively for the purpose of authorising the receipt of money payable on redemption under this Act shall be exempt from stamp duty

Naval Agency and Distribution Act
(27 & 28 Vict., Ch. 24).

S. 15 directs that shares of salvage and prize money, &c, shall be paid in such manner and subject to such provisic as may from time to time be directed by order in council

S. 16. All bills, orders, receipts, and other instruments, drawn, given, or made under the authority or in pursuance of any such order in council by, to, or upon any officer or person in the service of Her Majesty, or of the Lords of the Admiralty, shall be exempt from stamp duty

Naval and Marine Pay and Pensions Act
(28 & 29 Vict., Ch. 73).

S. 6. All bills, orders, receipts, and other instruments, drawn, given, or made under the authority or in pursuance of an order in council under this Act by, to, or upon any person in the service of Her Majesty or of the Admiralty shall be exempt from stamp duty

Parochial Clergy (Residence).
An Act to promote the Residence of the Parochial Clergy
(17 Geo. III., Ch. 53).

S. 15. No deed, bond, transfer, or other writing, instrument, or proceeding made, had, or done under the powers or authority of this Act shall be charged or chargeable with any stamp duty

This exemption is incorporated in the following Acts — 21 Geo III, Ch 66, 7 Geo IV, Ch. 66, 1 & 2 Vict., Ch 23, 28 & 29 Vict, Ch 69, 34 & 35 Vic., Ch 43 (Ecclesiastical Dilapidations Act), and 44 & 45 Vict, Ch. 25

Parochial Stipends (Scotland) Act
(50 Geo. III., Ch. 84).

S. 22. And be it enacted that the several precepts or warrants to be issued in manner before mentioned, and the receipts to be granted for the sums of money payable as hereinbefore directed, shall not be liable to any stamp duty

The Pawnbrokers Act, 1872
(35 & 36 Vict., Ch. 93).

S. 15. A pawnbroker shall, if required at the time of redemption, give a receipt for the amount of loan and profit paid to him, and such a receipt shall not be liable to stamp duty unless the profit amounts to forty shillings or more

S. 24. A special contract pawn ticket, or the duplicate thereof (following Form No VII in the Third Schedule to the Act), shall not be liable to any stamp duty

Pensions and Yeomanry Pay Act, 1884
(47 & 48 Vict., Ch. 55).

S. 5. Every order, receipt, affidavit, and document used in pursuance of any warrant, order, or regulation of Her Majesty, or a Secretary of State, whether made in pursuance of this Act or otherwise in relation to the payment of any pension in respect of military service, including service in any of the auxiliary forces, shall, unless otherwise provided by such warrant, order, or regulation, or by the regulations general or special of a Secretary of State, be exempt from stamp duty

Poor Law Act (England and Wales)
(4 & 5 Will. IV., Ch. 76).

S. 86. And be it further enacted that no mortgage, bond, instrument, or any assignment thereof, given by way of security, in pursuance of the rules, orders, or regulations of the said Commissioners, and conformable thereto, nor any contract or agreement or appointment of any officer made or entered into in pursuance of such rules, orders, or regulations, and conformable thereto, nor any other instrument made in pursuance of this Act, nor the appointment of any paid officer engaged in the administration of the laws for the relief of the poor or in the management or collection of the poor rate, shall be charged or chargeable with any stamp duty whatever

S. 87. And whereas by an Act passed in the twenty-second year of the reign of King George the Third, intituled *An Act for the Better Relief and Employment of the Poor*, the visitor and guardian of the poor of any parish, township, or place which shall adopt the provisions of the said recited Act are authorised thereby to borrow money at interest for the purposes mentioned in the said Act, and to secure such money by a charge upon the poor rates of such parish, township, or place, in sums not exceeding fifty pounds each, in a certain form contained in the Schedule to the said Act, or to that or to the like effect, and which security is directed and allowed to be assigned by indorsement on the back thereof in a certain form contained in the said Schedule, or to that or the like effect. And whereas doubts have arisen touching the liability of such securities as aforesaid, and the assignments or transfers thereof, to stamp duty, and it is expedient to remove the same. Be it therefore enacted and declared that no bond or other security at any time heretofore or to be at any time hereafter made or entered into in pursuance of the said recited Act, nor any assignment or transfer thereof, shall be charged or chargeable with or be deemed to be or to have been subject or liable to any stamp duty whatsoever, anything in any Act contained to the contrary thereof notwithstanding.

7 & 8 Vict., Ch. 101.

S. 61. No bond or any other security entered into in pursuance of this Act, or of the Act 59 Geo III., Ch 12, shall be charged or chargeable with or be deemed to be or to have been subject or liable to any stamp duty whatsoever.

By 5 & 6 Vict., Ch. 57, Sec 18, the Acts 4 & 5 Will IV, Ch 76, 5 & 6 Will IV, Ch 67, and 6 & 7 Will IV, Ch. 96, and the Acts there mentioned, are to be read as one Act, and to these was subsequently joined 7 & 8 Vict., Ch 101, Sec. 61. A contract for the sale of lands in pursuance of the order of the Local Government Board is within the exemptions (Guardians of Banbury Union v Robinson, 4 A & E, N. S 919, 12 L J, Q B 327.)

Poor Law Act (Scotland) (8 & 9 Vict., Ch. 83).

S. 22. And it shall be competent for any heitor, being a member of the parochial board, to appoint as heretofore, by a writing under his hand, any other person to be his agent or mandatory to act and vote for him at such board; and such appointment shall remain in force till recalled, and such writing or appointment is hereby declared to be valid and lawful, although the paper whereon it is written should not be stamped.

Poor Law Act (Ireland) (1 & 2 Vict., Ch. 56).

S. 96. And be it enacted that no charge, mortgage, bond, or instrument given by way of security, in pursuance of the orders of the Commissioners, and conformable thereto, nor any transfer thereof, nor any contract or agreement made or entered into in pursuance of such orders, and conformable thereto, nor any conveyance, demise, or assignment respectively to or by the Commissioners, nor any receipt for rate, nor any other instrument made in pursuance of this Act, nor the appointment of any paid officer engaged in the administration of the laws for the relief of the poor, or in the management or collection of the poor rate, shall be charged or chargeable with any stamp duty whatever

The Post Office Land Act, 1881 (44 & 45 Vict., Ch. 20).

S. 5. Every deed, instrument, receipt, or document made or executed for the purpose of the Post Office by, to, or with Her Majesty or any officer of the Post Office, shall be exempt from any stamp duty imposed by any Act, past or future, except where such duty is declared by the deed, instrument, receipt, or document, or by some memorandum endorsed thereon, to be payable by some person other than the Postmaster-General, and except so far as any future Act specifically charges the same

Post Office Orders Act (3 & 4 Vict., Ch. 96).

S. 38. And whereas the Postmaster-General hath, with the concurrence of the Commissioners of Her Majesty's Treasury, made regulations by which the public are enabled to remit small sums of money through the Post Office by means of money orders: be it enacted that such mode of transmitting money through the Post Office may have continuance so long as the Commissioners of Her Majesty's Treasury shall see fit

Although not in terms an exempting statute, this enactment has been held to render a stamp unnecessary upon a post office order. In Reg v Gilchrist (Car. & M. 224), Parke, B, in pronouncing the judgment of the Court, said, "The judges are of opinion that it is unnecessary to decide that point" (i.e whether a post office order is an instrument requiring a stamp) it being the practice to issue them unstamped, they were of opinion that it was sanctioned and legalised by the Statute 3 & 4 Vict., Ch. 96 And see "like other money orders" in the following Statute

Post Office (Money Orders) Act, 1880 (43 & 44 Vict., Ch. 33, Sec. 1).

To be construed as one Act with The Post Office (Money Orders) Act, 1848 (11 & 12 Vict., Ch. 88).

Subject to the Post Office regulations as defined by this Act, the Postmaster-General, with the consent of the Treasury, may, for the purpose of the transmission of small sums through the Post Office, authorise his officers, or any of them, to issue, in addition to the money orders already authorised by law, orders in the form set forth in the Schedule to this Act, and such orders shall be paid in the manner and subject to the conditions prescribed by the said regulations, and shall be deemed to be money orders within the meaning of the said regulations, and shall, like other money orders, be exempt from stamp duty

Public Health (Scotland) Act (30 & 31 Vict., Ch. 101.)

S. 130. All bonds, assignations, conveyances, instruments, agreements, receipts, or other writings made or granted by or to or in favour of the local authority under this Act shall be exempt from all stamp duties

Public Works Act (Ireland) (9 & 10 Vict., Ch. 86).

S. 8. And be it enacted that no obligation, contract, agreement, assignment, deed, conveyance, or other instrument whatever, taken or made to or by the said Commissioners for the execution of the said Act of the first and second years of the reign of His late Majesty King William the Fourth, for the extension and promotion of public works in Ireland, or any of the Acts amending the same, nor any affidavit, deposition, certificate, order, or receipt to be respectively taken or made under or by virtue of the said last mentioned Acts, or any of them, shall be liable to any stamp duty whatever, anything in any Act or Acts in force in Ireland to the contrary in anywise notwithstanding (9 & 10 Vict, Ch 101)

S. 47. And be it enacted that no bond or other security given to the Commissioners under this Act, and no certificate or other instrument made under this Act, shall be chargeable with any stamp duty

Review of Justices' Decisions Act, 1872 (35 & 36 Vict., Ch. 26).

S. 2. Whenever the decision of any Justice or Justices is called in question in any Superior Court of Common Law by a rule to show cause or other process issued upon an *ex parte* application, it shall be lawful for any such Justice to make and file in such Court an affidavit setting forth the grounds of the decision so brought under review, and any facts which he may consider to have a material bearing upon the question at issue. without being required to pay any fee in respect of filing such affidavit, or any stamp duty thereupon, and such affidavit may be sworn before a commissioner authorised to take oaths in Chancery, and may be forwarded by post to one of the Masters of the Court for the purpose of being so filed

Rules of the Supreme Court. Order XXXIV. (6).

The parties to a special case may, if they think fit, enter into an agreement in writing, which shall not be subject to any stamp duty, that on the judgment of the Court being given in the affirmative or negative of the questions of law raised by the special case, a sum of money fixed by the parties, or to be ascertained by the Court, or in such manner as the Court may direct, shall be paid by one of the parties to the other of them either with or without costs of the cause or matter.

Savings Banks Annuities Act (16 & 17 Vict., Ch. 46).

S. 29. No stamp duty whatever shall be paid or payable upon or in respect of any copy register of birth or baptism, or marriage or burial, or upon or in respect of any certificate of the payment of money for the purchase of an annuity or sum payable at death under this Act, or any power of or declaration to be made or taken in pursuance of this Act, or any certificate or other instrument whatsoever respecting attorney authorising the receipt, or any receipt for the payment of any such annuity or any part thereof, or for the payment of any sum of money payable at death

Savings Bank Consolidation Act (26 & 27 Vict., Ch. 87).

S. 50. No power, warrant, or letter of attorney granted to or to be granted by any person or persons, or trustee or trustees of any savings bank as aforesaid, nor any power, warrant, or letter of attorney given by any depositor or depositors in the funds of any such savings bank to any person or persons authorising him, her, or them to make any deposit or deposits of any sum or sums of money in the said funds on behalf of the said depositor or depositors, or to sign any document or instrument required, by the rules or regulations of such savings bank, to be signed on making such deposits, or to receive back any sum or sums of money deposited in the said funds, or the dividends or interest arising therefrom, nor any receipt nor any entry in any book of receipt for money deposited in the funds of any such savings bank, nor for any money received by any depositor, his or her executors or administrators, assigns or attorneys from the funds of such savings bank, nor any draft or order, nor any appointment of any agent or agents, nor any certificate or other instrument for the revocation of any such appointment, nor any surety bond, nor any submission to, or award, order, or determination of the said barrister, nor any other instrument or document whatever, required or authorised to be given, issued, signed, made, or produced in pursuance of this Act, shall be subject or liable to or charged with any stamp duty or duties whatsoever

Scotch Savings Banks.

Provisions of 59 Geo III, Ch 62, to continue in force as to all savings banks established before the passing of 26 & 27 Vict, Ch 87 (28th July, 1863), unless and until they shall conform to and be established under the provisions of that Act

Taxes Management Act, 1880 (43 & 44 Vict., Ch. 19).

S. 78. No bond or other security given under this Act by a collector or other person in respect of the collection, accounting for, or remitting of the land tax or the duties shall be liable to stamp duty

Telegraph Act (32 & 33 Vict., Ch. 73).

S. 22. No deed or other instrument which shall be made or executed by, to, or with Her Majesty's Postmaster-General, or otherwise, for any of the purposes of The Telegraph Act, 1868, or of this Act, shall be subject or liable to any stamp duty imposed by any Act now in force, nor to any stamp duty to be imposed by any future Act, unless such instruments be specially subjected to and specifically charged therewith by any future Act, and the fifth section of The Telegraph Act, 1868, shall be read and shall operate as if the words "duly stamped" had not been inserted therein

Tithe Commutation Acts.
6 & 7 Will. IV., Ch. 71.

S. 91. No agreement, award, or power of attorney made or confirmed or used under this Act shall be chargeable with any stamp duty

1 Vict., Ch. 69.

S. 12. No deed or declaration authorised by the said Act (6 & 7 Will IV, Ch 71) for the commutation, release, or merger of tithes shall be chargeable with any stamp duty

1 & 2 Vict., Ch. 64.

S. 2. No deed or declaration authorised by this Act for the merging of tithes shall be chargeable with any stamp duty

Voting Papers.

Voting papers used at the Parliamentary Election of the Universities —

OXFORD CAMBRIDGE DUBLIN	24 & 25 Vict., Ch. 53, Sec. 6.
LONDON	30 & 31 Vict., Ch. 102, Sec. 45.
EDINBURGH ST ANDREW'S GLASGOW ABERDEEN	31 & 32 Vict., Ch. 48, Sec. 39 (4).

Weights and Measures Act, 1878
(41 & 42 Vict., Ch. 19).

29 & 30 Vict., Ch. 82, *repealed*

S. 37. Indentures evidencing verification of local standards and indorsements upon such indentures or new indentures evidencing re-verification

Woods and Forests.
(10 Geo. IV., Ch. 50, continued by 14 & 15 Vict., Ch. 42, Sec. 2.)

S. 77. And be it further enacted that no memorandum, contract, or agreement to be made or entered into, by or with the Commissioners for the time being of His Majesty's Woods, Forests, and Land Revenues, under the powers and provisions of this Act, for the sale, purchase, or exchange of any estates, manors, lordships, messuages, lands, tenements, rents or hereditaments, or any term or interest therein, by the said Commissioners of His Majesty's Woods, Forests, and Land Revenues, nor any deed, receipt, or other instrument which shall be given, granted, entered into, executed or made for the purpose of carrying into effect any sale, purchase or exchange to be made by the said Commissioners of His Majesty's Woods, Forests, and Land Revenues under the powers and authorities of this Act, or which shall be incidental to or connected with any such purchase, sale or exchange, nor any grant by the said Commissioners under the authority of this Act, nor any lease or contract or agreement for any lease or leases, nor any counterpart of any lease to be entered into, made, executed or granted under the powers and authorities of this Act, nor any appointment of officers to be made by the said Commissioners under the authority hereof; nor any certificate for any gamekeeper appointed or to be appointed under the authority of this Act, nor any bond to be given by or for any receiver, as hereinafter mentioned, or by or for any other officer or agent, from or for whom security may be required by the said Commissioners, shall be subject or liable to any ad valorem or other stamp duty whatsoever imposed by any Act or Acts now in force, nor to any ad valorem or other stamp duty to be imposed by any future Act or Acts, unless the same be specially subjected thereto in and by such future Act or Acts

This exemption is extended to foreshore under the management of the Board of Trade by The Crown Lands Act, 1866 (29 & 30 Vict., Ch. 62, Sec 10)

8 & 9 Vict., Ch. 99.

S. 5. Licence or waiver of any forfeiture or power of re entry reserved in any lease heretofore granted, or hereafter to be granted, of the possessions or land revenues of the Crown

The provisions of the above section are applied by Section 2 of 15 & 16 Vict., Ch. 62, to any licence or waiver granted under the authority of that Act

TABLE OF STATUTES
in the foregoing Appendix.

	PAGE
BANKRUPTCY ACT (ENGLAND & WALES), 1883 (46 & 47 Vict., Ch 52, Sec 144)	242
BANKRUPTCY ACT (SCOTLAND), 1856 (19 & 20 Vict, Ch. 79, Sec 184)	243
BANKRUPTCY ACT (IRELAND), 1857 (20 & 21 Vict, Ch. 60, Sec. 400)	243
BARRACKS ACT, 1890 (53 & 54 Vict, Ch 25, Sec 11)	244
BUILDING SOCIETIES ACT, 1874 (37 & 38 Vict., Ch 42, Sec 41)	244
CARRIERS ACT (11 Geo IV & 1 Will IV, Ch. 68, Sec 3)	245
CESSIO BONORUM ACT (6 & 7 Will. IV, Ch 56, Sec. 20)	245
CHURCH BUILDING ACT (ENGLAND) (3 Geo IV, Ch. 72, Sec. 28)	245
CHURCH BUILDING ACT (SCOTLAND) (5 Geo IV, Ch 90, Sec. 10)	246
COMMON LAW PROCEDURE ACT, 1854 (17 & 18 Vict, Ch. 125, Sec 30)	246
COMMON LAW PROCEDURE AMENDMENT ACT (IRELAND), 1856 (19 & 20 Vict., Ch 102, Sec 36)	246
COMPANIES (COLONIAL REGISTERS) ACT, 1883 (46 & 47 Vict, Ch 30, Sec 7)	246
CONSECRATION OF CHURCHYARDS ACT, 1867 (30 & 31 Vict, Ch 133, Sec 6)	246
CONTAGIOUS DISEASES (ANIMALS) ACT, 1878 (41 & 42 Vict., Ch 56, Sec. 83)	247
COPYHOLD ACT, 1894 (57 & 58 Vict Ch 46), Sec 58	247
COPYRIGHT ACT (5 & 6 Vict, Ch 45, Sec 3)	247
COUNTY TREASURERS ACT (IRELAND) (1 & 2 Vict, Ch 53, Sec. 1)	247
CROWN LANDS ACT, 1866 (29 & 30 Vict., Ch 62, Sec 10)	262
CUSTOMS AND INLAND REVENUE ACT, 1889 (52 Vict, Ch 7, Sec 13)	247
DISPENSARY HOUSES (IRELAND) ACT, 1879 (42 & 43 Vict, Ch 25, Sec 14)	247
DRAINAGE ACT (9 & 10 Vict, Ch 101, Sec 47)	248
EAST INDIA LOAN ACT, 1893 (56 & 57 Vict, Ch 70, Sec 16)	248
EDUCATION (SCOTLAND) ACT, 1872 (35 & 36 Vict, Ch 62, Sec 39)	248

	PAGE
FRIENDLY SOCIETIES ACT, 1875 (38 & 39 Vict., Ch 60, Sec 15)	248
GLEBE LOANS (IRELAND) ACT, 1870 (33 & 34 Vict, Ch 112, Sec 8)	248
HACKNEY AND STAGE CARRIAGES (METROPOLITAN) ACT (6 & 7 Vict, Ch 86, Sec 23)	249
INCLOSURE ACT (8 & 9 Vict, Ch 118, Sec 163)	249
INCOME TAX ACT (5 & 6 Vict, Ch 35, Sec 179)	249
INDIAN PRIZE MONEY ACT (29 & 30 Vict, Ch 47, Sec 8)	249
LANDED PROPERTY (IRELAND) ACT, 1847 (10 & 11 Vict., Ch 32, Sec 59)	250
LAND TAX CONSOLIDATION AND AMENDMENT ACT (42 Geo III., Ch 116, Secs 68 and 81)	250
LAND TAX CONSOLIDATION AND AMENDMENT ACT (45 Geo III, Ch 7, Secs 1, 107, and 173)	250
LOAN SOCIETIES ACT (ENGLAND) (3 & 4 Vict, Ch 110, Secs 9, 12, and 14)	251
LOAN SOCIETIES ACT (IRELAND) (6 & 7 Vict., Ch 91, Sec 26)	251
LOCAL LOANS ACT, 1875 (38 & 39 Vict, Ch 83, Sec 19)	251
LORD TENTERDEN'S ACT (9 Geo IV, Ch 14, Sec 5)	252
MERCHANT SHIPPING ACT, 1894 (57 & 58 Vict., Ch. 60, Secs 108, 196, 309, 320, 342, 395, 563, 721	252
METROPOLITAN BOARD OF WORKS LOAN ACT (33 & 34 Vict, Ch 24, Sec. 5)	253
MILITARY FORCES LOCALISATION ACT 1872 (35 & 36 Vict, Ch 68, Sec 12)	253
MILITIA LAW AMENDMENT ACT, 1854 (ENGLAND AND WALES) (17 & 18 Vict, Ch. 105, Sec 20)	253
MUNICIPAL CORPORATIONS ACT (ENGLAND AND WALES) (5 & 6 Will IV, Ch 76, Sec 22)	253
NATIONAL DEBT REDEMPTION ACT, 1893 (56 & 57 Vict., Ch 64, Sec 4	254
NAVAL AGENCY AND DISTRIBUTION ACT (27 & 28 Vict., Ch 24, Secs 15 and 16)	254
NAVAL AND MARINE PAY AND PENSIONS ACT (28 & 29 Vict, Ch 73, Sec 6)	254
PAROCHIAL CLERGY RESIDENCES ACT (17 Geo III, Ch 53, Sec 15)	254
PAROCHIAL STIPENDS (SCOTLAND) ACT (50 Geo III., Ch 84, Sec. 22)	254
PAWNBROKERS ACT, 1872 (35 & 36 Vict, Ch 93, Secs 15 and 24)	255
PENSIONS AND YEOMANRY PAY ACT, 1884 (47 & 48 Vict, Ch 55, Sec 5)	255
POOR LAW ACT (ENGLAND AND WALES) (4 & 5 Will IV, Ch 76, Secs 86 and 87)	255

	PAGE
POOR LAW ACT (ENGLAND AND WALES) (7 & 8 Vict, Ch. 101, Sec 61)	256
POOR LAW ACT (SCOTLAND) (8 & 9 Vict, Ch. 83, Sec 22)	256
POOR LAW ACT (IRELAND) (1 & 2 Vict., Ch. 56, Sec 96)	256
POST OFFICE LAND ACT, 1881 (44 & 45 Vict., Ch. 20, Sec. 5)	257
POST OFFICE ORDERS ACT (3 & 4 Vict., Ch 96, Sec 38)	257
POST OFFICE (MONEY ORDERS) ACT, 1880 (43 & 44 Vict, Ch. 33, Sec 1)	257
PUBLIC HEALTH (SCOTLAND) ACT (30 & 31 Vict., Ch. 101, Sec 130)	258
PUBLIC WORKS ACT (IRELAND) (9 & 10 Vict., Ch 86, Secs 8 and 47)	258
REVIEW OF JUSTICES' DECISIONS ACT, 1872 (35 & 36 Vict., Ch. 26, Sec. 2)	258
RULES OF THE SUPREME COURT, ORDER XXXIV. (6)	259
SAVINGS BANKS ANNUITIES ACT (16 & 17 Vict, Ch 46, Sec. 29)	259
SAVINGS BANK CONSOLIDATION ACT (26 & 27 Vict., Ch. 87, Sec. 50)	259
SCOTCH SAVINGS BANKS	260
TAXES MANAGEMENT ACT, 1880 (43 & 44 Vict., Ch 19, Sec 78)	260
TELEGRAPH ACT (32 & 33 Vict., Ch. 73, Sec 22)	260
TITHE COMMUTATION ACTS (6 & 7 Will. IV., Ch. 71, Sec 91, 1 Vict., Ch. 69, Sec 12, and 1 & 2 Vict., Ch. 64, Sec. 2)	260
VOTING PAPERS (UNIVERSITIES) ACTS	261
WEIGHTS AND MEASURES ACT, 1878 (41 & 42 Vict., Ch. 19, Sec 37)	261
WOODS AND FORESTS ACTS (10 Geo IV, Ch. 50, Sec. 77; 8 & 9 Vict, Ch 99, Sec. 5, 14 & 15 Vict., Ch. 42, Sec. 2, 8 & 9 Vict, Ch 99; 15 & 16 Vict, Ch. 62, and 29 & 30 Vict., Ch 62, Sec 10)	261

DUTIES IMPOSED BY ACTS NOT OTHERWISE RELATING TO STAMP DUTIES.

	£ s d.
ARTICLES OF ASSOCIATION of a Company under The Companies Act, 1862 (25 & 26 Vict., Ch 89, Sec. 11) to be stamped as a deed	0 10 0
CERTIFICATE of DISTRICT AUDITOR. See **District Auditors Act, 1879.**	
CERTIFICATE of Incorporation under The Charitable Trustees Incorporation Act, 1872 (35 & 36 Vict., Ch 34, Secs 6 and 9)	0 10 0
CERTIFICATE of Registration of—	
(1) An alkali work	5 0 0
(2) Work required to be registered not being an alkali work	3 0 0
Alkali, &c, Works Regulation Act, 1881 (44 & 45 Vict, Ch 27, Sec. 11)	
DEEDS of ARRANGEMENT ACT, 1887 (50 & 51 Vict, Ch 57)	
Upon every deed of arrangement registered under the provisions of this Act	
For every £100 and fractional part of £100, computed as below (Section 6 [2])	0 1 0

S. 4 (2) A deed of arrangement, to which this Act applies, shall include any of the following instruments, whether under seal or not, made by, for, or in respect of the affairs of a debtor for the benefit of his creditors generally (otherwise than in pursuance of the law for the time being in force relating to bankruptcy), that is to say—

(a) An assignment of property;
(b) A deed of or agreement for a composition;

and in cases where creditors of a debtor obtain any control over his property or business—

(c) A deed of inspectorship entered into for the purpose of carrying on or winding up the business;

(d) A letter of licence authorising the debtor or any other person to manage, carry on, realise, or dispose of a business, with a view to the payment of debts; and

(e) Any agreement or instrument entered into for the purpose of carrying on or winding up the debtor's business, or authorising the debtor or any other person to manage, carry on, realise, or dispose of the debtor's business, with a view to the payment of his debts

S. 6 (2) No deed shall be registered under this Act unless the original of such deed, duly stamped with the proper inland revenue duty, and in addition to such duty a stamp denoting a duty computed at the rate of one shilling for every hundred pounds or fraction of a hundred pounds of the sworn value of the property passing, or, where no property passes under the deed, the amount of composition payable under the deed, is produced to the Registrar at the time of such registration.

The "proper inland revenue duty" is usually—

(1) Upon any instrument which contains a covenant or undertaking of the debtor with creditors or trustees for the payment of a composition, ad valorem duty (under the head "Mortgage," or "Bond, Covenant, or Instrument of any kind whatsoever") upon the amount of composition to be paid under the terms of the instrument.

	£ s. d.
(2) Upon an instrument under seal not containing such a covenant	0 10 0
(3) An instrument under hand not falling under (1)	0 0 6

But the forms of deeds of arrangement are so various that it is impossible to lay down a general rule

In ascertaining the "value of the property passing" the amount of debts secured by mortgages or other charges upon the property is deducted from the total gross value

DISTRICT AUDITORS ACT, 1879
(42 Vict, Ch 6, Sch 1)

(Upon the certificates of the District Auditor appointed by the Local Government Board, on the financial statement submitted to him by the local authority, the following stamp duties are payable)

Where the total of the expenditure comprised in the financial statement is—	£	s	d
Under £20	0	5	0
20 and under £50	0	10	0
50 ,, ,, 100	1	0	0
100 ,, ,, 500	2	0	0
500 ,, ,, 1,000	3	0	0
1,000 ,, ,, 2,500	4	0	0
2,500 ,, ,, 5,000	5	0	0
5,000 ,, ,, 10,000	10	0	0
10,000 ,, ,, 20,000	15	0	0
20,000 ,, ,, 50,000	20	0	0
50,000 ,, ,, 100,000	30	0	0
100,000 and upwards	50	0	0

For the audit of the accounts of the County Councils (*see* Local Government Act, 1888, 51 & 52 Vict, Ch. 41, Schedule) the above rates are thus extended —

	£	s	d
£100,000 and under £150,000	50	0	0
150,000 ,, ,, 200,000	60	0	0
200,000 and upwards, for every £50,000 or part thereof in addition	15	0	0

For the purposes of this Schedule the expenditure comprised in the financial statement shall be exclusive of any sum paid to another local authority in pursuance of a precept

	£ s. d.
LICENCE to keep a Retreat under The Habitual Drunkards Act, 1879 (42 & 43 Vict., Ch 19, Sec 14)—	
Upon every licence	5 0 0
And for every patient above ten whom it is intended to admit into the retreat	0 10 0

A licence is not to be granted for a period exceeding thirteen months (Section 6), and every renewal of a licence is to be impressed with a stamp of the same amount (Section 14).

LICENCE or Renewed Licence.—A house under 53 Vict., Ch 5 (The Lunacy Act, 1890)	0 10 0
MEMORANDUM OF ASSOCIATION of a company under The Companies Act, 1862 (25 & 26 Vict., Ch 89, Sec 11), to be stamped as a deed	0 10 0
NOTICE TO QUIT to be served on a tenant of a holding in Ireland, 33 & 34 Vict, Ch 46 (Irish Land Act), Sec 57	0 2 6

Charles v. Hill, 26 L R., Ir 603

EXAMPLE OF ASSESSMENT OF SETTLEMENT DUTY.

PARTIES
- A.—Husband's Father.
- B and C.—Wife's Parents
- D.—Husband.
- E.—Wife
- F and G.—Trustees

HUSBAND'S FUND

		£ s. d.	£ s. d.
£3,000 Consols at 97½	£2,925 0 0		
Other Stocks and Shares at prices of the day	3,618 0 0		
		6,543 0 0	
Life Policy for £1,000, dated 1883, covenant to pay premiums Bonus £73		1,073 0 0	
Covenant to insure for another £1,000 within three months, and pay premiums		1,000 0 0	
Policy for £1,000 on life of Smith, which was purchased by D in 1884. No covenant to keep up the same Surrender value at date of settlement		208 0 0	
Covenant by A for executors and administrators to pay £8,000 to trustees within six months after death		8,000 0 0	
Covenant by A to pay during life an annuity of	£400 0 0		
Deduct 4 per cent on £8,000 (Sec 105)	320 0 0		
	£80 0 0		

Proceeds of sale of leaseholds and furniture assigned to trustees by deed of even date

WIFE'S FUND.
(She is one of five children.)

Equal one-fifth or other share in fund, subject to trusts of parents' marriage settlement in absolute reversion, expectant upon decease of survivor of parents, who have the life interest therein

		£ s d
Value of stocks, &c., as if in possession, in which fund is invested at prices of the day	£6,248 0 0	
Policy on father's life included in settlement and bonus	1,053 0 0	
	£7,301 0 0	
One-fifth thereof		1,460 0 0

"Or other share" will bind any further sum that the wife may derive from the fund by the death of a brother or sister during infancy, but this is contingent, and not chargeable with ad valorem duty

Equal fifth share of another fund settled by a will, but subject to a power of appointment not yet exercised among children, parents having the life interest

Value of stocks, &c., as before, in which the fund is invested	£7,320 0 0	
One-fifth thereof		1,464 0 0

Appointment by B and C in execution of a power of one-fifth of £5,000 settled in trust for the children who she shall be living at the decease of survivor of them *

Contingent, charged with ad valorem duty   1,000 0 0

Appointment by B and C, in execution of a power, of E's one-fifth or other interest in fund settled by will of an uncle in trust for for his son (living, aged 18) when he shall attain the age of 21. Gift over in the event of his death during infancy, to children of B and C as they shall appoint

Contingent, not charged with ad valorem duty, but chargeable as "appointment in execution of a power with 10s"

---

* Before the decision in Onslow v. Commissioners, this would not have been included in the aggregate for ad valorem duty. Duty would have been assessed as "appointment in execution of a power 10s."

272 ASSESSMENT OF SETTLEMENT DUTY.

			£	s	d
Covenant of B and C to pay amount of £600 per annum during joint lives, and life of survivor		£600 0 0			
Deduct 4 per cent (Sec 10) on	£1,460 0 0 1,464 0 0 1,000 0 0				
	£3,924 0 0	157 0 0			
		£443 0 0	443	0	0

Covenant to settle other and after-acquired property, except property of value of £200.

On inquiry it is found that there is no other property to which she is now entitled within the terms of the covenant

The duties chargeable are—

		£	s	d
Ad valorem settlement duty at 5s per £100 on	£6,548 0 0 1,073 0 0 1,000 0 0 208 0 0 8,000 0 0 1,460 0 0 1,464 0 0 1,000 0 0			
	£20,788 0 0 =	52	0	0
Ad valorem covenant duty at 2s 6d for every £5 on	£80 annuity =	2	0	0
Ad valorem covenant duty at 2s 6d. for every £5 on £443 „	=	11	2	6
Appointment in execution of a power		0	10	0
And for other matter		0	10	0

Observe that one ten-shilling stamp covers the settlement as to all property not charged with ad valorem duty or appointed, and that the duties on the covenants are separately charged

DEATH DUTIES.

The Death Duties where the deceased died before the 2nd day of August, 1894, were—

1. **PROBATE AND ADMINISTRATION DUTIES,**
2. **ACCOUNT DUTY,**
3. **LEGACY DUTY,**
4. **SUCCESSION DUTY,**
5. **ESTATE DUTY,**

according to the Tables contained in the following pages

Following these Tables will be found the new Duties imposed by The Finance Act, 1894

1. PROBATE AND ADMINISTRATION DUTIES.

SCALE of STAMP DUTIES payable under Sec. 27 of the Act 44 Vict., Ch. 12, upon Affidavits for Probate or Letters of Administration in England or Ireland, or on the Inventory to be exhibited in Scotland.

Where the estate and effects for which the probate or letters of administration are to be granted, or whereof the inventory is to be exhibited, shall be above the value of £100 and not above £500 — At the rate of one pound for every full sum of £50, and for any fractional part of £50 over any multiple of £50.

Where such estate and effects shall be above the value of £500 and not above £1000 — At the rate of £1 5s for every full sum of £50, and for any fractional part of £50 over any multiple of £50.

Where such estate and effects shall be above the value of £1000 — At the rate of £3 for every full sum of £100, and for any fractional part of £100 over any multiple of £100.

Section 28 gives power to deduct debts and funeral expenses where deceased died domiciled in the United Kingdom.

Interest or other profits (whether actually received or not) apportioned to the date of the affidavit must be added.

2. ACCOUNT DUTY.

SCALE of STAMP DUTIES payable on Accounts under Sec. 38 of the Act 44 Vict., Ch. 12, as amended by Sec. 11 of the Act 52 Vict., Ch. 7.

Where the personal or moveable property included in an account is above the value of £100 and not above £500 — At the rate of one pound for every full sum of £50, and for any fractional part of £50 over any multiple of £50.

Where such personal and moveable property shall be above the value of £500 and not above £1000 ... — At the rate of £1 5s. for every full sum of £50, and for any fractional part of £50 over any multiple of £50.

Where such personal and moveable property shall be above the value of £1000 — At the rate of £3 for every full sum of £100, and for any fractional part of £100 over any multiple of £100.

3. LEGACY DUTY.

RATES of DUTY payable on LEGACIES, ANNUITIES, and RESIDUES by Statute 55 Geo. III., Ch. 184, and 51 Vict., Ch. 8.

NOTE.—If the deceased died on or after the 1st June, 1881, every pecuniary legacy or residue or share of residue, although not of the amount or value of £20, is chargeable by the Act 44 Vict., Ch. 12, Sec. 42.

	On real estate, if the deceased died *before* 1st July, 1888, and on personal estate	On apportioned value of real estate where deceased died on or *after* 1st July, 1888.
Children of the deceased, and their descendants, or the Father or Mother, or any lineal ancestor of the deceased, or the Husbands or Wives of any such persons	£1 per cent.	£1 10s per cent
Brothers and Sisters of the deceased, and their descendants, or the Husbands or Wives of any such persons	£3 ,,	£4 10s ,,
Brothers and Sisters of the Father or Mother of the deceased, and their descendants, or the Husbands or Wives of any such persons	£5 ,,	£6 10s ,,
Brothers and Sisters of a Grandfather or Grandmother of the deceased, and their descendants, or the Husbands or Wives of any such persons	£6 ,,	£7 10s ,,
Any person in any other degree of collateral consanguinity, or strangers in blood to the deceased	£10 ,,	£11 10s ,,

Persons otherwise chargeable with duty at the rate of £1 per cent. are exempt in respect of any legacy, residue, or share of residue payable out of or consisting of any estate or effects according to the value whereof duty shall have been paid on the affidavit or inventory, in conformity with the Act 44 Vict., Ch. 12

The husband or wife of the deceased is not subject to the duties on legacies, annuities, and residues

Relations of the husband or wife of the deceased are chargeable with duty at the rate of £10 per cent or £11 10s per cent, as the case may be, unless themselves related in blood to the deceased.

4. SUCCESSION DUTY.

Rates of Duty imposed by 16 & 17 Vict., Ch. 51, and 51 Vict., Ch. 8.

	Where the deceased died *before* the 1st July, 1888.	Where the deceased died *on or after* the 1st July, 1888.
Lineal issue or lineal ancestor of the predecessor	£1 per cent.	£1 10s. per cent.
Brothers and Sisters of the predecessor and their descendants	£3 ,,	£4 10s ,,
Brothers and Sisters of the Father or Mother of the predecessor and their descendants	£5 ,,	£6 10s ,,
Brothers and Sisters of a Grandfather or Grandmother of the predecessor and their descendants	£6 ,,	£7 10s ,,
Persons of more remote consanguinity or strangers in blood	£10 ,,	£11 10s. ,,

NOTE.—The higher rates are not payable upon the interest of a successor in leaseholds passing to him by will or devolution by law, or in property included in an account according to the value whereof duty is payable under The Customs and Inland Revenue Act, 1881 (44 Vict., Ch. 12)

Successors in leaseholds for years who would otherwise be chargeable with duty at the rate of £1 per cent. are exempt when the value of such leaseholds has been included in the affidavit or inventory, and duty has been paid thereon in conformity with the Act 44 Vict, Ch. 12

The husband or wife of the predecessor is not chargeable with duty, and a successor whose husband or wife is of nearer relationship to the predecessor is chargeable with duty at the rate at which such husband or wife would be chargeable. Relations of the husband or wife of the predecessor are chargeable with duty at £10 per cent. or £11 10s. per cent as the case may be, unless themselves related in blood to the predecessor

Interest at the rate of four per cent. per annum is chargeable upon all legacy and succession duty in arrear under the provisions of the Act 31 & 32 Vict., Ch. 124, Sec 9

5. ESTATE DUTY.

(Called Temporary Estate Duty in The Finance Act, 1894.)

Rates of Duty imposed by 52 Vict., Ch. 7, Part II.

Where personal estate passing under will or intestacy exceeds £10,000; or Where the value of the personal or moveable property included in an account delivered under the 27th Section of 44 Vict, Ch 12, exceeds £10,000; or Where the value of any succession, upon the death of any person dying after 1st June, 1889, exceeds £10,000 in value, or Where the value of any succession to real property, with any other benefit taken by the successor under the same will or intestacy, exceeds £10,000	A duty of £1 for every full sum of £100, and for any fraction of £100 over any multiple of £100 of such value.

DEATH DUTIES
Where the Deceased died on or after the 2nd day of August, 1894.

Section 1 of The Finance Act, 1894 (57 & 58 Vict., Ch. 30), Part I., imposes the new Estate Duty, and enacts that certain existing duties shall cease to be levied.

Grant of Estate Duty.

1. In the case of every person dying after the commencement of this Part of this Act, there shall, save as hereinafter expressly provided, be levied and paid, upon the principal value ascertained as as hereinafter provided of all property, real or personal, settled or not settled, which passes on the death of such person, a duty, called "Estate Duty," at the graduated rates hereinafter mentioned, and the existing duties mentioned in the First Schedule to this Act shall not be levied in respect of property chargeable with such Estate Duty. *[Grant of Estate Duty.]*

The date of the commencement of the Act is the 2nd day of August, 1894.

The First Schedule is as follows:—

FIRST SCHEDULE

EXISTING DUTIES REFERRED TO.

1. The stamp duties imposed by the Customs and Inland Revenue Act, 1881, on the affidavit to be required and received from the person applying for probate or letters of administration in England or Ireland, or on the inventory to be exhibited and recorded in Scotland. *[Probate and Administration Duties. 44 & 45 Vic. c. 12.]*

|||

Account Duty.
52 & 53 Vic. c. 7.

2. The stamp duties imposed by Section 38 of the Customs and Inland Revenue Act, 1881, as amended and extended by Section 11 of the Customs and Inland Revenue Act, 1889, on the value of personal or moveable property to be included in accounts thereby directed to be delivered.

Additional Succession Duties of 10s. per cent. for lineals and £1 10s per cent in all other cases.
51 & 52 Vic. c. 8.

3. The Additional Succession Duties imposed by Section 21 of the Customs and Inland Revenue Act, 1888.

Estate Duty

4. The Temporary Estate Duties imposed by Sections 5 and 6 of the Customs and Inland Revenue Act, 1889.

Legacy and Succession Duty of £1 per cent

5. The duty at the rate of one pound per cent. which would by virtue of the Acts in force relating to legacy duty or succession duty have been payable under the will or intestacy of the deceased, or under his disposition or any devolution from him under which respectively Estate Duty has been paid, or under any other disposition under which Estate Duty has been paid.

The Duties no longer charged are—

Probate and Administration Duties.

Account Duty.

Additional Succession Duties of 10s. per cent. for lineals, and £1 10s. per cent. in all other cases. (See p. 278.)

Temporary Estate Duty. (See p. 289.)

Legacy and Succession Duties of £1 per cent. where the New Estate Duty is paid.

The Duties now charged are—

1. **ESTATE DUTY.**
2. **LEGACY DUTY.**
3. **SUCCESSION DUTY.**

1. ESTATE DUTY.

SCALE of ESTATE DUTY under 57 & 58 Vict., Ch. 30, Section 17.

Where the Principal Value of the Estate		Estate Duty shall be payable at the Rate per cent of
£	£	
Exceeds 100	and does not exceed 500	£1 0s.
,, 500	1,000	£2 0s.
,, 1,000	10,000	£3 0s.
,, 10,000	25,000	£4 0s.
,, 25,000	50,000	£4 10s.
,, 50,000	75,000	£5 0s.
,, 75,000	100,000	£5 10s.
,, 100,000	150,000	£6 0s.
,, 150,000	250,000	£6 10s.
,, 250,000	500,000	£7 0s.
,, 500,000	1,000,000	£7 10s.
,, 1,000,000	- - - -	£8 0s.

In addition to these duties, **Settlement Estate Duty** at the rate of one per cent is charged upon settled property, by Section 5, which is as follows:—

5. (1) Where property in respect of which Estate Duty is leviable is settled by the will of the deceased, or having been settled by some other disposition passes under that disposition on

Settled Property.

the death of the deceased to some person not competent to dispose of the property,—

(a) A further Estate Duty (called Settlement Estate Duty) on the principal value of the settled property shall be levied at the rate hereinafter specified [*One per cent*, *Section* 17), except where the only life interest in the property after the death of the deceased is that of a wife or husband of the deceased; but

(b) During the continuance of the settlement the Settlement Estate Duty shall not be payable more than once

Foreign Property —Property passing on the death of the deceased, when situate out of the United Kingdom, is to be included in the aggregate for Estate Duty only if, under the law in force before the passing of the Act, Legacy or Succession Duty is payable in respect thereof, or would be so payable but for the relationship of the person to whom it passes

British Possessions —Section 20 of the Act may be applied by Order in Council to any British possession, and where the Commissioners of Inland Revenue are satisfied that in such British possession duty is payable by reason of a death in respect of any property situate in such possession, and passing by such death, they shall allow a sum equal to the amount of that duty to be deducted from the Estate Duty payable in respect of that property on the same death.

Small Estates —When the gross value of the estate, real and personal, in respect of which Estate Duty is payable on the death of the deceased does not exceed £300, the fixed duty is £1 10s.; and where the gross value exceeds £300, and does not exceed £500, the fixed duty is £2 10s (Section 16)

Allowances.—In determining the value of an estate for the purpose of Estate Duty, allowance is made for reasonable funeral expenses, and for debts and incumbrances

Interest—Interest at the rate of three per cent. per annum is to be paid from the date of the death up to the delivery of the Inland Revenue affidavit or account, or the expiration of six months after the death, whichever first happens, and is to form part of the Estate Duty.

Exemptions.

Estate Duty is not payable (Section 15) in respect of—

1. A single annuity not exceeding £25 purchased or provided by the deceased, either by himself alone or in concert or arrangement with any other person, for the life of himself and of some other person and the survivor of them, or to arise on his own death in favour of some other person.

2. Any such pictures, prints, books, manuscripts, works of art, or scientific collections, as appear to the Treasury to be of national, scientific, or historic interest, and to be given or bequeathed for national purposes, or to any university or to any county council or municipal corporation.

3. Any pension or annuity payable by the Goverment of British India to the widow or child of any deceased officer of such Government

4. Any advowson or church patronage which would have been free from succession duty under Section 24 of the Succession Duty Act, 1853.

2. LEGACY DUTY.

RATES of **DUTY** payable on **LEGACIES, ANNUITIES,** and **RESIDUES,** by Statute 55 Geo. III., Ch. 184, whether real or personal.

Children of the deceased, and their descendants, or the Father or Mother, or any lineal ancestor of the deceased, or the Husbands or Wives of any such persons	£1 per cent.
Brothers and Sisters of the deceased, and their descendants, or the Husbands or Wives of any such persons	£3 ,,
Brothers and Sisters of the Father or Mother of the deceased, and their descendants, or the Husbands or Wives of any such persons	£5 ,,
Brothers and Sisters of a Grandfather or Grandmother of the deceased, and their descendants, or the Husbands or Wives of any such persons	£6 ,,
Any person in any other degree of collateral consanguinity, or strangers in blood to the deceased	£10 ,,

The Legacy Duty at the rate of **one per cent.** is now payable only where the property is not liable to Estate Duty, or the Estate Duty has been returned.

The husband or wife of the deceased is not subject to the duties on legacies, annuities, and residues.

Relations of the husband or wife of the deceased are chargeable with duty at the rate of £10 per cent unless themselves related in blood to the deceased

3. SUCCESSION DUTY.

RATES of DUTY imposed by 16 & 17 Vict., Ch. 51.

Lineal issue or lineal ancestor of the predecessor £1 per cent.

Brothers and Sisters of the predecessor and their descendants . . . . £3 „

Brothers and Sisters of the Father or Mother of the predecessor and their descendants ... £5 „

Brothers and Sisters of a Grandfather or Grandmother of the predecessor and their descendants . . . . £6 „

Persons of more remote consanguinity or strangers in blood . . £10 „

The value for the purpose of Succession Duty of a succession to real property arising on the death of a deceased person shall, when the successor is competent to dispose of the property, be the principal value of the property after deducting the Estate Duty payable in respect thereof on the said death, and the expenses, if properly incurred, of raising and paying the same

The Succession Duty at the rate of **one per cent.** is now payable only where the property is not liable to Estate Duty, or the Estate Duty has been returned

The husband or wife of the predecessor is not chargeable with duty, and a successor whose husband or wife is of nearer relationship to the predecessor is chargeable with duty at the rate at which such husband or wife would be chargeable Relations of the husband or wife of the predecessor are chargeable with duty at £10 per cent unless themselves related in blood to the predecessor.

Interest at the rate of four per cent. per annum is chargeable upon all legacy and succession duty in arrear under the provisions of the Act 31 & 32 Vict., Ch. 124, Section 9

EXCISE LICENCES.

	Annual Duty.	Date of Expiration.
Appraisers (may act as house agents without further licence) . (8 & 9 *Vict.*, *Ch.* 76.)	2 0 0	July 5
Armorial Bearings, *see* **Establishment.**		
Auctioneers (may act as appraisers and house agents without further licence) (8 & 9 *Vict.*, *Ch.* 15)	10 0 0	July 5.

Exemptions under 8 & 9 Vict., Ch. 15, *Sec. 4.*

 Persons selling goods seized under a distress for nonpayment of rent or tithes to a less amount than £20

 Persons selling goods seized under the Acts for recovery of small debts specified in this section where the sum for which the process is enforced is under £20

By 33 & 34 Vict., Ch 32, no auctioneer's licence is required to sell fish by auction *upon the sea shore* where first landed.

The Commissioners allow sales by auction to be held by unlicensed persons in the following cases.—

 Sales by officers of ordnance under proper authority

 Sales of public stores by officers of the Admiralty.

 Sales by officers of the Court of Chancery under the order of the Court

 Sales of seizures by officers of customs or inland revenue

 Sales of the effects of deserters or of officers or soldiers dying in H. M. service by non-commissioned officers and soldiers under proper authority.

EXCISE LICENCES.

	Annual Duty.	Date of Expiration.
Sales of property for the benefit of the Crown by receivers and deputy receivers of wrecks appointed under The Merchant Shipping Act, 1894, and employed officially		
The letting of tolls to farm by the trustees or their clerks		
The letting of lands or any interest therein.		
Sales by ticket of mineral ore		
Beer (includes Cider and Perry)—		
Dealer (selling in quantities amounting to 4½ gallons, or equal to two dozen reputed quarts) (6 Geo IV, Ch 81; 3 & 4 Vict. Ch. 17)	3 6 1	July 5, Gt. B. Oct. 10, Ireland
Fairclough v Roberts, 54 J. P. 421.		
Dealers, additional or retail (i e, for sale in quantities less than above, not to be consumed on the premises) (26 & 27 Vict, Ch. 33; 43 & 44 Vict., Ch. 20)	1 5 0	July 5, Gt. B Oct. 10, Ireland.
Retailer (to be consumed on the premises), England (6 Geo IV, Ch. 81, 3 & 4 Vict., Ch. 17, 43 & 44 Vict, Ch. 20)	3 10 0	Oct. 10
Retailer (to be consumed off the premises), England (43 & 44 Vict, Ch 20)	1 5 0	Oct 10.
Retailer (Ireland) (6 Geo IV., Ch 81, 3 & 4 Vict., Ch 17; 43 & 44 Vict, Ch. 20)	3 10 0	Oct. 10.
Retailer (to be consumed on the premises), Scotland	3 10 0	May 15
Retailer (to be consumed off the premises), Scotland—		
Under £10	2 10 0	May 15.
£10 and upwards	4 4 0	May 15.
Retailer of Table Beer at a price not exceeding 1½d. per quart (24 & 25 Vict., Ch 21.)	0 5 0	July 5.

EXCISE LICENCES.

	Annual Duty.	Date of Expiration.
Retailers of Beer and Wine (to be consumed on the premises), United Kingdom	4 0 0	July 5
Retailers of Beer and Wine (not to be consumed on the premises), United Kingdom (43 & 44 Vict., Ch. 20.)	3 0 0	July 5.
Occasional Licences, for every day, not exceeding three days at one time (27 & 28 Vict., Ch. 18.)	0 1 0	
Brewers, vis.— Brewers brewing Beer for sale (43 & 44 Vict., Ch 20.) Howarth v. Minns, 51 J. P. 7.	1 0 0	Sept. 30.
Other Brewers,— *Not chargeable with Beer Duty.* Occupying houses exceeding the annual value of £8, but not exceeding £10	0 4 0	Sept. 30
Occupying houses exceeding £10, but not exceeding £15	0 9 0	Sept. 30.
Chargeable with Beer Duty. Farmers occupying houses exceeding the annual value of £10, brewing beer to give their labourers; and other persons occupying houses exceeding the annual value of £15 (43 & 44 Vict, Ch 20, 44 & 45 Vict., Ch 12, 48 & 49 Vict., Ch. 51.)	0 4 0	Sept. 30.
Exempt from Licence and Duty. Occupiers of houses of annual value not exceeding £8, brewing solely for their own domestic use. (49 & 50 Vict., Ch. 18, Sec 8.)		
Cards, see **Playing Cards**.		
Cider and Perry Retailer (to be consumed on or off the premises) (3 & 4 Vict., Ch 17; 43 & 44 Vict., Ch 20)	1 5 0	Oct 10.
Distillers, see **Spirits**.		

	Annual Duty.	Date of Expiration.

Dogs, licence to keep (Great Britain), for each dog
(30 & 31 *Vict.*, *Ch.* 5; 41 & 42 *Vict.*, *Ch.* 15.)
    Campbell *v* Strangeways, 3 L R., C P Div 105, 42 J. P 39
    James *v* Nicholas, 50 J. P 292.
	0 7 6	Dec 31.

Exemptions.

1. A shepherd, for one or two dogs used solely in his calling
2. A farmer, for one or two dogs used solely in tending sheep or cattle on his farm.
3. An occupier of land owning sheep feeding on unenclosed land, for three dogs if he has 400 sheep, four dogs if he has 1,000, and one additional dog for every 500 sheep over 1,000, for tending such sheep, but in no case more than eight dogs.

    A declaration must be made and a certificate of exemption obtained from the supervisor, in each of the above cases

4. A blind person, for one dog used for his or her guidance
5. A master of a pack of hounds, for young hounds up to the age of twelve months, and not entered in, or used with, a pack
6. All dogs less than six months old

    N B.—The use of a dog by a farmer or shepherd in taking rabbits or game will disentitle him to exemption
    Butchers and drovers who occupy land for their trade are not entitled to exemption

Establishment (Great Britain)
    (32 & 33 *Vict.*, *Ch.* 14, 51 & 52 *Vict.*, *Ch* 8

Exemptions from return and duty

1. Members of the Royal Family.
2. The sheriff of any county, or the

	Annual Duty.	Date of Expiration.

mayor or other officer in any corporation or royal burgh, serving an annual office therein, in respect of any servants or carriages kept by him for the purposes of his office during his year of service

3. Persons wearing by right of office any of the arms or insignia of members of the Royal Family, or of any corporation or royal burgh, in respect of the use of such arms or insignia.

4. Any person ordinarily residing in Ireland, and being a representative Peer for Ireland, or a member of the House of Commons, and not residing in Great Britain longer than during the Session of Parliament and forty days before and forty days after the Session; or any person ordinarily residing in Ireland, but residing in Great Britain by order of the Lord Lieutenant for the time being or of his chief secretary, for the purpose of public business, in respect of any servants, carriages, or armorial bearings employed, kept, or used by him, except in respect of any subject matter of duty which shall be employed or used by such person in Great Britain during his residence in Ireland

Armorial Bearings (if on carriage)	2 2 0	Dec 31.
Ditto (otherwise worn or used)	1 1 0	Dec 33

Exemptions

The proprietors of public stage carriages or hackney carriages licensed by local authority, in respect of any armorial bearings

	Annual Duty.	Date of Expiration.

marked thereon, or on the harness used therewith

The Commissioners of Inland Revenue do not require licences to be taken out in the following cases:—

1. By any shopkeeper in respect of the use of armorial bearings or devices, solely as trade marks, and in the course of trade.

2. By any municipal or other corporation, or any public company, in respect of the use of their corporate armorial bearings, or by any person using the armorial bearings of such a corporation or company by right of office

3. By any officer or member of a club, or society, using at the club, or on the business of the society, any armorial bearings for the use of which such club, or society, have taken out a licence

Carriages, viz —

	Annual Duty	Date of Expiration
Hackney carriages	0 15 0	Dec. 31.
All other carriages, i e. —		
With four or more wheels, and fitted to be drawn by two or more horses or mules, or by mechanical power	2 2 0	Dec 31.
With four or more wheels, and fitted to be drawn by one horse or mule only	1 1 0	Dec 31
With less than four wheels	0 15 0	Dec 31.

Half the foregoing rates charged on licences taken out between 1st October and 31st December

Barber v Callow, 41 J. P 823
Whitrow v Brown, 8 *Times* L R. 75, 56 J P. 374

	Annual Duty	Date of Expiration
Exemptions.		
1. Farm waggons or farm carts, duly inscribed, used on Sunday, Christmas Day, Good Friday, or any day of public fast or thanksgiving, to take the owner or his family to or from any place of divine worship (35 & 36 *Vict.*, *Ch.* 20.)		
2. Any carriage used without payment for the conveyance of electors to or from the poll at Municipal, County Council, and Parliamentary elections, and not otherwise used during the year (46 & 47 *Vict.*, *Ch.* 51, *Sec* 14.)		
3. Waggon, cart, or other such vehicle, which is constructed or adapted for use and is used *solely* for the conveyance of any goods or burden in the course of trade or husbandry, and which is inscribed as required with the Christian name, surname, and place of abode or business of the person keeping the same as required by the Act (51 *Vict.*, *Ch.* 8, *Sec.* 4.)		
The Commissioners of Inland Revenue do not require licences to be taken out for the following vehicles:—		
1 Carriages kept but not used at any time within the year.		
2 Horsebreakers' breaks, duly inscribed as required by the Act, and not adapted for ordinary use as a conveyance		
Hearses, if duly inscribed as required by the Act, and not used as, or forming part of, mourning coaches		

	Annual Duty.	Date of Expiration
4 Mail carts used under contract with the Post Office, and so made as not to carry any passenger		
5 Farm or trade carts lent to carry passengers (not the owner or his family) gratuitously on special occasions or holidays		
The licence for a carriage let for a period less than a year is to be taken out by the lettor, for a year or a longer period, by the hirer		
Male Servants ..	0 15 0	Dec. 31.

Exemptions under 32 & 33 Vict., Ch. 14.

Licences are not required in the following cases:—

By any officer in Her Majesty's army or navy for any servant employed by such officer in accordance with the regulations of Her Majesty's service.

By any person licensed by proper authority to keep or use any public stage or hackney carriage, for any servant necessarily employed by him to drive such carriage, or in the care of such carriage, or of the horses kept and used by him to draw the same

By any livery stable keeper, or person who keeps horses for hire, or for drawing any public stage or hackney carriage, for any servant employed by him in his business at his trade premises, where such person shall have made entry and complied with Sec 28 of 32 & 33 Vict, Ch 14, but duty must be paid for every servant em-

	Annual Duty.	Date of Expiration.

ployed to drive a carriage with any horse let for hire for any period exceeding 28 days

By any hotel-keeper, retailer of intoxicating liquor, or refreshment house-keeper, for any servant wholly employed by him for the purpose of his business

(36 & 37 Vict., Ch 18, Sec. 4.)

For a servant who, being *bonâ fide* employed in any capacity other than the capacities specified or referred to in Section 19 (3) of the Act 32 & 33 Vict., Ch. 14, is occasionally or partially employed in any of the said capacities, and for a person who has been *bonâ fide* engaged to serve his employer for a portion only of each day, and does not reside in his employer's house.
(39 Vict., Ch. 16, Sec 5)

NOTE — The Commissioners of Inland Revenue do not consider licences necessary for the following persons —

Game watchers who do not carry guns nor act as gamekeepers, attendants upon lunatics in asylums, labourers in gardens doing only spade labour and paid ordinary labourer's wages, sons while living with their parents and not receiving wages, grooms in public racing stables employed solely in taking care of racehorses.

The term "male servant" does not include a servant who, being *bonâ fide* employed in some other capacity, is occasionally

	Annual Duty	Date of Expiration.
or partially employed in any of the said duties, nor does it include a person *bonâ fide* engaged to serve for a portion only of each day, and who does not reside in his employer's house.		
But this does not exempt any servant chiefly employed in a taxable capacity		
Yelland *v* Vincent, 47 J P 230		
Yelland *v.* Winter, 50 J P 38		
Schulze *v* Steele, 54 J. P. 282		
Game, to kill.—		
If taken out after 31st July and before 1st November, to expire on the 31st July in the following year	3 0 0	July 31.
To expire on the 31st day of October in the same year in which taken out	2 0 0	Oct 31.
If taken out on or after 1st November, to expire on the 31st July following	2 0 0	July 31.
For a continuous period of fourteen days	1 0 0	
Gamekeepers in Ireland—same rates as foregoing		
Gamekeepers in Great Britain (23 & 24 *Vict.*, *Ch* 90, 46 & 47 *Vict.*, *Ch* 10)	2 0 0	July 31.

Exceptions and Exemptions under 23 & 24 Vict., Ch. 90, Sec 5

Exceptions.

1 The taking of woodcocks and snipe with nets or springes in Great Britain

2 The taking or destroying of conies in Great Britain by the proprietor of any warren or of any inclosed ground whatever, or

	Annual Duty.	Date of Expiration.

by the tenant of lands, either by himself or by his direction or permission.

3. The pursuing and killing of hares respectively, by coursing with greyhounds, or by hunting with beagles or other hounds.

4. The pursuing and killing of deer by hunting with hounds

5 The taking and killing of deer in any enclosed lands by the owner or occupier of such lands, or by his direction or permission

Exemptions

1. Any of the Royal Family

2. Any person appointed a gamekeeper on behalf of Her Majesty by the Commissioners of Her Majesty's woods, forests, and land revenues under the authority of any Act relating to the land revenues of the Crown

3 Any person aiding or assisting in the taking, &c., of any game, &c., in the company or presence, and for the use of another person, who shall have obtained in his own right a proper licence to kill game, and who shall by virtue of such licence then and there use his own dog, gun, &c., for the taking, &c., of such game, &c , and who shall not act therein by virtue of any deputation or appointment *See* Lewis *v* Taylor, 16 East 49.

4. As regards the killing of hares only, all persons who, under 11 & 12 Vict , Ch 29 & 30, are authorized to kill hares in England and Scotland respectively without obtaining an annual

	Annual Duty.	Date of Expiration
game certificate And *see* 40 & 41 Vict., Ch. 28, Sec. 4		
No licence or certificate is required to authorise the taking or killing of rabbits in Ireland (23 & 24 Vict., Ch 113, Sec. 43)		
The occupier of land, and the persons duly authorised by him as therein mentioned, are not required to obtain a licence to kill ground game (*i e* hares and rabbits), and he has the same power to sell as if he had a licence (43 & 44 Vict, Ch 47, Sec 4)		
Game, British or Foreign (to deal in), United Kingdom (23 & 24 Vict., Ch 90, 46 & 47 Vict, Ch 10, 56 Vict, Ch 7, Sec 2) Loome v Bailey, 3 L. T Rep. (N S) 406 Harnett v Miles, 48 J P. 455 Guyer v Reg, 59 J P. 436	2 0 0	July 1.
Gun (to use or carry), United Kingdom (33 & 34 Vict, Ch 57) Asquith v Griffin, 48 J P. 724.	0 10 0	July 31.

Exemptions

The penalty shall not be incurred by the following persons, viz —

1. By any person in the naval, military, or volunteer service of Her Majesty, or in the constabulary or other police force, using or carrying any gun in the performance of his duty, or when engaged in target practice
2. By any person holding an excise game licence or certificate
3. By any person carrying a gun by order of, for the use of, and

EXCISE LICENCES 301

	Annual Duty.	Date of Expiration.
belonging to a person having in force a game licence or certificate or gun licence, if the person carrying the gun shall, upon the request of any officer of Inland Revenue or constabulary, or any constable, owner or occupier of the land on which such gun shall be used or carried, give his true name and address and also the true name and address of his employer.		
By the occupier of any lands using or carrying a gun for the purpose only of scaring birds, or of killing vermin on such lands, or by any person using or carrying a gun for the purpose only of scaring birds, or of killing vermin on any lands, by order of the occupier thereof, who shall have in force a game or gun licence		
5 By any gunsmith or his servant carrying a gun in the ordinary course of the trade of a gunsmith, or using a gun by way of testing or regulating its strength or quality in a place specially set apart for the purpose.		
6 By any person carrying a gun in the ordinary course of his trade or business as a common carrier		
7. By any person using or carrying a gun in a dwelling-house or the curtilage thereof		
Hawker (United Kingdom) (51 & 52 Vict., Ch. 33.) Hudson v Shooter (55 J P 325)	2 0 0	March 31.

	Annual Duty.	Date of Expiration.

Exemptions (Licence unnecessary).

(a) By any person selling or seeking orders for goods, wares, or merchandise, to or from persons who are dealers therein, and who buy to sell again.

(b) By the real worker or maker of any goods, wares, or merchandise, and his children, apprentices, and servants, usually residing in the same house with him, selling or seeking orders for goods, wares, or merchandise made by such real worker or maker

(c) By any person selling fish, fruit, victuals, or coal.

(d) By any person selling or exposing for sale goods, wares, or merchandise in any public mart, market, or fair, legally established.

> This exemption does not free such person from compliance with local bye-laws Openshaw v Oakley, 53 J P. 740

House Agents — letting furnished houses at an annual rent exceeding £25 (may also act as Appraisers without further licence) .   2 0 0   July 5.
(24 & 25 Vic, Ch 21)

Medicines, *see* **Patent Medicines.**

Methylated Spirit Makers, *see* **Spirits.**

Methylated Spirit Retailers, *see* **Spirits.**

	Annual Duty.	Date of Expiration.
Passenger Vessels or Packet Boats on board which liquors or tobacco are sold	5 0 0	March 31
Passenger Vessels or Packet Boats on board which liquors or tobacco are sold, for one day only . .. (43 & 44 Vict, Ch 20.)	1 0 0	
Patent Medicine Vendors (Great Britain) . . (38 & 39 Vict., Ch 28)	0 5 0	Sept. 1.
Exemption from excise licence duty depends upon the question whether the article is chargeable with medicine stamp duty. (See "Handy Book of Medicine Stamp Duty," published by *The Chemist and Druggist*, 42 Cannon Street, E C.) Attorney-General v. Lamplough, 3 Ex. Div (C A.) 214 Smith v. Mason & Co., Ld [1894], 2 Q. B. 303, 58 J. P. 342		
Pawnbrokers (5 & 6 Vict, Ch 82) (17 & 18 Vict, Ch 83, Sec. 20 (I.) Reg. v Commissioners of Inland Revenue ; ex parte Garland, 7 Times L R. 121, ex parte Ohlson, 55 J. P. 117 *Exemption.* Loans above £10.	7 10 0	July 31.
Plate Dealers— Persons who trade in any article composed wholly or in part of gold or		

	Annual Duty.	Date of Expiration
silver, in respect of every house, &c., in which the business is carried on		
Where the gold is above 2 dwts and under 2 oz., or the silver is above 5 dwts and under 30 oz	2 6 0	July 5
Where the gold is 2 oz or upwards, or the silver is 30 oz or upwards	5 15 0	July 5
Hawkers' plate licence, same rates as above		
Pawnbrokers' plate licence	5 15 0	July 5
Refiners' plate licence	5 15 0	July 5

(30 & 31 Vict., Ch 90.)

Young v Cook, 41 J P. 824, 3 Ex. Div 101.

Exemptions

No licence is required for trading in gold or silver lace, or gold or silver wire, thread, or fringe.

(30 & 31 Vict., Ch 90, Sec. 4.)

Nor for the sale of watchcases by the maker.

(33 & 34 Vict., Ch. 32, Sec. 4.)

Playing Cards—Makers of	1 0 0	Sept. 1.

(25 & 26 Vict., Ch. 22.)

Refreshment House—

If the house and premises be under the rent or value of £30 a year	0 10 6	March 31.
If the rent or value be £30 or upwards	1 1 0	March 31

(23 & 24 Vict., Ch. 27,
23 & 24 Vict., Ch. 107 (I),
24 & 25 Vict., Ch 91).

Taylor v Oram, 10 W. R 800, 1 H. & C. 370, 31 L. J., M C, 252

Muir v. Keay, 23 W R 700, 44 L J, M C., 143, 10 Q. B 594

Howes v Inland Revenue, 24 W R 407 & 897; 45 L. J., M C, 86, 1 Ex Div. 385

Kelleway v McDougal, 45 J P 207

Spirits—

	Annual Duty.	Date of Expiration.
Distillers	10 10 0	Oct. 10.
Rectifiers	10 10 0	Oct. 10.
Dealers, not retailers	10 10 0	July 5
Dealers to retail foreign liquors (additional)	2 2 0	July 5
Dealers to retail spirits not less than a quart bottle (additional)	3 3 0	July 5
Methylated, makers of	10 10 0	Sept. 30
Methylated, retailers of	0 10 0	Sept 30
Retailers of spirits (publicans), including the right to sell beer, cider, perry, wine, and sweets, whose premises are rated under £10 per annum (United Kingdom)	4 10 0	England & Ireland Oct 10 Scotland May 15.
At £10 and under £15	6 0 0	
15 ,, 20	8 0 0	
20 ,, 25	11 0 0	
25 ,, 30	14 0 0	
30 ,, 40	17 0 0	
40 ,, 50	20 0 0	
50 ,, 100	25 0 0	
100 ,, 200	30 0 0	
200 ,, 300	35 0 0	
300 ,, 400	40 0 0	
400 ,, 500	45 0 0	
500 ,, 600	50 0 0	
600 ,, 700	55 0 0	
700 or upwards	60 0 0	

	Annual Duty.			Date of Expiration
Hotels and theatres of the value of £50 and upwards are liable to no higher amount of licence duty than	20	0	0	
Restaurants, under certain conditions, are liable to no higher amount of licence duty than	30	0	0	
Retailers of spirits and beer (grocers) in Scotland, whose premises are rated under £10 per annum	4	4	0	May 15.
At £10 and under £20	5	5	0	
20 ,, 25	9	9	0	
25 ,, 30	10	10	0	
30 ,, 40	11	11	0	
40 ,, 50	12	12	0	
50 or upwards	13	13	0	
Retailers of spirits (grocers) in Ireland, whose premises are rated under £25 per annum	9	18	5	Oct. 10.
At £25 and under £30	11	0	6	
30 ,, 40	12	2	6	
40 ,, 50	13	4	7	
50 or upwards	14	6	7	
Victualler's occasional, for every day not exceeding six	0	2	6	
Additional occasional licence for any further time not exceeding six days, 2s. 6d, per day; but duty for such additional licence shall not exceed 10s.				
(6 *Geo IV*, *Ch.* 81; 3 & 4 *Vict*, *Ch* 17, 24 & 25 *Vict*, *Ch.* 21, 27 & 28 *Vict*, *Ch* 18, 43 & 44 *Vict.*, *Ch.* 20)				
Stills and Retorts	0	10	0	Oct. 10.
(9 & 10 *Vict*, *Ch.* 90)				

EXCISE LICENCES.

	Annual Duty	Date of Expiration.
Sweets and made Wines—		
Dealers in	5 5 0	July 5
Retailers of	1 5 0	July 5
(6 Geo. IV., Ch. 81; 23 & 24 Vict., Ch. 113; 43 & 44 Vict., Ch. 20.)		
Richards v. Banks & Preston, 52 J. P. 28.		
Tobacco and Snuff—		
Manufacturers, not exceeding 20,000 lbs.	5 5 0	July 5.
Exceeding 20,000 lbs., and not exceeding 40,000 lbs.	10 10 0	
Exceeding 40,000 lbs., and not exceeding 60,000 lbs.	15 15 0	
Exceeding 60,000 lbs., and not exceeding 80,000 lbs.	21 0 0	
Exceeding 80,000 lbs., and not exceeding 100,000 lbs.	26 5 0	
Exceeding 100,000 lbs.	31 10 0	
Beginners	5 5 0 (and a surcharge).	
Dealers	0 5 3	July 5
Dealers Occasional licences for every day, not exceeding three days at one time	0 0 4	
(6 Geo IV., Ch 81; 3 & 4 Vict, Ch. 17.)		
Vinegar Makers	1 0 0	July 5.
(6 Geo. IV, Ch 81, 3 & 4 Vict., Ch 17; 52 & 53 Vict., Ch. 7.)		
Wine—		
Dealers in foreign wine, not having licences to retail spirits	10 10 0	July 5
Retailers selling wine to be consumed on the premises	3 10 0	March 31.

	Annual Duty	Date of expiration.
Retailers selling wine not to be consumed on the premises (England and Ireland)	2 10 0	March 31.
Grocers who sell wine not to be drunk or consumed on the premises in Scotland, having the Justices' Certificate to retail beer or spirits	2 4 1	May 15.
Occasional licences, for every day, not exceeding three days at one time	0 1 0	

(6 *Geo* IV, *Ch* 81, 3 & 4 *Vict.*, *Ch* 17, 39 & 40 *Vict.*, *Ch* 16, 43 & 44 *Vict.*, *Ch* 20)

Richards *v* Banks & Preston, 52 J P 23

Index.

	PAGE
ABSTRACT FOR ADJUDICATION	29
ACCESSORY OBJECT. (See "INSTRUMENT")	3
ACCOUNT DUTY, SCALE OF	275
ACKNOWLEDGMENT OF DEBT (See "AGREEMENT")	55, 56
ADHESIVE STAMPS (See "STAMPS")	
ADJUDICATION	27, 32
Commissioners may be required to assess duty	27
except on security without limit, &c	28
procedure on assessment	29
abstract to be furnished	29
contents of abstracts	30
Commissioners may call for evidence	28
effect of adjudication stamp	28
adjudication *ultra vires*	2, 29
instrument must be stamped in accordance with assessment	28
appeal against assessment	30
procedure and costs	30, 32
ADMINISTRATION BONDS	89
ADMINISTRATION DUTIES, SCALE OF	274
ADMISSIBILITY OF INSTRUMENTS IN EVIDENCE (See "INSTRUMENT")	
ADMISSION	44, 50
as Advocate, Barrister-at-Law, &c	44
as Fellow of the College of Physicians	46
as Doctor of Medicine in Scotland	47
as Burgess in England or Ireland	47
to ecclesiastical benefices exempt	48
to an office or employment exempt	48
how duty to be denoted	49
fine	50
ADMITTANCE TO COPYHOLD	127
AFFIDAVIT OR STATUTORY DECLARATION	50
exemptions	50, 51
"required by law"	50
for purposes of Companies Clauses Consolidation Act, 1845, Secs. 18 and 19	50
meaning of	50

	PAGE
AFFIDAVIT OR STATUTORY DECLARATION (*continued*)—	
on death of trustee, for transfer of stock held in trust	51
for purposes of Stamp Acts, before whom to be made	287
not to be used against person making for adjudication	29
voluntarily made for Commissioners	50
AGREEMENT UNDER HAND, accompanied with a deposit (*See* "MORTGAGE")	
for lease or tack (*See* "LEASE OR TACK")	
AGREEMENT FOR SALE OF PROPERTY (*See* "CONVEYANCE ON SALE")	
AGREEMENT UNDER HIGHWAY ACTS	52
AGREEMENT OR MEMORANDUM OF AGREEMENT UNDER HAND ONLY, or without clause of registration in Scotland	52, 61
exemptions	53
adhesive stamp may be used	53
how to be cancelled	53
must relate to a contract	53
signing immaterial	53
offer in writing	53, 60
memorandum required to satisfy Sec 4 of Statute of Frauds	54
memorandum required to satisfy Sec 17 of Statute of Frauds	59
guarantee	54, 58
independent memorandum of one party	54
contained in several letters	54
contained in separate instruments	54
I O U and acknowledgment of debt	55
receipt "in settlement of all claims"	56
attornment	56
cognovit	56
instrument described as "Policy"	2
acknowledgment of right to production of instruments	56
undertaking for safe custody of instruments	56
hire purchase	60
where value is under £5	56, 57
for hire of labourer, &c	57
menial servant	58
for sale of goods, wares, and merchandise	3, 58, 61
goods not yet completed	59
work and labour	59
growing crops	60
exemption under Lord Tenterden's Act	252
instrument of defeasance accompanied with deposit and securities transferable by delivery	61
relating to mortgage of registered stock or security	61

	PAGE
ALKALI WORK, CERTIFICATE OF REGISTRATION OF	267
ALLOTMENT. (*See* "LETTER OF ALLOTMENT.")	
ALLOWANCE FOR STAMPS (*See* "STAMPS")	
ALTERATION OF INSTRUMENT. (*See* "INSTRUMENT")	
ANNUITY. (*See* "CONVEYANCE," "MORTGAGE, &c.," "BOND, COVENANT, &c.," "SUPERANNUATION ANNUITY.")	
APPEAL AGAINST ASSESSMENT (*See* "ADJUDICATION")	
APPOINTMENT TO AN ECCLESIASTICAL BENEFICE, OR AN OFFICE OR EMPLOYMENT. (*See* "ADMISSION.")	
APPOINTMENT—	
in execution of a power	62
of a gamekeeper	134
of trustee under Settled Land Acts	62
" " Married Women's Property Act, 1882	63
of valuer under Lands Clauses Consolidation Act	124
OF A NEW TRUSTEE	63
interpretation of term	62
several appointments by one instrument	63
with conveyance, &c of trust property	63
at a meeting by resolution	63
conveyance made upon	123
(*See also* "DISCHARGE OF TRUSTEE")	
APPRAISEMENT OR VALUATION	63, 66
exemptions	64
for probate &c.	65
to be written on stamped paper	65
fine in default	65
definition of "Appraiser"	65
for Copyhold Commissioners	66
APPRAISER (*See* "APPRAISEMENT")	
APPRENTICESHIP	66
definition	66
exemptions	66
of certain persons to employment in colonies	203
APPROPRIATED STAMPS (*See* "STAMPS")	
ARMS, GRANT OF	140
ARRANGEMENT, DEED OF	266, 267
ARTICLES OF ASSOCIATION OF A COMPANY	268
ARTICLES OF CLERKSHIP	67, 68
renewed	69
penalties on stamping	42, 64, 68
service under unstamped articles not computed	68
in Ireland account of duty	68
ASSESSMENT OF DUTY (*See* "ADJUDICATION")	
ASSIGNMENT. (*See* "CONVEYANCE" and "MORTGAGE")	
ASSIGNMENT OF LIFE POLICY (*See* "CONVEYANCE")	

INDEX.

	PAGE
ASSURANCE OR INSURANCE. (*See* "POLICY.")	
ATTESTED COPY (*See* "COPY.")	
ATTORNEY, LETTER OR POWER OF. (*See* "LETTER OF ATTORNEY")	
ATTORNEY, WARRANT OF. (*See* "MORTGAGE.")	
ATTORNMENT—	
not liable to duty	56, 145
in a mortgage (*See* "MORTGAGE")	
AUXILIARY SECURITY (*See* "MORTGAGE, COLLATERAL, &c, SECURITY")	
AWARD OR DECREET ARBITRAL	69
difference between and appraisement	70
decision of an umpire not an award	70
arbitration under Common Law Procedure Act, 1854, exempt	70
BACK BOND (*See* "MORTGAGE")	
BANKER—	
definition	70
fine for issuing bank note not duly stamped	71
BANK NOTE	70, 71
definition	70
may be reissued without further duty	71
unstamped, fine	71
BANK OF ENGLAND STOCK, TRANSFER OF	100
BANKRUPTCY ACT, 1883—	
exemption	242
to what documents it applies	242, 243
BILL OF EXCHANGE PAYABLE ON DEMAND—	
rate of duty	71
duty may be denoted by adhesive stamp	22, 80
definition in Bills of Exchange Act, 1882	80
duty on, drawn abroad, how to be paid	80
certain orders for payment of money liable to duty as	75
fine for issuing, &c, unstamped	83
provision for stamping with adhesive stamp on presentation	83
BILL OF EXCHANGE AND PROMISSORY NOTE—	
rates of duty	72
stamps are appropriated stamps	26
cannot be stamped after execution	83
except when stamped with stamp of sufficient amount but improper denomination	83
penalty on stamping in such case	83
sum payable must be a "sum certain"	76, 78
definition of "sum certain"	76
interest bygone or future	76, 77
sum payable by instalments	79
fine for issuing or dealing with, &c, unstamped	82

INDEX.

	PAGE
BILL OF EXCHANGE AND PROMISSORY NOTE (*continued*)—	
purporting to be drawn abroad, to be so deemed	82
(*See* "BILL OF EXCHANGE PAYABLE ON DEMAND.")	
BILL OF EXCHANGE—	
exemptions of, for bankers and official purposes	72, 74
coupon attached to a security—	
upon issue or renewal thereof	74
not applicable to coupon attached to scrip certificate	74
definition of, for purposes of stamp duty	75
embraces definition in Bills of Exchange Act, 1882	76
order for payment of money, definition	77
difference between, and assignment of debt under Judicature Act	77
cheque is a bill of exchange	75, 77
post-dated	77
when stamp is *functus officio*—	
on ordinary bill	78
on accommodation bill	78
bills drawn in a set	84
(And *see* "BILL OF EXCHANGE PAYABLE ON DEMAND.")	
PROMISSORY NOTE—	
definition of, for purposes of stamp duty	78
considered in Court of Appeal	79
includes definition in Bills of Exchange Act, 1882	78
for payment from fund which may not be available	78
on a condition or contingency	78
examples of doubtful promissory notes	79, 80
may have coupons attached	80
many cases under old stamp laws misleading	80
incorrectly adjudicated as liable to duty as agreement	2, 29
memorandum endorsed upon, effect of	17
BILL OF EXCHANGE AND PROMISSORY NOTE drawn or made out of the United Kingdom—	
definition for purposes of stamp duty	82
differs from definition in Bills of Exchange Act, 1882	82
duties to be denoted by adhesive stamp	81
such stamps are appropriated stamps	81
when stamp to be affixed	81
proviso for protection of *bonâ fide* holder	81
bonâ fide holder may perfect cancellation of stamp	81
cancellation of stamp may be effected at any time	82
"present for payment," interpretation of	81
"presentment for acceptance" is not "negociation"	81
penalty for dealing with unstamped, how far applicable	83
meaning of "duly stamped," with relation to	84
drawn in a set	84
(*See* "BILL OF EXCHANGE PAYABLE ON DEMAND.")	

	PAGE
BILL OF LADING	84
not to be stamped after execution	84
fine	84
definition	85
does not extend to inland navigation	85
BILL OF SALE (See "CONVEYANCE" and "MORTGAGE")—	
original must be produced duly stamped on registering	85
(See "DEEDS OF ARRANGEMENT.")	
BOND (See "MORTGAGE," "MARKETABLE SECURITY," and "CONVEYANCE OR SALE" [Sec 75])	
BOND, COVENANT, OR INSTRUMENT—	
for securing an annuity or periodical payments	85, 88
interest on unsecured loan	87
annuities in settlements (See "SETTLEMENT")	
weekly sums	87
fine for not stamping with proper duty	40
BOND FOR PAYMENT OF EXCISE OR CUSTOMS DUTIES	88
BOND ON OBTAINING LETTERS OF ADMINISTRATION	89
BOND NOT SPECIFICALLY CHARGED	90
BOND ACCOMPANIED WITH DEPOSIT (See "MORTGAGE")	
BOOK DEBTS—	
agreement for sale of	16, 55, 119
(And see "CONVEYANCE")	
BOTTOMRY BOND EXEMPT	203
BUILDING SOCIETIES ACT, 1874—	
exemption	175
construction of	244
as to receipts	245
as to mortgages	244
as to reconveyance	245
CANADIAN STOCK (INSCRIBED), TRANSFER OF	100
on appointment of new trustees	123
CANCELLATION OF ADHESIVE STAMP (See "STAMP.")	
Case stated (See "ADJUDICATION")	
CAPITAL DUTY	204
CERTIFICATE—	
for obtaining drawbacks of customs	95
of births, deaths, and marriages. (See "COPY")	95
of district auditors (See "DISTRICT AUDITORS ACT, 1879.")	
of incorporation of charitable trustees	266
of registration of an alkali work	266
CERTIFICATE OF SOLICITORS, &c	90, 95
Law List, when not evidence	94
fine for practising without	92, 94
proceedings may be set aside	92

	PAGE
CERTIFICATE OF SOLICITORS, &c. (continued)—	
solicitor or officer of public department	92
fine for drawing instrument without	92
exceptions	92, 93
uncertificated solicitor cannot recover costs	93
"acting and practising" within ten miles radius	93
regulations as to taking out	94
CHARITABLE TRUSTEES—	
certificate of incorporation of	266
CHARITY. (See "APPRENTICESHIP.")	
CHARGING ORDER	170
CHARTER-PARTY	96
duty may be denoted by adhesive stamp	22, 96
partly executed out of the United Kingdom	96
wholly executed out of the United Kingdom	97
stamping after execution	96
CHARTER OF RESIGNATION, &c, IN SCOTLAND	95
CHEQUE (See "BILL OF EXCHANGE")—	
drawn by Friendly Society	248
CLARE CONSTAT	97
CLAUSE OF REGISTRATION IN SCOTLAND	50, 132
COLLATERAL SECURITY (See "MORTGAGE")	
COLONIAL GOVERNMENT SECURITY (See "MARKETABLE SECURITY")	
COLONIAL STOCK (INSCRIBED) TRANSER OF	100
on appointment of new trustees	123
COMMISSION—	
officers in the army, navy, and royal marines	97
COMMISSION (Scotland) (See "LETTER OF ATTORNEY" and "FACULTY")	
COMPANIES CAPITAL DUTY	204
companies constituted under Companies Acts	204
companies constituted otherwise	204
amount of nominal share capital	205
COMPANIES' CLAUSES CONSOLIDATION ACT, 1845—	
declaration made on transmission of an interest	50
COMPOSITION FOR STAMP DUTY ON—	
(1) transfers, share warrants, and stock certificates of county council, corporation, or company	205, 210
foreign stocks inscribed at Bank of England	206
agreement to be made with Commissioners	207
accounts	207
rules	213
fine for non-payment of composition	208
exemption upon payment of composition	207
(2) accident policies	209
rules	216

COMPOSITION FOR STAMP DUTY ON (*continued*)—	
(3) Canadian stock, transfers	205
(4) Colonial stock, transfers	205
CONDITIONAL SURRENDER (*See* "MORTGAGE")	
CONDITIONS OF SALE (*See* "CONVEYANCE.")	
CONGE D'ELIRE (*See* "GRANT")	
CONSIDERATION (*See* "INSTRUMENT," "CONVEYANCE," and "LEASE")	
CONSTAT OF LETTERS PATENT (*See* "EXEMPLIFICATION")	
CONSTRUCTION OF EXEMPTIONS	3, 13, 14, 15, 16, 244
CONSTRUCTION OF STAMP LAWS	1
effect of general regulations	16
special regulations	16
Stamp Acts are *in pari materiâ*	15
CONTINUATION NOTE (*See* "CONTRACT NOTE")	
CONTRACT (*See* "AGREEMENT")	
CONTRACT FOR SALE LIABLE TO CONVEYANCE DUTY (*See* "CONVEYANCE ON SALE")	
CONTRACT NOTE—	
definition	98, 99
rates of duty	98
by what stamps to be denoted	98, 99
cancellation	98, 99
separate duties for each sale and purchase	98
fines	98, 99
brokerage not recoverable unless note duly stamped	98, 99
when liable to duty as an agreement	99
continuation note	100
CONVEYANCE OR TRANSFER, WHETHER ON SALE OR OTHERWISE—	
Bank of England stock	100
Canadian stock or colonial stock inscribed	100
CONVEYANCE ON SALE	100, 122
applies to marketable securities	156
definition	101
fine and penalty for not stamping with proper duty	40
must be "on sale"	103
family arrangement not a sale	104
transfer of business from father to son	104
partition	104
division of partnership assets	113
surrender of lease	104
redemption of ground annual and feu duty	104
compulsory sale under Lands Clauses Consolidation Act	106
"property," definition of	104

INDEX 317

CONVEYANCE ON SALE (continued)— PAGE
    enfranchisement award under Copyhold Act, 1894 . . 102
    grant of right - 105
    licence to use patent &c. - 105
    goodwill - 105
    letters patent and trade marks - 105
    interest in partnership - 112, 113
    several conveyances in one instrument . . . 101, 108
    separate interests - 101, 105
    legal estate outstanding - 105
    community of interest 19
    in separate parcels - 114
    on sub-sale - 116
    creation of annuity or other right 121
    creation of superannuation annuity by one payment . 88
    several instruments of title - 114
    freeholds and copyholds sold together . . . 122
    covenant to surrender equitable estate in copyholds - 129
    contracts for sale of certain property to be charged as
        conveyances 116, 121
        what property excepted 116, 120
        sub-contract - 116
        subsequent conveyance 116
        example of assessment of duty on . . . 120
        made upon reconstruction of company . . 121
    consideration—
        duty must be paid on true consideration . . 105
        for all property passing by conveyance . . 106
        overriding rent charge or ground rent . . 106
        on premium in articles of partnership . . 107
        consideration not ascertained 107
        contingent consideration - 107
        apportionment of consideration . . . 114, 119
        stock or security, or marketable security . . 108
        periodical payments - 109
        annuity 109
        debt 110
        natural love and affection - 104
    subject to mortgage or other debt, or interest, or future
        payments 109, 111, 120
        mortgage to building society 112
        partnership liabilities 112, 113
        rent charges or annuities - 112
    in foreclosure action 112
    release of equity of redemption to mortgagee . . 112
    on dissolution of partnership - . . . 112, 113
    order for payment of money when chargeable as conveyance 107

	PAGE
CONVEYANCE ON SALE (continued)—	
of property abroad	34, 116
of bankrupt's estate	248
assignment of life policy must be stamped	210
otherwise duty and penalty to be a debt due to the Crown	211
practice thereon	211
conditions of sale as to stamp duty void	210
all deeds of title should be duly stamped	210
CONVEYANCE NOT ON SALE OR MORTGAGE	122
for nominal consideration	123
subject to mortgage	112
for effectuating appointment of new trustee	128
CONVEYANCER (See "CERTIFICATE.")	
CONVEYANCING ACT, 1881—	
Sec 6, what passes by conveyance	106
Sec 24, appointment of receiver	152
Sec 32, discharge of trustee	63
Sec 34, declaration vesting property in new trustee	63
Sec. 65, enlargement of long term	123
COPY (ATTESTED) OR EXTRACT	123
duty does not apply to examined copy	37, 125
COPY (CERTIFIED)—	
from Register of Births, Deaths, and Marriages	125
COPYHOLD ACT, 1894—	
certificate of charge	170
transfer thereof	170
enfranchisement award	102
COPYHOLDS, INSTRUMENTS RELATING THERETO (See "CONVEYANCE OF SALE," "MORTGAGE," and "LEASE")—	
upon any other occasion	126
rules to be observed by stewards, and fines	128, 128
COPYRIGHT—assignment of, exempt	247
COST BOOK MINES (See "TRANSFER")	
COUNTERPART. (See "DUPLICATE.")	
COUPON. (See "BILL OF EXCHANGE" and "POLICY.")	
COVENANT (See "MORTGAGE, &c.," "BOND, &c.," "CONVEYANCE," and "SUPERANNUATION ANNUITY.")—	
separate deed of covenant	129
COVENANT TO SURRENDER—	
equitable estate in copyhold on sale	129
containing mortgage clauses	129
CRIMINAL PROCEEDINGS—	
unstamped instrument admissible in all	33, 87
offences relating to stamps	230, 236
CROWN PROPERTY—instruments relating to	212
CUSTOMARY ESTATES. (See "COPYHOLDS")	

INDEX.

	PAGE
DEATH DUTIES where deceased died on or after 2nd August, 1894	281
DEBENTURE. (See "MORTGAGE" and "MARKETABLE SECURITY.")—	
trust deed for securing	165
renewal of, by endorsement	165
what is a debenture	170
when not a marketable security	173
for principal sum and bonus	170
for drawback or bounty	180
DECLARATION. (See "AFFIDAVIT.")	
DECLARATION OF USE OR TRUST	130
DECREET ARBITRAL (See "AWARD")	
DEED OF ARRANGEMENT	266, 267
DEED OF FURTHER ASSURANCE. (See "MORTGAGE.")	
DEED OPERATING AS A MORTGAGE OF STOCK. (See "MORTGAGE")	
DEED NOT SPECIALLY CHARGED	131
certain instruments under seal not deeds	131
clause of registration in Scotland	131
instrument under seal of company in England or Ireland	132
DEFEAZANCE, INSTRUMENT OF. (See "MORTGAGE" and "AGREEMENT.")	
DEFINITIONS AND INTERPRETATIONS—	
"amount of nominal share capital"	205
appraiser	65
"average rate"	142
bank note	70
banker	70
bill of exchange	75, 82
payable on demand	75, 80
bill of lading	85
cheque	77
Commissioners	213
Colonial Government security	160
contract note	98
conveyance on sale	101
"definite and certain"	169, 198
delivery order	132
die	238
"duly stamped"	23, 34, 84
for foreign bills and notes	86
equitable mortgage	163
"executed" and "execution"	213
foreign bill or note	78
foreign security	159
"goods, wares, and merchandise"	59, 61

	PAGE
DEFINITIONS AND INTERPRETATIONS (*continued*)—	
instrument	213
"issue" of a security	161
marketable security	100, 214
material	213
money	213
mortgage	167
negotiate	81
order for payment of money	77
policy of insurance	177
policy of insurance against accident	188
policy of insurance (life, &c.)	188
,, ,, (sea)	177
"present for payment"	81
promissory note	78, 82
property	104
public officer	43
receipt	187
sale	108
"stamp" and "stamped"	213
statutory declaration	50
steward	214
stock	213
sum certain	76
superannuation annuity	86
"transferable by delivery"	159
warrant for goods	201
DELIVERY DUTY. (*See* "MARKETABLE SECURITY")	
DELIVERY ORDER AND WARRANT FOR GOODS	132
adhesive stamp	133
by whom duty payable	133
definition	132
es	133
DENOTING STAMPS	27
regulations on applying for	27
DEPOSIT OF SECURITY TRANSFERABLE BY DELIVERY, INSTRUMENT RELATING TO. (*See* "AGREEMENT.")	
DEPOSIT OF TITLE DEED. (*See* "MORTGAGE.")	
DEPUTATION OR APPOINTMENT OF GAMEKEEPER	134
DISCHARGE OF TRUSTEE—	
instrument effecting	63
DISCLAIMER	3
DISPENSATION (*See* "FACULTY.")	
DISPOSITION IN SCOTLAND. (*See* "CONVEYANCE ON SALE" and "MORTGAGE")—	
not otherwise described	134

	PAGE
DISTRICT AUDITORS ACT, 1879—	
duty on certificate	268
DOCK WARRANT (See "Warrant for Goods")	
DOCKET	135
DRAFT FOR MONEY. (See "Bill of Exchange")	
DRAFTSMEN IN EQUITY (See "Certificate")	
DUPLICATE OR COUNTERPART	135
denoting stamp	135
not applicable to counterpart lease	135
"DULY STAMPED" meaning of	23, 34, 84
DUTY when a debt to the Crown	222
how recoverable	222
on capital of companies	204
EIK TO A REVERSION. (See "Mortgage")	
EQUITABLE MORTGAGE (See "Mortgage")	
ESCROW	42
ESTATE DUTY, TEMPORARY	280
grant of	281
table of	283
EVIDENCE, ADMISSIBILITY OF INSTRUMENTS (See "Instrument")	
EXCHANGE OR EXCAMBION	136
when consideration for equality exceeds £100	136
EXCISE LICENSES, TABLE OF	289
EXEMPLIFICATION OR CONSTAT	137
EXEMPLIFICATION of record or proceedings	137
EXEMPTIONS (See Table of, Appendix)	242, 265
general exemptions from all stamp duties	203
rule as to construction of	9, 15, 16
in statutes not Stamp Acts	242, 265
onus of proof on person claiming	16
EXTRACT (See "Copy")	
FACTORY (See "Letter of Attorney.")	
FACULTY—	
as notary public	137
relating to consecrated building, &c (licence)	153
of any other kind	137
(And see "Licence")	
FAMILY ARRANGEMENT. (See "Conveyance on Sale")	
FEU CONTRACT (See "Conveyance on Sale")	
FINE how to be recovered	212, 288
powers of Commissioners to mitigate	212
FIXTURES (See "Agreement," "Lease," and "Conveyance on Sale")	
FORECLOSURE (See "Conveyance on Sale")	

	PAGE
FOREIGN CURRENCY, HOW CHARGEABLE	21
FOREIGN PROPERTY—	
conveyance of	34
contract for sale of	116
FOREIGN SECURITY—	
definition	159
transfer of	156
penalty for issuing &c. not duly stamped	161
what is "issue"	161
may be stamped without penalty	161
former rates of duty	160
(And see "MARKETABLE SECURITY.")	
FOREIGN OR COLONIAL SHARE CERTIFICATE. (See "MARKETABLE SECURITY.")	
FOREIGN STATE—	
revenue laws of, not noticed here	35
FORGERY OF STAMPS	230, 236
FREIGHT OF SHIPS—	
instrument relating to, exempt	203
FRIENDLY SOCIETIES—	
exemption and cases	248, 249
FURTHER CHARGE OR FURTHER SECURITY (See "MORTGAGE")	
FURTHER VALUABLE CONSIDERATION. (See "INSTRUMENT")	
GAMEKEEPER—	
deputation or appointment of	134
GOODS, WARES, AND MERCHANDISE—	
instrument relating to sale of	58, 60, 116, 119, 120
GOODWILL—	
agreement for sale of	16, 55, 119
(And see "CONVEYANCE")	
GRANT OF AN OFFICE (See "ADMISSION")	
GRANT OF COPYHOLDS. (See "CONVEYANCE OF COPYHOLDS")	
GRANT OF CUSTODY OF A LUNATIC	140
GRANT OR LICENCE to take arms or use surname	140
GRANT OR WARRANT OF PRECEDENCE	140
GRANTS OF HONOURS AND DIGNITIES	138
GUARANTEE (See "AGREEMENT")	
HABITUAL DRUNKARDS ACT, 1879 (See "LICENCE.")	
HERITABLE BOND. (See "MORTGAGE")	
HIGHWAY ACTS—	
list of	52
agreement or contract under	52
under seal of County Council	52

	PAGE
ILLEGAL CONSIDERATION—	
instrument made for	37
INFORMER—	
power of Commissioners to reward	212
INSPECTION OF ROLLS, BOOKS &c.—	
power of Commissioners	43
INSTRUMENT—	
definition	213
includes "post letter" for Section 9	25
relating to Crown property	212
property situate abroad	32, 34, 116, 120
executed abroad to be acted on here	34
executed here to be acted on abroad	34, 35
must be stamped according to legal effect and intention	2
according to tenor	2
according to substance of the transaction	2
must be stamped for leading object	3
duty not affected by accessory matter	3
misdescription o instrument	2
expression of that which the law allows	4
exempt, not rendered liable by accessory matter	3
stamp to appear on face of instrument	17
several instruments on same material	17
relating to several distinct matters	18
examples	18
other examples—	
appointment of new trustee and conveyance	63
discharge of new trustee and conveyance	63
conveyance on sale, and other matter not incidental to conveyance	108
conveyance on sale, and acquisition of legal estate outstanding on stranger	108
conveyance in consideration of rentcharge, operating also as a substituted security	165
lease with option of purchase of other property	143
lease with contract for sale of fixtures	143
mortgage operating also as a conveyance and *vice versâ*	110, 173
settlement of money and after-acquired property	194, 270, 272
valuation of separate properties	65
further valuable consideration	18
duty payable on true consideration	105
facts affecting liability to be fully stated	20
fine in default	20
ascertainable by reference to another instrument	20
duty chargeable in respect of foreign currency	21
stock or marketable security	21

INSTRUMENT (*continued*)—

	PAGE
effect of statement of current rate of exchange or average price	21
duties to be denoted by impressed stamps except &c	16
stamping after execution, general provisions	38, 43
instruments executed abroad	42
subject to express provisions, list of	41
cases in which penalty is usually imposed	41
Commissioners may remit penalties	40
may return penalties	42
penalties for not stamping certain instruments within thirty days	39
list of such instruments, and persons liable to penalties	40
date of execution, what is	34, 42
alteration of date, requirements of Commissioners	42
escrow	42
payment of penalty to be denoted by a stamp	40
evidence—	
insufficiently stamped instrument may not be given in evidence	32, 38
except—	
in criminal proceedings	38
in penal proceedings	37
to prove fraud	37
to prove a collateral fact	37
an instrument made for an illegal consideration	37
a forged instrument	37
on payment of duty and penalty	32
unstamped transfer invalid	36
ruling of judge as to stamp duty, rule of Supreme Court	33
when such ruling is not final	33
objection to duty	34
duty of judge	34
as to examined copy	37
instrument lost or destroyed, rule	36
not produced on notice	37
obliterated stamp	37
alteration of instrument, when fresh stamp required	38
when made *in fieri*	38
registration of insufficiently stamped instrument, fine	43

(See also "STAMP")

I O U (See "AGREEMENT")

"ISSUE" OF A SECURITY — 161

LAW AGENT (SCOTLAND) (See "ADMISSION" and "CERTIFICATE")

		PAGE
LEASE		140, 148
from week to week or month to month		141
for rent and premium		141
release of a debt as premium		141
"of any kind whatsoever"		142
at will or for lives		142
what is "average rate" of rent		142
for rent reducible on punctual payment		143
for rent and gas or garden gate		143
for rent and royalty		143
for rent not stated but ascertainable		143
with option of purchase of property demised		3, 18, 143
other property		3, 18, 143
with surety for payment of rent		3, 143
with contract for sale of fixtures		3, 143
of hereditaments and furniture		143
in consideration of produce or goods		145
in consideration of surrender		146
covenant relating to the matter of the lease		146, 147
in articles of partnership		145
penal rent		147
instrument increasing rent		146
of several parcels by one instrument		144
by ecclesiastical corporations		146
by Trinity College, Dublin		146
of dwelling-house &c under £10		147
furnished dwelling-house or apartment		147
adhesive stamp		148
fine		148
agreement for lease for term not exceeding thirty-five years		144
chargeable as a lease		144
lease made in conformity with		144
with variation of terms		145
with option for further terms		144
at rent and further valuable consideration		145
at uncertain rent		145
agreement for "taking" only		144
attornment		4, 145
LEGACY DUTY, TABLES OF		276, 286
LETTER OF ALLOTMENT OR RENUNCIATION		148
LETTER OF CREDIT (See "BILL OF EXCHANGE")		
LETTER OF ATTORNEY &c		150, 153
proxy to vote at one meeting		150
to receive dividends		151
voting papers		200
fines		153

	PAGE
LEASE (continued)—	
appointment of receiver under Conveyancing Act, 1881	152
to be acted on abroad	35
he s, executed abroad	35
LETTERS PATENT—	
assignment of	105
licences to use and vend	105
duty in respect of royalty	107
LETTERS OF MARQUE AND REPRISAL	153
LETTER OF REVERSION IN SCOTLAND (See "MORTGAGE")	
LETTER OF RENUNCIATION	148
adhesive stamp may be used	148
LICENCE TO DEMISE UNDER HAND	55
LICENCE FOR MARRIAGE	153
LICENCE, ECCLESIASTICAL	154, 155
for any matter relating to a consecrated building or ground	155
LICENCE TO ACT AS NOTARY PUBLIC. (See "FACULTY.")	
LICENCE TO KEEP A RETREAT (HABITUAL DRUNKARDS ACT, 1879)	269
LICENCE UNDER LUNACY ACT, 1890	269
LICENCE TO USE SURNAME OR ARMS. (See "GRANT.")	
LICENCE TO USE AND VEND PATENT (See "CONVEYANCE")	
LICENCE TO USE PATENTED INVENTION	87
advertise on tramcars &c	87
fix bookstalls &c.	87
LUNATIC—	
grant of custody of estate or person of	140
MANDATE (See "LETTER OF ATTORNEY.")	
MARRIAGE LICENCE (See "LICENCE FOR MARRIAGE")	
MARRIAGE SETTLEMENT. (See "SETTLEMENT.")	
MARKETABLE SECURITY	155, 162
definition of "marketable security"	160, 214
rates of duty	155, 158
what is included for purposes of duty	159
foreign security	159
(And see "FOREIGN SECURITY.")	
Colonial Government security, definition	160
security transferable by delivery, and substituted security	156
fine	161
"transferable by delivery," definition	159
transfer of marketable security liable to conveyance duty	156
"ISSUE" OF A SECURITY	161

	PAGE
MEMORIAL	163
MEMORANDUM OF AGREEMENT (See "Agreement.")	
MEMORANDUM OF ASSOCIATION OF A COMPANY	269
MEMORANDUM ENDORSED OR WRITTEN ON INSTRUMENT	17
"MONEY" IN FOREIGN OR COLONIAL CURRENCY	21

MORTGAGE, BOND, DEBENTURE &c.—
    not being a marketable security - 163, 175
    stamping compulsory - 40
    interpretation of "mortgage" - 167
    must be for a "definite and certain sum" - 167
    meaning of "definite and certain" - 169
    chargeable with duty on principal sum only - 169
    conveyance in trust for sale intended only as a security - 167
        for the benefit of creditors - 168, 170
        apparently absolute - 168
    instrument under seal accompanying deposit of title deeds - 171
    charge of portions - 169
    assignment of debts in trust to collect &c. - 170
    attornment - 4
    certificate of charge under Copyhold Act, 1894 - 170
    recognisance - 170
    charging order - 170
    to indemnify a security - 169
    to secure contingent payments - 169
    of policy of insurance - 170
    security for transfer or retransfer of stock - 172
    for further advances where amount is limited - 172
    security without limit
        not subject for adjudication - 28
        good for amount covered by stamp - 29, 174
        provision for increasing duty - 174
        what may be included in amount - 169, 170
        policy mortgaged as - 210
    security for account current - 174
        repayment by periodical payments - 172
    transfer and further charge - 172
    further charge with additional security for original advance - 172
    of copyholds alone - 172
        with other property - 173
    covenant to surrender copyholds containing mortgage clauses - 129, 173
    with conveyance of equity of redemption - 173
    building society not incorporated, exemption - 175, 244, 245
    following equitable mortgage - 166

COLLATERAL &c SECURITY—
    duty and description - 164

MORTGAGE, BOND, DEBENTURE &c. (continued)—
 not applicable to equitable mortgage under hand   165
 fee farm rent in lieu of land   166
 formal mortgage under seal following equitable mortgage   166
 "duty paid" stamp required   166
 reconveyance of   166
 EQUITABLE MORTGAGE—
  duty   164
  definition   168
  must be under hand   168
  for amount without limit   174
  not applicable to bills of lading or dock warrants   171
 TRANSFER OF MORTGAGE &c   164
  of marketable security on sale   156
  of certificate of charge under Copyhold Act, 1894   170
  duty payable on amount transferred   166
   not current interest   164, 166
 RECONVEYANCE &c   164
  of part of mortgaged property   166
  of collateral security   166
  of mortgage to building society   245
  of mortgage to friendly society   245
  warrant to vacate   167
   copyholds mortgaged alone   167
   in several manors   167
   mortgaged with freeholds   167
  of instrument of defeazance chargeable as an agreement   62
 MORTGAGE OF STOCK OR MARKETABLE SECURITY   168
  ad valorem duty when by deed   168
  by instrument under hand and transfer   61
   duty on transfer of registered stock &c   61
   release or discharge of   61
 SECURITY TRANSFERABLE BY DELIVERY   (See "MARKETABLE SECURITY")

MUTUAL DISPOSITION   174

NOTARIAL ACT   174
 adhesive stamp   175
 executed abroad, when liable   175
NOTARY PUBLIC, FACULTY   137
 annual certificate   90
NOTICE TO QUIT (IRELAND)   260

OBJECTION TO DUTY   (See "INSTRUMENT")
ORDER FOR PAYMENT OF MONEY   (See "BILLS OF EXCHANGE" and "CONVEYANCE ON SALE.")

	PAGE
PAPER USED FOR STAMP DUTIES—	
forgery of	232
illegal possession	233
PARTITION OR DIVISION (*See* "Exchange")—	
of partnership assets not a sale	113
PARTNERSHIP, INSTRUMENTS RELATING TO. (*See* "Conveyance on Sale" and "Lease")	
PASSPORT	176
PATENT—	
assignment and licence to use and vend	105
duty in respect of royalty	107
(And *see* "Conveyance")	
PENAL PROCEEDINGS, ADMISSIBILITY OF INSTRUMENT	87
PENALTY ON STAMPING INSTRUMENT OUT OF DATE. (*See* "Instrument")	
power of Commissioners to remit, mitigate, or return	42, 212
POLICY OF INSURANCE—	
definition	177
POLICY OF LIFE INSURANCE—	
rates of duty	182
re-insurance	182
definition	183
fine for not making out policy duly stamped	184
assignment of, must be duly stamped	210
POLICY OF INSURANCE AGAINST ACCIDENT AND FOR PAYMENT DURING SICKNESS OR BY WAY OF INDEMNITY—	
rate of duty	182
definition	182
combined accident and sickness policy to be charged one duty only	182
adhesive stamp may be used	183
fine	183
composition for duty	209
POLICY OF SEA INSURANCE—	
rates of duty	176
re-insurance	182
definition	177
must specify risk	178
exceptions	178, 179
time for stamping	179
legal alterations may be made	180
for voyage and time, two duties	179
several vessels under one policy	178
fines	180, 182
brokerage may not be charged unless policy duly stamped	181

	PAGE
POST LETTER—	
definition	25
POST OFFICE ORDER	257
POWER, APPOINTMENT IN EXECUTION OF	62
PRECEPT OF CLARE CONSTAT	184
PREMIUM (See "Conveyance on Sale" and "Lease")	
PROBATE DUTIES, TABLE OF	274
PROCURATION	184
PROMISSORY NOTE (See "Bank Note" and "Bill of Exchange")	
PROSPECTUS—	
should be stamped if relied on as a contract	55
PROTEST OF A BILL OR NOTE	185
PROXY (See "Letter of Attorney")	
RECEIPT	185, 190
definition	187
exemptions	185, 187
adhesive stamp	187
for cheque, liable	188
for contribution to charity	189
for counsel's fee	189
given by officer of county court	189
ready-money transactions	189
terms upon which may be stamped after execution	189
signed abroad	189
fines	190
"in settlement of all claims"	188
in bankruptcy proceedings	243
by building society	245
by friendly society	249
RECEIVER, APPOINTMENT OF, UNDER CONVEYANCING ACT, 1881	152
RECONVEYANCE (See "Mortgage")	
RECOGNISANCE	170
REGISTRATION OF INSTRUMENT NOT DULY STAMPED	43
Clause of (Scotland) (See "Deed.")	
RE-INSURANCE	182, 183
RELEASE OR RENUNCIATION OF PROPERTY	191
RENTCHARGE, CREATION OF (See "Conveyance on Sale," 114, and "Bond &c." 83)	
RENUNCIATION, LETTER OF	191
REPLEVIN BOND (IRELAND)	203
RESIGNATION, INSTRUMENT OF (SCOTLAND)	191
REVOCATION OF USE OR TRUST	191
REWARD, POWER OF COMMISSIONERS TO	212

	PAGE
RIGHT NOT BEFORE IN EXISTENCE (*See* "Conveyance on Sale")	
ROYALTY—	
duty in respect of	107
SALE OF STAMPS. (*See* "Stamps.")	
SCRIP CERTIFICATE AND SCRIP	149
SEARCH WARRANT FOR FORGED DIES, STOLEN STAMPS &c.	234
SECURITY WITHOUT LIMIT (*See* "Mortgage.")	
SECURITY TRANSFERABLE BY DELIVERY. (*See* Marketable Security.")	
SECURITY TO BEARER. (*See* "Marketable Security")	
SEISEN, INSTRUMENT OF	191
SETTLED LAND ACTS—	
appointment of trustee	62
SETTLEMENT	192, 197
stamping compulsory	40
"definite and certain sum"	193
of reversionary interests	193
of contingent interest	193
other and after-acquired property	194
real estate, furniture &c	194
policy of life insurance	195
accident policy	196
"single premium" policy	195
covenants for payments of annuities in	196
several instruments	197
example of assessment of duty	270, 272
SHARE CERTIFICATE, FOREIGN AND COLONIAL. (*See* "Marketable Security.")	
SHARE WARRANT (THE COMPANIES ACT, 1867) AND STOCK CERTIFICATE TO BEARER	198
penalty for issuing unstamped	198
definition of stock certificate	198
(And *see* "Composition")	
SHIP, INSTRUMENTS RELATING TO	203
SOLICITOR'S CERTIFICATE (*See* "Certificate")	
SPECIAL PLEADER. (*See* "Certificate")	
STAMP—	
adhesive stamps, list of instruments for which they may be used	22
how to be cancelled	23
when more than one stamp is used	23
unless properly cancelled, instrument not duly stamped	23
fine for refusing to cancel	23

	PAGE
STAMP (continued)—	
when to be affixed to specified instruments	24
unless affixed at proper time, instrument not duly stamped	23
defacement prohibited	235
Postage and Inland Revenue stamps may be used to limit of 2s 6d.	22
fines for fraud in relation to	25, 236
appropriated stamps, list of	26
not to be used for other instruments	26
licences for sale of stamps	223
fines for unauthorised sale	224
hawking stamps	225
discount	226
spoiled stamps, allowance for—	
general regulations	226, 230
misused stamps, allowance	230
Commissioners may repurchase stamps not required	229
forgery of and offences relating to stamps	230, 238
(And see "INSTRUMENT")	
STAMPING (See "INSTRUMENT")	
STATEMENT OF CAPITAL (See "COMPANIES' CAPITAL DUTY")	
STATUTES CONTAINING SPECIAL EXEMPTIONS FROM STAMP DUTY	242, 262
TABLE OF	263, 265
STATUTORY DECLARATION (See "AFFIDAVIT")	
STOCK, HOW TO BE VALUED	21
STOCK CERTIFICATE TO BEARER. (See "SHARE WARRANT")	
SUBSTITUTED SECURITY. (See "MORTGAGE, COLLATERAL SECURITY")	
SUCCESSION DUTY, TABLE OF	278, 287
SUPERANNUATION ANNUITY	86
stamping compulsory	40
SURNAME, LICENCE TO USE	140
SURRENDER—	
of copyholds (See "COPYHOLDS.")	
in any other case	199
TACK OF LANDS, &c, IN SCOTLAND. (See "LEASE")	
TACK OF SECURITY. (See "MORTGAGE.")	
TRANSFER (See "CONVEYANCE)—	
of share in or at book mine	199
charge of duty	199
adhesive stamp	200
fine	200

	PAGE
TRANSFER (*continued*)—	
of shares in Government or Parliamentary stocks or funds, exemption	203
TRUST DEED FOR SECURING DEBENTURES	165
debenture stock	165
TRUSTEE, APPOINTMENT OF NEW	62
for Settled Land Acts, &c	62
discharge of, under Conveyancing Act, 1881	63
VALUATION (*See* "APPRAISEMENT.")	
VOTING PAPER. (*See* "LETTER OF ATTORNEY")	
WADSET (*See* "MORTGAGE")	
WARRANT OF ATTORNEY (*See* "MORTGAGE")	
WARRANT FOR GOODS OR DOCK WARRANT	201, 202
exemptions	201
definition	201
adhesive stamp on	202
fine	202
WARRANT TO VACATE (*See* "MORTGAGE" and "RECONVEYANCE.")	
WARRANT UNDER SIGN MANUAL	202
WORDS. (*See* "DEFINITIONS.")	
WRIT OF ACKNOWLEDGMENT (SCOTLAND)	202
WRIT OF RESIGNATION AND CLARE CONSTAT	202
WRITER TO THE SIGNET (*See* "ADMISSION" and "CERTIFICATE.")	

JORDAN & SONS,

STAMPING DEEDS AND OTHER DOCUMENTS.

Attention is particularly called to recent alterations in the Law relating to the Stamping of Agreements, Contracts, Deeds, and other Instruments. Until the passing of The Customs and Inland Revenue Act, 1888, the time allowed for Stamping an Agreement under Hand was Fourteen Days, and for an Instrument under Seal Two Months. In default of payment of duty within the prescribed time, until the passing of that Act, the Commissioners of Inland Revenue had power to remit the penalty chargeable on default up to Twelve Months after the date of the Instrument being executed. Under existing Law, Instruments under Seal or chargeable with *ad valorem* duty must now be stamped within Thirty Days after execution; and if not properly stamped the Commissioners have no power to remit penalties after Three Months. The time allowed for Stamping Agreements under Hand remains the same as before—viz., Fourteen Days.

JORDAN & SONS give particular attention to the proper Stamping of Agreements, Deeds, and other Instruments. All documents forwarded to them for that purpose are carefully examined, and, if necessary, submitted for adjudication as to the Duty chargeable thereon.

As Duties have to be paid in cash, JORDAN & SONS must request that they be remitted with the Documents to be stamped.

JORDAN & SONS are in daily attendance at the Companies' Registration Office, the Inland Revenue Department, the Registry of Wills, the Legacy and Succession Duty Offices, and the Registries of Births, Marriages, and Deaths, and give their immediate attention to all matters entrusted to them in connection with those Departments.

Company Registration Agents, Printers, and Stationers,
120 CHANCERY LANE, AND 8 BELL YARD, LONDON, W.C.

JORDAN & SONS,

INCORPORATION OF COMPANIES &c.

JORDAN & SONS will be happy to render assistance in all matters connected with the Formation, Management, and Winding Up of Public Companies. Their large practical experience in business of this nature, extending over many years, frequently enables them to be of service to Solicitors and others who entrust them with the supervision and printing of Prospectuses, Memorandums and Articles of Association, Contracts, Special Resolutions, Notices, and other Documents

All papers put into their hands are printed with the utmost care and expedition, and in conformity with the requirements of the Companies Acts and the Registrar of Joint Stock Companies

MEMORANDUMS AND ARTICLES OF ASSOCIATION

and other Documents sent to them to be Stamped and Registered are immediately attended to, and the Certificates of Incorporation obtained and forwarded as soon as issued

JORDAN & SONS are in daily attendance at the Companies' Registration Office, the Inland Revenue Department, the Bills of Sale Office, the Registry of Wills, the Legacy and Succession Duty Offices, and the Registries of Births, Marriages, and Deaths, and will give their immediate attention to all matters entrusted to them in connection with those Departments.

Company Registration Agents, Printers, and Stationers,
120 CHANCERY LANE, AND 8 BELL YARD, LONDON, W.C.

JORDAN & SONS,

DRAFT FORMS
OF
Memorandums and Articles of Association.

JORDAN & SONS beg to announce that, in compliance with numerous requests, they now supply Draft Forms of Memorandums and Articles of Association suitable for various kinds of Joint Stock Companies. In order that these Drafts shall be as reliable as possible, they have been carefully settled by Mr. F. GORE-BROWNE, M.A., of the Inner Temple, Barrister-at-Law, Author of "Concise Precedents under the Companies Acts," and Joint Author of "A Handy Book on the Formation, Management, and Winding Up of Joint Stock Companies."

In each Draft the Objects Clauses of the Memorandum of Association have been set out in the most comprehensive manner, in order that, in this important particular, the amplest powers may be secured to meet every likely contingency in carrying on the Company's business; and in the Articles all the regulations are introduced which a wide experience of the working of the Companies Acts has shown to be necessary or desirable.

The object of the Drafts is twofold—first, to provide suitable Precedents on which the Practitioner may base the Memorandum and Articles of any Company whose documents he may have to prepare, and, secondly, to save the labour, delay, and risk of error which attend the writing out of

---

Company Registration Agents, Printers, and Stationers,
120 CHANCERY LANE, AND 8 BELL YARD, LONDON, W.C.

JORDAN & SONS,

such lengthy documents as Memorandums and Articles of Association frequently now are. The forms will also be useful for laying before Promoters and proposed Directors with a view to taking instructions as to the clauses to be actually adopted

The series comprises three sets of forms, as follows :—

Form A.—A full form, containing a complete set of Articles entirely superseding Table A, and suitable for Limited Companies generally.

Form B.—To be used where Table A is adopted with modifications, setting out the clauses usually added or substituted A copy of Table A, foolscap size, accompanies this form

> The clauses given in this form show the principal variations from Table A which are found useful in practice, but they may be shortened by omitting those which are considered unnecessary for any particular Company

Form C.—A form suitable for Single Ship Companies, containing in the Articles of Association special clauses as to Management A copy of Table A also accompanies this form

The Drafts are printed on one side of the paper, in such form that alterations can be made to meet the circumstances of each particular case, and wherever necessary explanatory foot-notes are added There is also appended a Table of Stamp Duties and Fees payable on Registration of Companies Limited by Shares.

The price of each Draft is Three Shillings and Sixpence, post free on receipt of remittance.

Company Registration Agents, Printers, and Stationers,
120 CHANCERY LANE, AND 8 BELL YARD, LONDON, W.C.

JORDAN & SONS,

Price 10s 6d.; for Cash with Order 8s 6d; by Post 6d. extra.

CONCISE PRECEDENTS
UNDER
THE COMPANIES ACTS.
BY
F. GORE-BROWNE, M.A.,
OF THE INNER TEMPLE, BARRISTER-AT-LAW,
JOINT AUTHOR OF
"A HANDY BOOK ON THE FORMATION, MANAGEMENT, AND WINDING UP OF JOINT STOCK COMPANIES."

Containing numerous Precedents of Memorandums and Articles of Association, Agreements with Vendors, and other Preliminary Contracts, Underwriting Letters, Commission Notes, &c., Forms of Debentures and Trust Deeds, Schemes of Winding Up and Reconstruction of Companies and Arrangements with Creditors, Forms of Resolutions and Petitions to Reduce Capital, to alter Memorandum of Association, and to Wind Up, Notices of Motion and Summons, Pleadings in Actions, and many other Forms for various purposes

"This book aims at supplying a real business want by providing such short and clear forms as are constantly being required by both lawyers and laymen who have to do with the formation the management, and the winding up of companies. With great skill the Author has kept the promise of his title page, and given us Precedents that are Concise, and to anyone who knows how much easier it is to be prolix and diffuse in such matters this is a great gain. Besides the numerous Precedents adapted to all kinds of companies and ready for actual use, the Author has, by way of introductory remarks to each chapter and numerous notes throughout, kept his object clearly in view, and explained everywhere all practical points as they arise, with the addition of useful hints which are evidently the outcome of experience. We have thus in one handy, well printed volume of 550 pages for half-a-guinea a clearly arranged series of Precedents, noted up with cases down to date, and applicable to the Formation, Carrying Out, and Winding Up of a Company We begin with the Memorandum of Association, and go right through company business, ending even with Pleadings in Actions, and containing in its Addenda a mass of useful matter in the way of Stamps, Fees, Rules of the Stock Exchange, and the Companies Acts, all dealing with and completing the subject treated."—*Manchester Guardian*

"For those who desire a book moderate in size and price, containing a good deal of accurate information, this handy and well printed treatise will be very serviceable"—*Law Journal*

Company Registration Agents, Printers, and Stationers,
120 CHANCERY LANE, AND 8 BELL YARD, LONDON, W.C.

JORDAN & SONS.

Seventeenth Edition. Price 3s. 6d. net; by Post, 3s. 9d.

A HANDY BOOK

ON THE

FORMATION, MANAGEMENT, AND WINDING UP

OF

JOINT STOCK COMPANIES.

BY

WILLIAM JORDAN,

Registration and Parliamentary Agent,

AND

F. GORE-BROWNE, M.A.,

Of the Inner Temple, Barrister-at-Law, Author of "Concise Precedents under the Companies Acts."

EXTRACTS FROM PREFACE

The issue of the Seventeenth Edition of a Law Book is an event sufficiently uncommon to justify its Authors in feeling some gratification, and in holding the opinion that their work is not without its use. Definite references to decided cases (which has been my part of the work) were first included in the Fourteenth Edition, which appeared in April 1891, and as each succeeding year has seen a new edition the book may now almost be considered an "Annual". Should any reader take the trouble to compare any one edition with its immediate predecessor he will find that no edition is a mere reprint of the previous one, but that revision and annotation take place each year. The volume has by this means grown from 184 pages to its present size, for, besides the case law included, the practical information which was the distinguishing feature of earlier editions has been all retained, and in many places extended by Mr William Jordan.

The aim of the book is to be a trustworthy guide to Shareholders, Directors, Promoters, Secretaries, Officers, Liquidators and Creditors of Companies as to their duties and rights, and the methods of performing those duties and enforcing those rights, while Lawyers will find references to the authorities which establish or elucidate the propositions set forth.

A few new Rules as to winding up have been published, and these are incorporated in their proper places. It has been necessary also to add upwards of seventy references to cases reported during 1891 and January 1894. It is hoped that the fact of thus bringing the statement of the law down to the latest possible date will make this a useful book of reference even to those who possess the larger text books on the Companies Acts published three or four years ago.

2 Plowden Buildings, Temple,   F. GORE BROWNE.
February, 1894.

**Company Registration Agents, Printers, and Stationers,
120 CHANCERY LANE, AND 8 BELL YARD, LONDON, W.C.**

JORDAN & SONS,

cond Edition, Price 5s net, by Post 5s 6d

SECRETARY'S MANUAL
ON THE
Law and Practice of Joint Stock Companies
WITH FORMS AND PRECEDENTS.
BY
JAMES FITZPATRICK,
SECRETARY OF PUBLIC COMPANIES, AND ACCOUNTANT,
AND
V. de S. FOWKE,
OF LINCOLN'S INN, BARRISTER-AT-LAW.

"This is the best book of the sort that we have yet seen. It explains the duties and responsibilities of a Secretary from the very commencement, including matters concerning the prospectus and all things prior to allotment. The various books that are required are set out in detail, and every act in the life of a company, until its winding up, is described."—*Financial News.*

Price 5s net, by Post 5s 6d.

THE COMPANIES ACTS, 1862 to 1890;
THE LIFE ASSURANCE COMPANIES ACTS, 1870 TO 1872;
THE STANNARIES ACTS, 1869 & 1887;
THE FORGED TRANSFERS ACTS, 1891 & 1892;
AND
Other Statutes and Statutory Enactments relating to or affecting Joint Stock Companies formed under The Companies Acts, 1862 to 1890, with Cross References and a full Analytical Index.

BY
V. de S. FOWKE,
Of Lincoln's Inn, Barrister-at Law, Author of "Reminders of Company Law," and Joint Author of "The Secretary's Manual on the Law and Practice of Joint Stock Companies"

"This is intended to be a companion volume to the popular books on Company Law issued by the same Publishers—the 'Handy Book on the Formation, Management, and winding Up of Joint Stock Companies' and 'The Secretary's Manual.' The size of those works forbids the inclusion of the text of the Statutes, and the present volume supplies the omission. All the Statutes bearing on Companies are printed in full, numerous cross references are given, and occasionally also the more important decisions are noted. The Editor appears to have performed his task very judiciously, and the book will be found convenient to have at hand for reference."—*Solicitors' Journal*

Company Registration Agents, Printers, and Stationers,
20 CHANCERY LANE, AND 8 BELL YARD, LONDON, W.C.

JORDAN & SONS,

IMPORTANT WORK ON THE NEW LAW OF TRUSTS.

Price 6s. net; by Post 6s. 6d.

THE

TRUSTEE ACT, 1893:

AN ACT

Consolidating Enactments Relating to Trustees,

TOGETHER WITH

The Trustee Act, 1888,

AND

The Trust Investment Act, 1889,

With Explanatory Notes, the Rules of the Supreme Court under the New Act, Numerous Forms, and a Complete Index.

BY

ARTHUR REGINALD RUDALL,

OF THE MIDDLE TEMPLE, BARRISTER-AT LAW,

AND

JAMES WILLIAM GREIG, LL.B, B.A. LOND.,

OF LINCOLN'S INN, BARRISTER AT LAW

(SCHOLAR IN REAL AND PERSONAL PROPERTY LAW, LINCOLN'S INN, 1882)

"This is a valuable work on an Act which came into force on the 1st of January. The Authors, Messrs Rudall and Greig, are experienced writers on the Law of Trusts, and their work on 'The Duties, Powers, and Liabilities of Trustees,' published in 1889, was well received. The new Act is a consolidation of the many hitherto existing Statutes relating to Trusts and Trustees, and as the book, besides giving the text of the Act, summarises a vast amount of case law reaching down to the date of going to press, and also contains the Rules of Court issued under the new Act, it should be of considerable value both to the legal practitioner and to the large number of persons who have accepted the responsible office of trustee."—*Financial News*.

Company Registration Agents, Printers, and Stationers,

120 CHANCERY LANE, AND 8 BELL YARD, LONDON, W.C.

JORDAN & SONS,

Price 6s. net, by Post 6s. 6d.

THE LAW

AS TO

COPYHOLD ENFRANCHISEMENT

UNDER

THE COPYHOLD ACT, 1894,

CONTAINING THE TEXT OF THE ACT, WITH EXPLANATORY
NOTES, COMPARATIVE TABLES OF REPEALED STATUTES,
MINUTES OF THE BOARD OF AGRICULTURE, SCALES
OF COMPENSATION, NUMEROUS FORMS, AND
A FULL ANALYTICAL INDEX.

BY

ARTHUR REGINALD RUDALL,

OF THE MIDDLE TEMPLE,

AND

JAMES WILLIAM GREIG, LL.B., B.A. LOND.,

OF LINCOLN'S INN,

*Joint Authors of a Treatise on the Law of Trusts under
The Trustee Act, 1893, etc.*

Company Registration Agents, Printers, and Stationers,
120 CHANCERY LANE, AND 8 BELL YARD, LONDON, W.C.

JORDAN & SONS,

Demy 8vo. strongly bound in Buckram, pp. xxiv.—488, Price 15s., for Cash with Order 12s. 6d; by Post 6d. extra.

A

Practical Treatise

ON

PATENTS, TRADE MARKS

AND

DESIGNS,

WITH A

Digest of Colonial and Foreign Patent Laws;

THE TEXT OF THE

PATENTS, DESIGNS, AND TRADE MARKS ACTS,

1883 to 1888, CONSOLIDATED;

The Rules, Fees, and Forms relating to Patents, Designs, and Trade Marks (Consolidated); the International Convention for the Protection of Industrial Property, Precedents of Agreements, Assignments, Mortgages, &c, and a full Analytical Index.

BY

DAVID FULTON, A.M.I.C.E.,

Fellow of the Chartered Institute of Patent Agents, and of the Middle Temple,

BARRISTER-AT-LAW.

Company Registration Agents, Printers, and Stationers,
120 CHANCERY LANE, AND 8 BELL YARD, LONDON, W.C.

JORDAN & SONS,

Price 3s 6d; by Post 3s. 9d.

PROVISIONAL ORDERS

OF THE

BOARD OF TRADE

IN REFERENCE TO

GAS AND WATER, TRAMWAY,
PIER AND HARBOUR, AND ELECTRIC LIGHT
UNDERTAKINGS:

BEING

A MANUAL OF PRACTICE FOR PROMOTERS,
OPPONENTS, AND OTHERS

BY

FRANCIS J. CROWTHER,

PARLIAMENTARY AGENT

SECOND EDITION.

"Local Authorities anxious to secure Provisional Orders of whatever nature, whether they apply to gas, water, tramway, pier and harbour, or electric light undertakings, will find in Mr CROWTHER's handbook on 'Provisional Orders of the Board of Trade' an invaluable guide. Mr CROWTHER's experience as a Parliamentary Agent befits him to speak on the subject with which he deals, and whether we want Provisional Orders, or are anxious to oppose, Mr CROWTHER's book lucidly sets forth the procedure to be observed."—*Local Government Journal*

Company Registration Agents, Printers, and Stationers,
120 CHANCERY LANE, AND 8 BELL YARD, LONDON, W.C.

JORDAN & SONS,

Third Edition. Demy 8vo, Cloth, Price 7s. 6d.

THE
PARISH COUNCILLOR'S GUIDE
TO THE
LOCAL GOVERNMENT ACT, 1894,
WITH
Introductory Chapters, the Full Text of the Act with Explanatory Notes, and the Rules and Forms issued by the Local Government Board.

BY

H. C. RICHARDS,

Of Gray's Inn and the Middle Temple, Counsel to Her Majesty's Postmaster-General, c c c, etc.,

AND

J. P. H. SOPER, B.A., LL.B.,

Of Lincoln's Inn.

"A treatise of which we fancy the bewildered parish councillor will sorely stand in need, and which seems to be lucidly and carefully written."—*The Times.*

"The chapters relating to 'Affairs of the Church and Ecclesiastical Charities' and 'The Vestry' are specially interesting to those who have the welfare of the Church at heart."—*The National Church.*

"The book is handy in size and price, deals with a very important topic in a straightforward manner, contains a good deal of accurate information, is well printed, and forms a really useful companion to the Act.—*Law Students' Journal.*

"When we consider the immense number of persons interested in parish affairs who will have to master the Act we are convinced that this book will find a ready and large sale. The publishers' name alone is a guarantee of its value, as the public have by this time become aware that any book of this sort published by Messrs. Jordan may be relied on to give full, clear, and accurate information."—*Investors' Guardian.*

"The book is well laid out, and the explanation of the Act from an ecclesiastical point of view is very lucid, and easily understood. It is one of the best works yet issued on the subject, and certainly the very best for use by the clergy, church wardens, and trustees of charities."—*Local Government Journal.*

"The authors write mainly for those who view parish matters from within the church porch. On the position of the parson, the trusteeship of charities, the shrunken powers of the vestry, they write fully and clearly."—*Daily Chronicle.*

Company Registration Agents, Printers, and Stationers,
120 CHANCERY LANE, AND 8 BELL YARD, LONDON, W.C.

JORDAN & SONS,

Second Edition, Price 2s. 6d.; by Post 2s. 9d.

THE
CANDIDATES' AND AGENTS' GUIDE
IN
CONTESTED ELECTIONS:
BEING A
Complete Vade Mecum for Candidates, Agents, and Workers in Parliamentary and Municipal Elections,

By H. C. RICHARDS,
Of Gray's Inn and the Middle Temple, Barrister-at-Law.

Also by the same Author, Price 2s. 6d., by Post 2s. 9d.

The Corrupt and Illegal Practices Prevention Act,
ANNOTATED AND EXPLAINED,

With Notes of Judicial Decisions in Cases of Bribery, Treating, Undue Influence, Personation, &c., and a Copious Index.

One of Her Majesty's Judges writes:—"Many thanks for the book on Contested Elections which you were kind enough to send me. It is a most useful book, and will probably relieve me, as an Election Judge, of many an Election Petition, for Candidates will now be fairly warned of pitfalls in their paths, and clearly shown how to avoid them."

LORD SALISBURY writes:—"Hatfield House, Dec. 24, 1893. Dear Mr RICHARDS,—I am much obliged to you for the copy of your two little works on Election Law. I have been glad to receive them, for they contain a large amount of very useful information put together in a very accessible form.—Believe me, yours faithfully, SALISBURY."

"For the political worker we can imagine no more useful guides than these two publications, and they ought to be in the hands of every Unionist Parliamentary Candidate and Election Agent in the country."—*Yorkshire Post.*

Company Registration Agents, Printers, and Stationers,
120, CHANCERY LANE, AND 8 BELL YARD, LONDON, W.C.

JORDAN & SONS,

Bound in Boards, with Leather Back, 2s 6d ; in Cloth Boards, gilt lettered, 5s , by Post 6d. extra.

THE COMPANIES'
Diary and Agenda Book.

COMPILED BY
JAMES FITZPATRICK,
Fellow of the Incorporated Society of Accountants and Auditors, Joint Author of "The Secretary's Manual on the Law and Practice of Joint Stock Companies."

This Diary is issued in November, in readiness for the ensuing year. It is compiled for the use of Secretaries, Directors, and other Company Officials, and contains a large amount of special information relative to their duties.

The book is of foolscap folio size. the Diary having a full page for each week A few pages are provided for Memoranda and Reminders of a permanent nature, and a quire of ruled foolscap for Agenda, Rough Minutes of Proceedings at Board and General Meetings, and for use as a Note Book at other times as necessity arises

The following are some of the items of information given —

Memoranda of Requirements of the Companies Acts
Responsibility of Officers of Companies
Table of Stamp Duties and Fees on Registering a Company Limited by Shares
Stamp Duties on Transfers, Bonds, Debentures, &c.
General Provisions as to Stamping
Precedents for Special and Extraordinary Resolutions
Annual Returns of Capital and Members, with Examples
The full Text of The Directors' Liability Act, 1890, and The Forged Transfers Acts, 1891 and 1892
Bills of Sale. Deeds of Arrangements for Benefit of Creditors Postal Regulations Transfer and Dividend Days Trust Investments Table of Interest on Investments at various Rates. Foreign Moneys, with Equivalents in British Currency. Interest Ready Reckoner Discount Table, &c

Company Registration Agents, Printers, and Stationers,
120 CHANCERY LANE, AND 8 BELL YARD, LONDON, W C.

JORDAN & SONS,

The following are the Principal Books, &c., required on the Formation of a Company, all of which may be obtained of JORDAN & SONS:—

1. **Agenda Book** (for entering particulars of business to be transacted at Board and General Meetings)
2. **Directors' Minute Book** (for records of the proceedings [at] Board Meetings)
3. **General Minute Book** (for records of the proceedings at General Meetings)
4. **Letters of Allotment** (which have to be *impressed* with Penny Stamps)
5. **Allotment Book.**
6. **Numerical Register of Shares.**
7. **Register of Members and Share Ledger** (to comply with the requirements of Section 25 of The Companies Act, 1862).
8. **Register of Transfers.**
9. **Annual List and Summary** (to comply with the requirements of Section 26).
10. **Common Seal** (usually fitted to lever press, and enclosed in case with two locks, or secured with bolt or clamp and two locks).
11. **Share Certificates.**
12. **Notices of Call.**
13. **Forms for Returns of Capital and Members.**
14. **Guard Book** (for keeping Transfers, Forms of Proxy, &c.).

Besides the ordinary Books of Account—such as Cash Book, Day Book, Journal, Ledger, &c.

All Registers and other Books and Forms supplied by Jordan & Sons may be relied upon as being prepared strictly in accordance with the requirements of the Companies Acts.

Railway, Banking, Insurance, Gas, Water, and other Companies' Books and Forms kept in stock, or Ruled and Printed to order on the shortest notice

---

Company Registration Agents, Printers, and Stationers,
120 CHANCERY LANE, AND 8 BELL YARD, LONDON, W C

JORDAN & SONS

Make a Speciality of the Printing of

Memorandums and Articles of Association,

PROSPECTUSES, TRUST DEEDS, AGREEMENTS, &c.,

And Legal and Company work of all kinds

ESTIMATES GIVEN

FOR THE

Printing and Publication of Legal Works, and Books in General Literature.

REGISTERS, ACCOUNT BOOKS, &c.,

Required by Corporations and Companies kept in Stock, or Special Rulings prepared to order in a few days.

TELEGRAMS —"CERTIFICATE LONDON"

JORDAN & SONS,

CORPORATE & COMPANIES' SEALS.

JORDAN & SONS are noted for the high quality and artistic design of Corporate and other Seals designed and engraved by them.

In consequence of their special facilities for the rapid execution of this branch of Art, they are enabled to supply Seals where necessary at exceedingly short notice.

Designs drawn free of charge where an order for engraving the Seal is given; otherwise a small charge is made for drawing the Sketch.

Japanned Cases for the safe custody of Seals, with two good lever locks and duplicate keys, 12/6, 15/-, and 17/6, according to size of Press.

Mahogany case, with two patent locks and duplicate keys, 30/-.

Lettering name of Company on Case in gold or white, average cost 2/- extra.

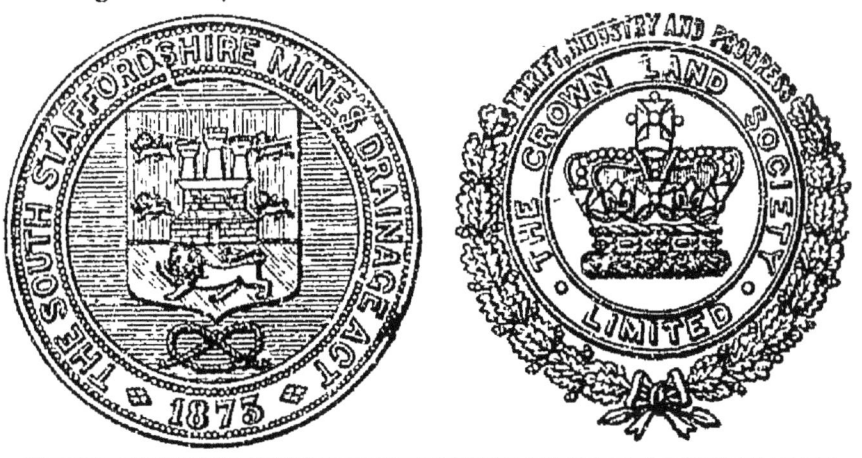

Company Registration Agents, Printers, and Stationers,
CHANCERY LANE, AND 8 BELL YARD, LONDON, W.C.

JORDAN & SONS,

Specimens of Seals designed and engraved by
JORDAN & SONS.

Company Registration Agents, Printers, and Stationers,
120 CHANCERY LANE, AND 8 BELL YARD, LONDON, W.C.

JORDAN & SONS,

JAPANNED CASES
For Corporate and Companies' Seals

These Cases are for the purpose of securing Corporate and Companies' Seals from use by unauthorised persons, to keep them free from dust, and to enable them to be easily carried from place to place. They are fitted with two good lever locks, with duplicate keys to each, and are stocked in three sizes, at the following prices —

No 1	No. 2	No 3
(9 by 6¾ by 4¼ ins)	(10¼ by 8¼ by 4¾ ins)	(11¼ by 9 by 5¼ ins)
12/6	**15/-**	**15/-**

Other sizes made to order

Lettering on front with name of Corporation or Company involves a small extra charge, according to length of name

---

Company Registration Agents, Printers, and Stationers,
120 CHANCERY LANE, AND 8 BELL YARD, LONDON, W C

Ingram Content Group UK Ltd.
Milton Keynes UK
UKHW050825190423
420422UK00008B/499